INDIA'S GOVERNANCE

BOOKS BY MADHAV GODBOLE

1. *The Babri Masjid-Ram Mandir Dilemma: An Acid Test for India's Constitution*, Konark Publishers, New Delhi, 2019
2. *Indira Gandhi—An Era of Constitutional Dictatorship*, Manas Publications, New Delhi, 2018
3. *Secularism: India at a Crossroads*, Rupa & Co., New Delhi, 2016
4. *The God who Failed: An Assessment of Jawaharlal Nehru's Leadership*, Rupa & Co., New Delhi, 2014
5. *Good Governance: Never on India's Radar,* Rupa & Co., New Delhi, 2014
6. *India's Parliamentary Democracy on Trial,* Rupa & Co., New Delhi, 2011
7. *The Judiciary and Governance in India,* Rupa & Co., New Delhi, 2008
8. *The Holocaust of Indian Partition: An Inquest,* Rupa & Co., New Delhi, 2006
9. *Public Accountability and Transparency—The Imperatives of Good Governance,* Orient Longman, New Delhi, 2003
10. *The Changing Times—A Commentary on Current Affairs,* Orient Longman, New Delhi, 2000
11. *Unfinished Innings—Recollections and Reflections of a Civil Servant,* Orient Longman, New Delhi, 1996
12. *Rural Employment Strategy—A Quest in the Wilderness,* Himalaya Publishing House, Mumbai, 1990
13. *Public Expenditures in Maharashtra—A Case For Expenditure Strategy,* Himalaya Publishing House, Mumbai, 1989
14. *Industrial Dispersal Policies—A Case Study of Maharashtra,* Himalaya Publishing House, Mumbai, 1978

INDIA'S GOVERNANCE

An incisive commentary on some burning issues

Madhav Godbole

Konark Publishers Pvt Ltd
New Delhi · Seattle

Konark Publishers Pvt. Ltd
206, First Floor,
Peacock Lane, Shahpur Jat,
New Delhi - 110 049
Tel: +91-11-41055065
Mob: +91-93552 93900, +91-93552 94900
e-mail: india@konarkpublishers.com
website: www.konarkpublishers.com

Konark Publishers International
8615, 13th Ave SW,
Seattle, WA 98106
Phone: (415) 409-9988
e-mail: us@konarkpublishers.com

ISBN: 978-81-942-0182-3

Jacket Design by Dushyant Parasher

Typeset by Saanvi Graphics, Noida

Printed and bound at Thomson Press (India) Ltd

For
Rahul and Dakshina
&
Meera and Mahesh

CONTENTS

PART TWO
GOOD GOVERNANCE MUST BE A FUNDAMENTAL RIGHT

PART THREE
PUBLIC LIFE – A DOWNHILL JOURNEY

PART FOUR
RHETORIC OF ZERO TOLERANCE FOR CORRUPTION

PART FIVE
RULE OF LAW, THE POLICE AND THE CBI

PART SIX
ECONOMIC REFORMS GONE ASTRAY

PART SEVEN
NATIONAL SECURITY – INCREASING CONCERNS

PREFACE

I AM DELIGHTED TO place this second collection of my selected essays in the hands of the readers. The first was, *The Changing Times: A Commentary on Current Affairs* (2000). During the intervening years, a great deal has changed in India but the government's image, approach, functioning and sensitivities have largely remained the same. As they say, more the things change, more they remain the same. As for the society at large, the situation is even worse, with pronounced regression in several respects!

Apart from writing several books, I have made it a point to write extensively on current issues having long-term implications. I believe that this is important for empowering the people and strengthening democracy in the country. But, writings published in newspapers and periodicals, and even well- known journals, are not easily accessible after a time, though the issues continue to be relevant, and may have even become explosive in the meantime. Placing such a compilation in the hands of the readers helps in maintaining a credible record of significant happenings, enabling their in-depth analysis and evaluation of actions and inactions.

Over the last 27 years since my 'retirement', I have written more than 450 articles in English and Marathi of which seven collections of Marathi articles and one of English articles have been published so far. Some essays have also been published in the books on the relevant subjects. For me, this has been a very satisfying way of reaching a large cross-section of readers.

The present compilation consists of 36 selected essays written during 2006 to January 2019. It is divided into seven sections: Is India secular?; Good governance must be a fundamental right; Public Life – A downhill journey; Rhetoric of zero tolerance for corruption; Rule of law, the police and the CBI; Economic reforms gone astray; and National security – Increasing concerns. In each section, articles are arranged chronologically for facilitating understanding of issues in perspective. Each section is preceded by a short introduction bringing out historical background and important issues.

It may be noted that these articles and essays had appeared in a wide range of publications, often representing different ideologies and both in the print and online media. They comprise leading national dailies, weeklies and other periodicals. It has been my conscious effort to reach as large a cross-section of society as possible, without getting bogged down in the narrow compartments of ideologies.

The writings bring out some notable points. Illustratively, there is a growing divide between the precepts of secularism laid down in India's Constitution and the ground realities. Governance in the country has deteriorated markedly. Public life in the country has been muddied significantly. Economic reforms have been grossly politicised and have no takers. And the rule of law on which the Indian Constitution lays so much emphasis has lost its sheen. This broad-brush survey should impel us to introspect about what the future holds.

I would like to place on record the help and encouragement given by my wife Sujata in all my writing endeavours. She would not like me to thank her formally, but I will be failing in my duty if I do not acknowledge her debt. I am obliged to my Coordinating Editor Jiza Joy and Editorial Associate Lekshmi Parameswaran for diligently going through the manuscript and giving it the finishing touches. I must also place on record my deep appreciation for the keen interest taken by K.P.R. Nair in bringing out the book speedily and elegantly.

Madhav Godbole
Pune

PART ONE

Is India Secular?

SECULARISM – CHASING A DREAM?

WHEN INDIA BECAME independent, it consciously rejected the option of becoming a Hindu *Rashtra* and opted to be a secular, democratic union of states. After the Lok Sabha elections in 2014 and the Bharatiya Janata Party (BJP) came to power at the Centre, and the thumping renewed mandate it received in 2019 elections, India's secularism is being seriously questioned and demands are being voiced for declaring India a Hindu state. This raises a number of serious questions since India is a multi-religious, multi-cultural, multi-ethnic and multi-lingual country, with nearly 20 per cent of its population comprising religious minorities.

The Indian Constitution contains a number of forward-looking provisions on secularism. Secularism is also a part of the Preamble of the Constitution. More importantly, the Supreme Court has declared secularism as a part of the basic structure of the Constitution which Parliament has no powers to dilute. The Supreme Court has also opined that non-adherence to secularism will be akin to failure of the constitutional machinery in the state under Article 356 of the Constitution and the state government can be dismissed and President's rule imposed. But in a fractious polity, these sanctions are difficult to enforce.

The most outstanding example of this was the demolition of the Babri Masjid in 1992 by frenzied mob of lakhs of volunteers, with the BJP government in Uttar Pradesh (UP) being not just a mute spectator but an abettor! In spite of the advice of the Ministry of Home Affairs to dismiss the UP government in pre-emptive action and to impose President's rule, the then Prime Minister P.V. Narasimha Rao preferred to watch the situation helplessly. I was Union Home Secretary at the time and, after the demolition of the Masjid, in sheer disgust, I opted for premature retirement. The relevant legal and constitutional issues are discussed in the articles and essays in this section. My essay in the *Economic and Political Weekly* (EPW) clearly brings out that the plea taken by the then Prime Minister P.V. Narasimha Rao that he could not have acted under Article 356 of the Constitution to dismiss Kalyan Singh government was not tenable. It was clearly a case of lack of political will to act.

Safeguarding and promoting the interests of minorities is the legitimate responsibility of the majority community. Unfortunately, this subject has become highly controversial with charges and counter-charges of sham secularism, minority appeasement and vote-bank politics. On the one side, this has meant pandering to the demands of Muslim extremists and fundamentalists, and, on the other, neglecting the interests of the poor and deprived sections of minority communities. Answers must be found to this conundrum.

Yet another evidence of declining secular values is the increasing communal violence in the country. The ban on cow slaughter, which is against the precept of secularism, is being enforced by almost all state governments. The decision of the Supreme Court upholding the ban by reversing its own earlier decision on the subject, which held sway for several years, has made the position more complex. Several instances of mob violence due to rumours of cow slaughter or transportation of animals for slaughter created shock waves in the country. Time and again, India virtually became *Lynchistan*, tarnishing its image irretrievably.

The social and political atmosphere in the country has become so intolerant that any talk of secularism is frowned upon. Open dialogue, debate and discussion, which are the hallmarks of democracy, are disappearing. One example of this was the B.G. Deshmukh memorial lecture which I was to give at the Mumbai branch of the Indian Institute of Public Administration. The event was to be held in the conference hall of Mantralaya, the Maharashtra State Secretariat. I was asked by the organisers to send an advance copy of my speech so that it could be circulated to the invitees and the media. I had decided to speak on, *Is India A Secular Nation?* The lecture was cancelled on the specious plea that the State Assembly session was on! Extracts of the speech were however widely reported in the media. A full text of the speech is given in this book.

As discussed in my book, *Secularism: India at a Crossroads (2017)*, if secularism is to be upheld, the Constitution will need to be amended to increase the credibility of secularism. Further, these amendments will also have to include shifting the entries 'police' and 'public order' from the State List to the Concurrent List of the Seventh Schedule, and empowering the Union to deploy the central police forces for law and order duties in any state. Otherwise, the Union government will be as helpless in upholding secularism and dealing with serious communal situations, as at the time of the demolition of the Babri Masjid in 1992 and later during the Godhra communal riots in 2002.

In the final analysis, mere constitutional provisions will not make India secular. It will call for a new mindset. The Indian society and the people at large will have to adopt and embrace secular values. Secularism must become a way of life.

1

AYODHYA AND INDIA'S MAHABHARAT – CONSTITUTIONAL ISSUES AND PROPRIETIES

P. V. NARASIMHA RAO was the Prime Minister (PM) when India's secular foundations were shaken by the wanton demolition of the Babri Masjid. The ensuing communal holocaust led to 2,026 persons being killed and 6,957 injured, widened the communal divide and left visible scars of communal bitterness and hatred. Since this was one of the most shocking events in the history of independent India, it was expected that Rao's book *Ayodhya: 6 December 1992* (Penguin India, 2006) would shed new light on the relevant issues. These expectations were reinforced since Rao wanted the book to be published only after his death. The book has belied these expectations.

After the First World War, a French general is stated to have written a glowing account of how well his troops had fought and won a battle in which their forces had actually suffered

---

Economic and Political Weekly, 27 May 2006.

an ignominious defeat. The general gave the account to his second-in-command and asked him to dispatch it to the army headquarters. The next day the general asked him whether he had done so. The officer said, 'Sir, I have not sent it since the account which you have written is quite the opposite of what actually happened.' The general coolly told him, 'Ami, c'est pour l' histoire (Friend, it is for history).' The same can be said of Rao's book.

Far from the Truth

Rao's version of the events has come more than 13 years after the catastrophic event. According to the publisher's note, Rao wrote this account after he stepped down as PM in 1996 and made revisions to the manuscript till a few days before his death in December 2004. Since Rao has so little to add to what was already contained in the central government's 'White Paper on Ayodhya' (1993), it is not clear why he wanted to have it published only after his death. Was he afraid of people questioning him closely and joining issues with him?

Rao has stated, 'I held a large number of meetings with individuals and groups directly concerned with the dispute, as well as journalists, political, religious and social leaders' (p 95). These discussions are stated to have 'facilitated a better understanding of the position of the parties concerned and enabled various sections of them to put forward their own insights into the various facets of the problem' (p 96). Rao has stated, 'No specific proposal or suggestion for a solution was put forward on behalf of the government.' The book is silent on what transpired in these countless meetings in which only Rao had participated.

The book sheds no light on the decision-making process in the government. When a Prime Minister writes an account of a unique historical event, it is not unreasonable to expect that he would elucidate the discussions which took place at the official and political levels and the considerations which weighed with him in taking the decisions. This is more so since, according to Rao, not taking a decision was also a decision! Rao claims, 'the officers told me again and again that whatever was being done for queering the pitch was for political reasons and not based on what obtained on the field. They said they had studied the field and were quite clear that the "kar seva" would be peaceful. This was the situation (p 185).' This was true only in respect of some officers. His assertion that, 'today's hindsight was not available to anyone in the government of India on those dates... The formidable snag is that no one at that crucial time knew *how it was going to happen*' (emphasis in the original) (p 171), is also far from true. While none could have precisely known 'how it was going to happen', there were serious apprehensions of the forthcoming calamity among some of Rao's cabinet colleagues and some senior officers. This has been fully brought out in the memoirs of this author who was then the union home secretary [Godbole 1996].

Self-Defence

We shall now turn to the discussion of the constitutional issues and proprieties on which Rao has rested his self-defence. The constitutional provisions for dealing with states which are remiss in fulfilling their constitutional obligations are Articles 256, 355, 356 and 365, aptly described as New Delhi's Long Arm [Austin 1999]. We shall examine the extent to which recourse to these could have been and was actually taken by the Rao government. Article 256 states, 'The executive power of every state shall be so exercised as to ensure compliance with the laws made by Parliament and any existing laws which apply in that state and the executive power of the Union shall extend to the giving of such directions to a state as may appear to the government of India to be necessary for that purpose.' This article has been rarely invoked by the Centre. Attention of the states of Kerala and West Bengal was, however, invited to the provisions of this article in 1968 when these states had declined to deal firmly with the central government employees' strike and give adequate protection to the central government offices and public sector undertakings. In the agitation leading to the demolition of the Babri Masjid, no formal directions were issued to the Government of Uttar Pradesh (GoUP) but scores of letters, faxes and telephonic messages were sent to the state government at the level of union home minister and senior officers to urge that adequate precautions should be taken to protect the disputed structure. These communications served the same purpose as directions under Article 256. It must be noted that issuing a direction under Article 256 implies that if it is contravened, it can lead to the dismissal of the state government and imposition of President's Rule as provided in Article 365. In the explosive situation prevailing in UP, issuing a formal direction would have alerted the state government of the possible action under Article 356 and this could have been used as a pretext by kar sevaks and the ruling party activists to bring about the demolition of the masjid. The BJP could have then blamed the central government for it, as Kalyan Singh, chief minister, had been repeatedly threatening to do. Thus, in the extraordinary situation in UP, the use of Article 256 had its own limitations and could have been counterproductive.

It is important to understand the extent to which Article 355 could have come handy in dealing with the situation. Article 355 states that 'It shall be the duty of the Union to protect every state against external aggression and internal disturbance and to ensure that the government of every state is carried on in accordance with the provisions of this Constitution'. Noorani has commented that 'Article 355 was not entirely born in sin, but was conceived in murky circumstances', mainly to protect the thrones of princely rulers who wanted the Union's protection lest neighbouring provinces of the former British India or their own people rose in revolt in the altered circumstances [Noorani 2000]. As compared to similar provisions in the constitutions of the US and Australia, the provision in Article 355 does not contain a requirement of a request from the state government for protection and intervention by the Centre. It is, however, important to note that the US Supreme Court has, as far back as in 1895, held that if internal disturbance in any state interfered with the operation of the national government itself or with the movement of interstate commerce, the Centre can send force on its own initiative, without waiting for application from the state authorities. After this ruling, the requirement of an application by the affected state for aid for suppression of internal violence has lost its importance. In 1963, the US federal government did not hesitate to deploy the national militia in Little Rock to quell racial disturbances, and to enforce the decision of the Supreme Court on racial integration. This was done very much against the wishes of the state government. [Jain 2005]

Misleading Statements

The term 'internal disturbance' used in this article is much broader than the term 'armed rebellion' used in Article 352 and can cover a wide variety of situations. The Sarkaria Commission has observed that 'the scope of the term "internal disturbance" is wider than "domestic violence". It conveys the sense of "domestic chaos" which takes the colour of a security threat from its associate expression "external aggression". Such a chaos could be due to various causes. Large-scale public disorder, which throws out of gear the even tempo of administration and endangers the security of the state, is ordinarily one such cause.' The commission also observed that 'Article 355 not only imposes a duty on the Union but also grants it, by necessary implication, the power of doing all such acts and employing such means as are essentially reasonably necessary for the effective performance of that duty' [GoI 1988]. The situation in UP leading to the demolition of the Babri Masjid in 1992 was fully in keeping with the interpretation of the term 'internal disturbance' given by the Sarkaria Commission.

Rao refers at more than one place (pp 125, 151) to the contingency plan prepared by the central government to deal with the situation, but says that it was only to assist GoUP to deal with the situation effectively and 'ensuring compliance with the orders of the court'. This is far from true. In fact, it is a travesty of the truth. Rao has himself stated that 'As a measure of abundant caution, however, the central government had stationed 195 companies of central paramilitary forces (CPMFs) near Ayodhya in November 1992 so that these could be made available at short notice if and when required by the state government *or for any other contingent purpose*' (emphasis added) (p 125). But, Rao has deliberately kept silent about the other contingent purpose, namely, dismissal of GoUP and imposition of President's rule. Rao has made much of the fact that 'the central government did not have even a toe-hold anywhere in UP at the time. In the absence of such a hold, the Centre could not have found it feasible to take an extremely crucial step like the imposition of President's rule in the teeth of determined resistance by an entrenched state government' (p 173). But, the comprehensive contingency plan prepared by the ministry of home affairs (MHA) was meant to deal with any such eventuality effectively and to ensure protection of the Babri Masjid by swift action by commando units and paramilitary forces as a surprise move in the middle of the night, followed by imposition of President's rule. The union home minister, in his reply to the marathon debate in the Lok Sabha on 3 December 1992, had clearly stated that 'the

Centre could easily resort to Article 355 of the Constitution' (p 136). This was based on the contingency plan which the MHA had prepared. Since Rao did not want to take action under Article 356 coupled with a pre-emptive action under Article 355, the contingency plan became infructuous so far as the original objective was concerned.

The statement in the book that 'it was not the position of the state government that they would not use the CPMFs even if it became necessary to do so' (p 141) is factually incorrect and misleading. The resolve of GoUP not to use CPMFs was amply evident by its refusal to deploy these forces in and near the masjid even though they were stationed in Faizabad and other nearby locations from 24 November 1992, the deliberate delay in calling the CPMFs on 6 December after the demolition of the structure began, and its refusal to provide magistrates to escort the CPMFs which led to their returning to the barracks. Further, since the GoUP had all along declared its intentions of not using force to deal with the kar sevaks, the CPMFs were not useful even as a show of force. As a result, the largest ever CPMF of about 20,000 men and women mobilised from all over the country and stationed just a few kilometres away from Ayodhya and other elaborate advance planning—procurement of rubber bullets, training of commando units, dog squads, bomb disposal squads, hundreds of requisitioned vehicles, water cannons, tonnes of concertina wire, firefighting equipment and vehicles—was of no use and the CPMFs had to watch helplessly when the structure was demolished. Rao prefers to keep this shocking reality away from the reader.

By the 42nd Amendment of the Constitution in 1976, a new Article 257A was added empowering the Centre to deploy any central force for dealing with a grave situation of law and order in any state without its concurrence. Any such force was to act subject to the control and directions of the Centre and not of the concerned state government. This provision was deleted by the 44th Amendment due to the fears voiced by states, but Entry 2A still remains a part of the Union List. Even if Article 257A had continued to be a part of the Constitution, it would not have made any difference to the handling of the situation in UP since Rao government lacked the political will to act.

Non-invocation of Article 356

The third most potent instrument could have been Article 356 under which the state government could have been dismissed and President's rule imposed. Rao has stated that 'from millions of people has come the inevitable and irresistible question: Why did the President of India not impose President's rule under Article 356 of the Constitution of India and save the structure in time?[1] The central government certainly owes a full explanation to the people. It has been given several times, but it would be proper to consolidate the reply to the question in all its relevant aspects, to stand witness to history and throw light on the future' (sic) (p 166). Rao's arguments for non-invocation of Article 356 are curious and hardly convincing. His assertion that 'it was not possible to identify the stage, event or moment that could fit in the above description (ie., when it could be said that the government of the state could not be carried out according to the provisions of the Constitution) had not arisen' (p 169) is preposterous. This is amply borne out by the central government's repeated pleadings before the Supreme Court—the solicitor general telling the court on 24 November 1992 that 'the situation on the ground is escalating day by day' (p 111), the attorney general telling the court on 25 November 1992 that 'the situation in Ayodhya had reached a boiling point' and warning that 'even one day of adjournment could prove costly'. He had also told the court that the state government had clearly stated that 'use of force to prevent kar seva will not be appropriate' (p 113). 'The deficiencies in the existing security arrangements (made by GoUP) which were pointed out by the central government were taken note of by the court' (p 124). Rao has himself underlined that 'the law and order implications of the Ram Janmabhoomi-Babri Masjid (RJB-BM) dispute had always been serious' (p 124). Rao has further admitted that 'Based on past experience and the continuing undercurrent of communal tension on account of the RJB-BM dispute, serious apprehensions existed about the outbreak of fresh violence in various parts of the country, particularly if any untoward incident took place in Ayodhya during the proposed kar seva' (p 125). All this and much more evidence which was available with the Centre was adequate to justify the dismissal of GoUP. But, Rao has asserted: 'It is clear that on a correct construction of Article 356, it is not possible to invoke the provision to serve a preventive purpose in time. This is not a happy situation and calls for a relook at the language of Article 356, if it is to be provided with any legally valid "teeth" to serve a preventive purpose' (p 179). This too does not hold water as can be seen from the observations of Sawant and Kuldip Singh, JJ, in the *Bommai* case: 'A reasonable prognosis of events to come and of their multifarious effects to follow can always be made on the basis of the events occurring, and if such prognosis led to the conclusion that in the circumstances, the governments of the states could not be carried out in accordance with the provisions of the Constitution, the inference cannot be faulted.'[2] Equally relevant are the observations of Jeevan Reddy and Agrawal, JJ, 'The situation was an extraordinary one; its repercussions could not be foretold at that time. Nobody could say with definiteness what would happen and where? The situation was not only unpredictable, it was a fast evolving one. The communal situation was tense. It could explode anywhere at any time.'[3] Though these observations were made by the court to uphold the dismissal of the governments of MP, HP and Rajasthan, they could have been made with even greater force to dismiss GoUP. And this is what MHA was repeatedly urging. The ministry of law had also concurred in the cabinet note prepared for the dismissal of GoUP.

On President's Rule

Rao has claimed that he could not have taken action to impose President's rule when the Supreme Court was holding hearings on almost day-to-day basis. However, the court itself had pointed out on November 25, 1992 that 'the central government is, of course, at liberty to make its own assessment of the matter and take such action on its own as may appear to it proper and permissible' (p 115). It had declined to direct the central government to withdraw CPMFs from Ayodhya by saying, 'neither of the court's (previous) orders had prevented any constitutionally elected government from performing its duty in accordance with the law' (p 130). Rao's argument that 'the Supreme Court's refusal even to make the central government a receiver (as pleaded by one of the petitioners) for the limited and specific purpose of giving adequate protection to the disputed structure at Ayodhya is also a meaningful pointer; it only translates into a "hands off the state" directive to the Centre' (p 180) which is breathtaking. The fact that the central government did not even have a 'toe-hold in UP' (words used by Rao in p 173) must have weighed with the court in not casting the responsibility of receivership on the Centre. This author too had advised Rao that if the court appointed the central government as a receiver, such a responsibility could be discharged only if the state was taken under President's rule.[4] Rao's self-serving and untenable interpretation of the Supreme Court's position on receivership is a desperate attempt to justify his indecision and inaction.

Rao has made much of the advice given by the Governor against imposition of President's rule on the specious plea that 'the Governor is in charge of the state' (p 170). The Governor is in charge of a state only when the state is under President's rule. At other times, he is the constitutional head of a state. In the situation obtaining in UP and brought out, day after day, by the Intelligence Bureau reports to which Rao was privy, it was abundantly clear that the Governor had not kept himself informed of the rapidly deteriorating situation. It is nowhere laid down that the central government must go by the assessment of the Governor. Article 356 clearly states, 'If the President, on receipt of a report from the Governor of a state *or otherwise* is satisfied...' (emphasis added). This was particularly so in the instant case. After the Babri Masjid was demolished, the central government took the decision to dismiss not just GoUP, but also the BJP governments in MP, HP and Rajasthan to retrieve its secular credentials. This was in spite of the advice of MHA that the law and order situation in these states was much better than the Congress-ruled states of Maharashtra, Gujarat and Karnataka and these states were faithfully implementing central government orders, including action against banned organisations such as the RSS, VHP and Bajrang Dal. After taking the decision to dismiss these governments, the Governors were told to send suitable reports for the purpose. So much for Rao's avowed faith in constitutional proprieties!

In his speech in the Constituent Assembly, Ambedkar had hoped that 'the proper thing we ought to expect is that such articles (emergency provisions) will never be called into operation and that they would remain a dead letter.' This hope was belied by the Centre making blatant misuse, over the years, of Article 352 by declaration of emergency and of Article 356 by imposition of President's rule in states on nearly hundred occasions. Against this background, it was supremely tragic that Article 356 remained a dead letter on perhaps the only occasion when its use would have made all the difference. Noorani has stated that in spite of the pious intentions of the founding fathers of the Constitution, 'Article 356 is a weapon of first resort' (op cit, p 261). Unfortunately, in the instant case, it was not used even as an instrument of last resort. In fact, it was not used at all! Rao has referred to the judgment of the Supreme Court in the *Bommai* case for justifying his decision not to take recourse to Article 356. But, a close scrutiny of the judgment would show that none of the principles laid down by the court in that case would have been contravened if GoUP had been dismissed in November 1992. It may be pertinent to note that one of the very first cases of the use of Article 356 was the dismissal of Kerala government in 1959 on the ground of its failure to maintain law and order in the state. The same reasoning was used for dismissing some other state governments including the Tamil Nadu government in 1991. In all these cases, the gravity of the failure was much less as compared with the situation in UP in November 1992. Clearly, it was not the Constitution which was found wanting as averred by Rao. It was the failure of the national leadership during this critical period. In this light, Rao's assertion that 'any prudent President or Prime Minister would not have gone ahead and clamped Article 356 under these circumstances' (p 180) will not have many takers. A reference may also be made to Rao's own observation that 'Constitutional pundits, administrators and others understand that in some critical situations, time is of the essence in taking a decision' (p 181).

Rao's handling of the RJB-BM dispute and its disastrous outcome proves its validity decisively. A nagging question still remains. It is difficult to believe that Rao, who had spent a lifetime in national politics, was a close confidant and adviser of Indira Gandhi and Rajiv Gandhi, was a central minister for decades before he became Prime Minister, and was appropriately known as Chanakya, did not realise that it was imperative to take recourse to Articles 355 and 356 if the impending disaster was to be avoided. What then were his political compulsions for not doing so? Was he worried about the Hindu backlash if the Congress party was seen to be opposing the construction of the Ram temple? Rao was well aware that, keeping in view of the importance of not alienating the Hindus, Rajiv Gandhi took the initiative to have the locks of the Ayodhya temple in the Babri Mosque opened in 1986 and permitted 'shilanyas' on the land in dispute in 1989. Rajiv Gandhi had also commenced his party's election campaign in 1989 from Ayodhya promising to establish 'Ram Rajya' [Gill 1996]. It is believed that in Rao's wide-ranging confabulations, the fears of Hindu backlash were repeatedly voiced. Beneath the veneer of secularism of the Congress party, there was a growing concern regarding the implications of opposing the Ayodhya agitation on the electoral fortunes of the party. When the Centre' s strategy of kid-glove treatment of Ayodhya agitation failed and the masjid was demolished by kar sevaks leading to a severe backlash not just from the Muslims and secular sections, but even large sections of Hindus, the Congress party made Rao the pariah and he was not even given a party ticket in the Lok Sabha election. It is perhaps in this sense that Rao has cryptically stated that, 'They (his colleagues) were playing either for success, or an alibi through a scapegoat in case of failure! It was a perfect strategy. They could loudly proclaim later that the Muslim vote did not come to the Congress after the demolition of the Babri Masjid solely because of me. It remains to be seen whether the future will vindicate me in this regard' (p 188). For a lay reader, these political manoeuvrings and games of one-upmanship are difficult to fathom. Rao could have guided the reader through this maze by bringing out the political confabulations, their nuances and his political compulsions but he has preferred to remain silent for ever as a true Congressman! By indulging in legalistic sophistry rather than recording what actually happened behind the scenes, he has wasted the valuable opportunity to clear his name.

Lessons for the Future

We shall now turn to the lessons for the future. The main question is whether the Constitution needs to be amended in any way as advocated by Rao. While Rao presumably wanted to have the emergency powers of the Centre enlarged, the states are keen on their curtailment. The Sarkaria Commission and the Commission to Review the Working of the Constitution have, on the contrary, recommended certain precautionary measures to prevent the misuse of these articles by the Centre [Kashyap 2004]. But, clearly, no one had visualised that the country will be faced with a situation, as in UP, in which a recalcitrant state government, belonging to a major national party, would be bent on flouting all constitutional norms and proprieties, and disregarding the unequivocal commitments given by it to the central government, the National Integration Council, the High Court and the Supreme Court. Similar eventualities cannot be ruled out in the future and the Centre's discretion under the emergency provisions must not be circumscribed in any way. After the stringent safeguards of judicial review laid down by the Supreme Court in *Bommai* case, there need be no fears of misuse of these powers by the Centre.

Austin has presented an alarmist and exaggerated assessment of rapidly expanding CPMFs and the fears of central intervention generated thereby among states [Austin op cit: 599-600]. It is important to note that except for the Central Reserve Police Force, all other central forces have been created for specific purposes such as border guarding, protection of railways and central industrial and other establishments, etc, and are diverted and deployed in aid of civil power only when inescapable. While the Centre is urging the states to augment their police strength and reduce their dependence on central forces, it is the states which have been clamouring for support of CPMFs. In spite of the wide discretion given to the Centre by Article 355, this power was used by the Centre only once in 1968 in Assam, West Bengal and Kerala and that too only to give protection to the central government offices and the central public sector undertakings. Though the CPMFs and armed forces have been stationed in various parts of the country, they have not been deployed by the Centre on its own at any time to contain 'internal disturbance'. Invariably, the CPMFs have been placed at the disposal of the state governments whenever requested by them. During such deployment, they operate only under the control of the state government.

It is difficult to believe but though Article 257A was repealed by the 44th Amendment, even the National Democratic Alliance (NDA) government wanted its provisions to be reintroduced! The group of ministers on reforming the national security system had recommended that a supporting legislation, in pursuance of Article 355, may be passed by Parliament to provide for: '(a) Suo motu deployment of central forces, if the situation prevailing in the states so demands; (b) Defining powers, jurisdiction, privileges and liabilities of the members of the central forces while deployed in states in accordance with Entry 2-A of the Union List; and (c) Specifying situations construed as failures/break-down of constitutional machinery in a state in which the central government can intervene to advise or direct, as the case may be, a state government and violation of these advisories/ directions would invite action under Article 365/352' [GOI 2001]. It is often said that public memory is short. But, even the BJP had conveniently forgotten its own postures and threats during the critical period in November-December 1992 when it had stoutly opposed the central government taking recourse to Articles 355 and 356 in UP.

A reference may be made to the critique of the *Bommai* judgment by Soli Sorabjee. As he has rightly stated, the decision of the Supreme Court will go a long way in minimising the Centre's frequent onslaught on states, but some of the observations of the judges made in the course of arriving at the conclusions are of serious concern. According to Justices Jeevan Reddy and Agrawal, 'if a political party espousing a particular religion comes to power, that religion tends to become, in practice, the official religion. All other religions come to acquire a secondary status, at any rate, a less favourable position.' They further held that 'under our Constitution, no party or organisation can simultaneously be a political and a religious party. It has to be either'. There is no dissent or qualification or reservation by any of the other judges on this part of the judgment. Accordingly, the legal position enumerated by Justices Jeevan Reddy and Agrawal can be regarded as the law laid down by the apex court. It is impossible to describe them as obiter dicta. Sorabjee has rightly stated that 'these propositions are over-broadly stated' (Journal section (1994) 3 SCC, p 30). The law laid down by the apex court is questionable and is bound to become a minefield though it has escaped public attention so far.

The final chapter in the history of this momentous event will unfold when the Liberhan Commission submits its report. But, the painful memories of the demolition of the Babri Masjid, which signified a monumental failure of governance of the country, will linger for a long time. Making Constitution the scapegoat, as Rao has tried to do, will not take us anywhere. This national tragedy calls for sincere introspection on the part of all political parties, the civil society and all those who have the interest of the country at heart. The tragedy showed how fragile the Constitution can be in such crisis situations. It highlighted the weaknesses of the major pillars of democracy. But, this was due to the failure of political leadership at various levels. Almost all those responsible, in one way or another, for the tragedy have got away. The foremost of them was Kalyan Singh who incredibly got away with only a token punishment of one day's imprisonment and a fine of Rs 2,000 for contempt of the highest court of the country!

Notes

1. Legally speaking President's rule is not imposed by the President of India, but by the central government with the approval of the President.
2. S R. Bommai vs Union of India and Others (1994) 3 SCC. p 9.
3. Ibid. p 11.
4. Ibid. pp 380-81.

References

Gill, S. S. (1996). *The Dynasty: A Political Biography of the Premier Ruling Family of Modern India.* HarperCollins India, pp 416-17.

Godbole, Madhav (1996). *Unfinished Innings: Recollections and Reflections of a Civil Servant.* Orient Longman, New Delhi.

GOI (1988). *Report of the Commission on Centre-State Relations.* Part I. Government of India, pp 165-69.

GOI (2001). *Recommendations of the Group of Ministers on Reforming the National Security System,* p 43.

Granville, Austin (1999). *Working a Democratic Constitution: The Indian Experience.* Oxford University Press. New Delhi.

Jain, M.P. (2005). *Indian Constitutional Law,* fifth edition, Wadhwa and Company, Nagpur, p 682.

Kashyap, S.C. (2004). 'Report of the National Commission to Review the Working of the Constitution' in S.C. Kashyap, *Constitution Making since 1950: An Overview,* Universal Law Publishing Company, New Delhi, pp 421-27.

Noorani, A.G. (2000). *Constitutional Questions in India,* Oxford University Press, New Delhi, p 272.

2

IS INDIA A SECULAR NATION?

Introduction

AT THE OUTSET, I must say how happy I am to have this opportunity to address this august gathering in the memory of Late B.G. Deshmukh, one of the most illustrious civil servants of India. I had the privilege of working closely with him in the state and at the Centre. It was because of him that, as Principal Finance Secretary, I could initiate and vigorously implement zero-base budgeting in the state and earned, what some of the detractors believed, the ignominious, but what I am ever proud of, nickname of 'Mr No'. I am glad to know that this 'glorious' tradition of Finance Secretary being the 'punching bag' has continued in Maharashtra to this day! If only all states had more 'Mr Nos', the state governments would have done a yeoman service by enhancing the rate of growth of the states and ensuring more productive public expenditures. B.G., as he used to be fondly and reverentially known, was brutally frank and

---

Late B.G. Deshmukh Memorial Lecture 2016 by Dr Madhav Godbole on 4 April 2016 at Mantralaya in Mumbai, which was cancelled.

open in tendering his advice to his colleagues and political executives. He achieved the rare distinction of occupying the three highest and most coveted positions in the civil service of Chief Secretary of a state, Cabinet Secretary and Principal Secretary to Prime Minister. He personified the best in the 'endangered species' of the civil service.

I am going to speak today on whether India is a secular nation. I have deliberately framed the question so as not to restrict it to 'India as a secular state'. For, I believe, it is not enough if the Indian state is secular, which it is not. It is equally, if not more, important that we are a secular society, a secular nation. I believe this question needs to be asked, reflected upon and answered truthfully.[1] My latest book, *Secularism—India at a Crossroads,* on this subject is being brought out shortly. It is perhaps the first book totally devoted to operationalisation of secularism and comprehensively looks at the constitutional, statutory, policy and administrative issues in the light of the experience of the working of secularism gained over the last 66 years since the adoption of the Constitution.

The Backdrop

At the outset it must be stated that I am a firm believer in the concept of secularism. It is my conviction that India's survival as a multi-religious, multi-lingual, multi-racial, multi-cultural society will depend on how successful it is in working its secularism. Presently, religious minorities constitute about 20 per cent of India's population, with Muslims accounting for 14.2 per cent. According to some estimates, in a few years, this percentage is likely to stabilise at a little over 25, with Muslims accounting for 20 per cent. With extremist and radical external forces such as Islamic State of Iraq and Syria (ISIS) and Inter-Services Intelligence (ISI) of Pakistan, to name just two, bent on disturbing the peace and tranquillity in the country, it will be foolhardy to neglect the welfare of minorities. No society can prosper or be at peace with itself if one-fourth of its population feels neglected, deprived and unwanted.

There is a great deal of talk in the country about the appeasement of minorities in general and Muslims in particular, but socio-economic indicators of Muslims brought out by Justice Sachar Committee bring out convincingly how this so-called 'vote-bank' of some political parties has remained at the margin all these years. It is shocking to see that Parliament did not have time to discuss the findings of this report as also the major recommendations of Justice Ranganath Misra Commission Report. Both these high-level expert groups were appointed by the then United Progressive Alliance (UPA) government. Many in this distinguished gathering are aware of the predecessor-successor complex which is so common in civil services. Unfortunately, studies of expert committees and commissions too have been afflicted by this virus. Secularism was expected to bring about the integration of the diverse elements of Indian society. But it is a travesty that the majority community as well as the minorities are dissatisfied with it. In fact, the concept of secularism has lost all credibility.

It must be stated that India would not have been either a parliamentary democracy or a secular nation, to whatever degree it is, without the firm commitment of Jawaharlal Nehru and Vallabhbhai Patel to these precepts. The Indian Constitution is one of the most explicitly secular Constitutions in the world though the founding fathers of the Constitution could not agree on calling it 'secular' for fears that it would be perceived as anti-religious or irreligious in the Western sense of the term. It was felt that by calling it secular, the Constitution would be denuded of the ethical and moral underpinning of the religious precepts which are so necessary for the governance of the country. This deficiency was made good during the Emergency in 1976 by the Forty-second Amendment by the inclusion of the word 'secular' in the Preamble of the Constitution.

It is disconcerting to see that, in recent times, serious questions are being raised about India's secularism. It is for the first time since independence that the *Hindu Rashtra* ideology is being talked about so openly, defiantly and persistently. It is interesting to note that Jawaharlal Nehru had made his position clear on *Hindu Rashtra* way back on 6 September 1951:

> It may sound very nice to some people to hear it said that we will create a *Hindu Rashtra* etc...Hindus are in a majority in this country and whatever they wish will be done. But the moment you talk of *Hindu Rashtra* you speak in a language which no other country except one can comprehend and that country is Pakistan because they are familiar with this concept. They can immediately justify their creation of an Islamic nation by pointing out to the world that we are doing something similar. *Hindu Rashtra* can only mean one thing and that is to leave the modern way and get into a narrow, old fashioned way of thinking, and fragment India into pieces. *Those who are not Hindus will be reduced in status.* You may say patronisingly that you will look after the Muslims or Christians or others as in Pakistan they say that they will look after the Hindus. Do you think any race or individual will accept for long the claim that they are looked after while we sit above them?[2]

If the Supreme Court had not categorically declared in *S.R. Bommai* v. Union of India {(1994) 3 SCC 1} that secularism is a part of the basic structure of the Constitution and Parliament has no powers to dilute it in any way, concerted efforts would have been made by some political parties to amend the Constitution to dilute its secular tenets.

In retrospect, it is fortunate that the proposal of the Janata government contained in the Forty-fourth Amendment Bill, 1978, for effecting amendment of the Constitution by holding a referendum on certain important matters such as its secular or democratic character, abridging or taking away fundamental rights, prejudicing or impeding free and fair elections on the basis of adult suffrage, and compromising the independence of the judiciary, did not find acceptance in the Rajya Sabha. Otherwise, attempts would even have been made to rally public opinion in favour of doing away with the secular characteristics of the Constitution and I would not be surprised if, in the present polarised political atmosphere in the country, it would have found a majority support. The Supreme Court itself has expressed apprehensions in this regard: 'India till now is a secular country...we do not know for how long it will remain a secular country.' (*Indian Express*, 10 February 2015: 1)

Against this background, it is necessary to examine what needs to be done to safeguard secularism from political turmoil and vicissitudes and to ensure that it will continue to be an important ingredient of the basic structure of the Constitution. In this context, it will be appropriate to recall what Jefferson, the statesman who played a great part in the making of the American Constitution, had stated: 'We may consider each generation as a distinct nation, with [a] right, by the will of the majority, to bind themselves, but none to bind the succeeding generation, more than the inhabitants of another country.' I hope proposals made hereafter would be looked at in this light.

Secularism - Constitutional Precepts and Reality

A series of articles in the Constitution underline the precepts of secularism. These include: Article 14—equality before law; Article 15—prohibition of discrimination on grounds of religion, race, caste, sex or place of birth; Article 16—equality of opportunity in matters of public employment which, inter alia, lays down that no citizen shall, on grounds of religion, race, caste, etc. shall be ineligible for, or discriminated against in respect of employment or office under the state; Article 19—protection of certain rights regarding freedom of speech and expression, to assemble peaceably and without arms, to form associations or unions, to move freely throughout the territory of India, to reside and settle in any part of the territory of India, and *to practice any profession, or to carry on any occupation, trade or business*; Article 21—protection of life and personal property; Article 25—freedom of conscience and free profession, practice and *propagation of religion*; Article 26—freedom to manage religious affairs; Article 27—freedom as to payment of taxes for promotion of any particular religion; Article 28—freedom as to attendance at religious instruction or religious worship in certain educational institutions; Article 29—protection of interests of minorities; and Article 30—right of minorities to establish and administer educational institutions. Reference must also be made to the two provisions in the Directive Principles of State Policy which have considerable significance in sustaining secularism in the country. These are Article 44—uniform civil code for the citizens, and Article 48—organisation of agriculture and animal husbandry which has been invoked for banning cow slaughter in a number of states. Particular attention may also be invited to Article 51A on fundamental duties which, in clause (e), lays down the duty to promote harmony and the spirit of common brotherhood amongst all people of India transcending religious, linguistic and regional or sectional diversities; and to renounce practices derogatory to the dignity of women; and clause (f) to value and preserve the rich heritage of our composite culture.

The reality is however quite disappointing. The majority community as also the minorities are totally disillusioned with the working of secularism. Instead of being the cementing force, secularism has led to alienation of all communities. This is borne out by series of failures in important areas. These include grievance of Hindus that rules, regulations and restrictions are being prescribed only for their religious institutions; non-implementation of the uniform civil code; passage of Muslim Women's Divorce Act to appease the radical, orthodox and conservative Muslim elements, totally disregarding the liberal and reformist Muslim view; propagation of religion by Muslims and Christians leading to large-scale conversions, particularly in the tribal areas and of persons below the poverty line, and unjustified protection given to minority educational institutions.

Equally disconcerting are some other signposts which raise serious doubts about how secular India is. Most important of these are non-separation of religion from politics, wanton demolition of the Babri Masjid, anti-Sikh riots in Delhi and other places in 1984, horrific riots in Mumbai in December 1992 and January 1993, and unbelievable atrocities in riots in Godhra and other cities in Gujarat 2002, continued widespread communalism and communal violence in several parts of the country which led to 8,449 communal incidents resulting in 7,229 deaths and 47,321 persons injured in a brief span of 1954 to 1985, and banning of cow slaughter leading to curtailment of freedom of persons about what to eat and restricting their freedom to carry on any profession and trade.

Due to constraints of time and space, I shall briefly deal with only a few of these features. What is striking is the total lack of political will on the part of all political parties to address these critical issues, thereby raising serious doubts about their real commitment to secularism, whatever may be the rhetoric indulged in by them for public consumption.

There are two very strong views in the country regarding enactment of a uniform civil code. It needs to be noted that while an impression was created by the speeches of Vallabhbhai Patel, Nehru and others in the Constituent Assembly that Muslims had agreed to go along with the provision for uniform civil code, careful reading of the debates clearly shows that all Muslim members, without an exception, were stoutly opposed to making a provision for a uniform civil code even in the Directive Principles of State Policy and had in fact pressed for deleting it altogether. There has been no change in the stand of the Muslims since then. It is clear that no political party, including the BJP, will be able to get such a bill passed in Parliament. In my soon-to-be released book on secularism, I have elaborately brought out the strong opposition of Hindus which had to be resisted while enacting the Hindu Code and how there was a persistent cry of Hindu religion being in danger. Even prominent leaders of the Congress party itself, like Rajendra Prasad, who was the President of the Constituent Assembly and also the President of India later, were stoutly opposed to the reforms in Hindu law. We, as a nation, should be eternally grateful to Jawaharlal Nehru for standing firm and having the relevant enactments passed. It is, however, unfortunate that Nehru did not show similar courage in initiating enactment of a uniform civil code. If reforms in Muslim personal law had been pursued, the social and religious ethos of the country would have undergone significant changes by now. Having lost the golden opportunity at that time, it will be impossible to enact a uniform civil code now, irrespective of the exhortations of the Supreme Court, unless there is a strong reformist and liberal move from within the Muslim community. Sadly, all political parties are remiss in encouraging modern, scientific, enlightened, progressive and liberal leadership among the Muslims.

While enactment of a uniform civil code will thus have to inevitably wait, separation of religion from politics is of such urgency that no time should be wasted in bringing this about. It is interesting to note that the Constituent Assembly (Legislative) had passed an explicit resolution on the subject as far back as 3 April 1948. In fact, it was perhaps the first major resolution passed by the Assembly. The resolution moved by Ananthasayanam Ayyangar read as under:

> Whereas it is essential for the proper functioning of democracy and the growth of national unity and solidarity that communalism should be eliminated from Indian life, this Assembly is of opinion that no communal organisation which by its constitution or by the exercise of discretionary power vested in any of its officers or organs, admits to or excludes from its membership persons on grounds of religion, race and caste, or any of them, should be permitted to engage in any activities other than those essential for the bona fide religious and cultural needs of the community, and that all steps, legislative and administrative, necessary to prevent such activities should be taken.

Nehru had welcomed the resolution and assured that the government 'wished to do everything in their power to achieve the objective which lies behind this resolution... The only alternative is civil conflict. We have seen as a matter of fact how far communalism in politics has led us; all of us remember the grave dangers through which we have passed and the terrible consequences we have seen...' The resolution slightly amended to permit any activities other than those essential for the bona fide religious, cultural, social and educational needs of the community was passed by the Constituent Assembly.[3]

But, though Nehru was Prime Minister for 17 years, he failed to take any action on the resolution. The only other time when any political party enjoyed two-thirds majority in the Lok Sabha, so as to be able to see through such a constitutional amendment, was when Indira Gandhi and Rajiv Gandhi were in power. But they too did not find it politically expedient to act on the resolution. It was only after the demolition of the Babri Masjid, when the secular credentials of the Congress party were being seriously questioned in India and abroad, that P.V. Narasimha Rao government brought the Constitution (Eightieth Amendment) Bill and a bill for amendment of the Representation of People Act before Parliament in 1993 to bring about separation of religion from politics. However, no effort was made by the government to take other political parties into confidence and to build a national consensus and create pressure of public opinion on the subject. The bills were so shoddily piloted in Parliament as to raise serious doubts whether the government wanted them to be passed at all or whether it was meant to be just a window-dressing exercise. As a result, the bills failed to receive adequate support and had to be withdrawn. Though over two decades have elapsed since then and though the Congress or the UPA led by that party was in power for most of this period, no effort was made to revive the proposal. This once again brings out the hollowness of the commitment of so-called secular parties to secularism. With the BJP in power at the Centre since 2014, it will be futile to expect any action in the near future. But, unless this issue is addressed seriously, India's secular credentials will continue to be questioned.

Demolition of the Babri Masjid is a shameful chapter in India's recent history raising serious doubts about its secularism. I was destined to live through this ignoble chapter at close quarters as the Union Home Secretary. All efforts made by the Ministry of Home Affairs to avert the tragedy by resorting to action under Article 355 (Duty of the Union to protect States against external aggression and internal disturbance) for taking possession and safeguarding the Babri Masjid by central forces, followed by imposition of President's Rule in Uttar Pradesh under Article 356 (Provisions in case of failure of constitutional machinery in States) of the Constitution were frustrated due to the disinclination of the Prime Minister to act. I have brought out the happenings of the period at length in a 80-page chapter titled 'The Ayodhya Debacle' in my memoirs *Unfinished Innings* published by Orient Longman way back in 1996.[4] I have also dealt at length in my article in the *Economic and Political Weekly*,[5] with the untenable defence given by P.V. Narasimha Rao in his book *Ayodhya: 6 December 1992* published by Penguin/Viking, posthumously, in 2006, in which Rao has claimed that he was unable to take any action due to the restrictive provisions of the Constitution and that he was made a scapegoat by the Congress party. This must be the only case of its kind in history in which the Prime Minister has alleged of being made a scapegoat! Otherwise, it is the well accepted prerogative of Prime Ministers to find a scapegoat for each of their lapses!

The Ayodhya debacle has several other firsts to its credit. Prime Minister Rao's assurance of 'rebuilding the mosque' given immediately after its demolition on 6 December 1992 has remained on paper. Kalyan Singh, who was the Chief Minister of Uttar Pradesh (UP) at the time and who had given assurances to the National Integration Council, the Government of India and the Supreme Court to fully safeguard the Babri Masjid, has been elevated as a Governor by the NDA government. Earlier, the Supreme Court, before which he was hauled up for contempt of court for actions taken after assuming charge as chief minister in 1991, gave punishment of imprisonment till the rising of the court and a token fine of Rs 2,000! The judicial commission of inquiry under the chairmanship of Justice M. Liberhan, set up within a week of the demolition of the mosque, created a world record by taking 17 years to complete the inquiry and effectively found no one guilty! The CBI cases against the perpetrators of the crime are still languishing though 22 years have elapsed. It is this callousness and connivance which goes to show how sham is India's commitment to secularism. On this background, to call secularism a part of the basic structure of the Constitution makes no sense.

Equally disconcerting is the manner in which perpetrators of crimes in the widespread communal riots have been casually and leniently handled by the respective state governments. Despite appointing dozens of committees and commissions to identify those responsible in the anti-Sikh riots in Delhi, hardly any action has been taken against the leaders of the Congress party who are alleged to have instigated the riots. These riots took place under the benign leadership of the central government and were therefore all the more shocking. The riots in Mumbai in December 1992 and January 1993 is another can of worms. Justice Srikrishna Commission has commented on them at great length. But the political parties and persons responsible have been permitted to go scot-free. The usual adage of the law taking its own course has been held to ridicule. The Godhra riots were qualitatively different in that it was the state-sponsored violence against the minorities. The National Human Rights Commission and the Supreme Court have done a yeoman service in upholding the rule of law but the main issue of the urgency of reorganisation of police administration which has been highlighted by the judicial commissions as also the citizens' commissions again and again has been overlooked. Even the directions of the Supreme Court issued as far back as 2006 in a public interest litigation have remained on paper. What kind of a robust and vigilant democracy are we if even the orders of the highest court in the country are not to be implemented?

Finally, the question has to be asked whether banning cow slaughter is in keeping with the concept of secularism. The Supreme Court upholding the constitutional validity of these enactments by a majority decision of 6:1 on 26 October 2005 [(2005) 8 SCC 534] has closed all options, at least for the present. It proves the adage that the Supreme Court is supreme only because there is no appeal over its decision. As one of the judges of the Supreme Court had said, 'If there were an appellate court over us, probably a majority of our judgments would be upset.' It would also be worth recalling what Justice Brennan, a judge of the US Supreme Court, had said, 'The Supreme Court [of United States] is not final because it is infallible; the court is infallible because it is final.'[6]

In a secular state, religion is expected to be a purely personal and private matter and is not supposed to have anything to do with the governance of the country. The Supreme Court had observed in the *Bommai* case that if religion is not separated from politics, religion of the ruling party tends to become the state religion. This seems to be coming true. The BJP and its affiliate parties have given to the prevention of cow slaughter sanctity of Hindu religious precept. But this is hardly justified. Further, the Fundamental Right of persons to practise any profession or to carry on any occupation, trade or business contained in Article 19 (1) (g) of the Constitution has been over-ridden by Article 48, one of the Directive Principles of State Policy. In the scheme of the Constitution, Directive Principles are not supposed to over-ride the Fundamental Rights. But it has now become a sacrilege to even raise such questions. Economic justification for enforcing cow slaughter is also highly questionable. It is unfortunate that though Nehru was staunchly opposed to prevention of cow slaughter, he did not oppose the inclusion of this provision in the Constitution. In fact, the discussion in the Constituent Assembly shows that a political decision to incorporate this provision was taken in the Congress party meeting and it was merely formalised in the Constituent Assembly by putting forth spacious and unconvincing arguments. This is yet another instance of the ambivalence of the Constitution on secularism.

Constitution Making – Inevitably an Exercise in Give and Take

The gigantic, complex and highly emotive exercise of uniting and integrating this continental sized country, including, apart from British India, more than 550 princely states, and comprising multiplicity of religions, languages, cultures, customs, traditions, political and social divisions was attempted for the first time in the history of India and credit must be given to the founding fathers of the Constitution for carrying all these diverse elements with them and unanimously agreeing on such an epoch-making Constitution. Though the Congress party alone had an overwhelming presence all over the country, due to Mahatma Gandhi's foresight, eminent persons representing different viewpoints were elected to the Constituent Assembly with the support of the Congress party. One of them was Dr B.R. Ambedkar, who was also made the Chairman of the Drafting Committee. Understandably, the Constitution was a compromise document. This is particularly evident in the provisions pertaining to secularism.

Nehru and Patel were particularly keen on doing away with the communal electorates and the reservation of seats in legislatures on the basis of the strength of religious communities. Once this objective was achieved with the concurrence of the minorities, the Congress party was prepared to concede the other demands of minorities as a compromise. As a result, provisions were made in the Constitution to include right to propagation of religion as a Fundamental Right, at the instance of Muslims and Christians on the ground that propagation was a part of their religion. The right of minorities to establish and administer educational institutions was also similarly recognised as a Fundamental Right, in spite of reservations expressed by several members including Jayaprakash Narayan and Rajkumari Amrit Kaur.

Operationalising Secularism

As stated earlier, India's future is intrinsically tied up with secularism. To make a real success of it, time has come to seriously examine its working during the last 66 years since the adoption of the Constitution. There are no political compulsions any longer. I have made an objective and dispassionate attempt to look at the relevant issues in the discussion hereinafter. Since the proposals are aimed at strengthening secularism, they are not adversely affected by the injunction of the Supreme Court on non-amendability of the provisions pertaining to secularism.

Define the word 'secular'

It is best to start the exercise with the basics. As stated earlier, the founding fathers of the Constitution had reservations about the word 'secular'. But, as the Constituent Assembly debates bring out, there was no doubt in anyone's mind that India was giving itself a secular Constitution. But, the definition of the word 'secular' was never debated or agreed upon. Even Nehru seemed ambivalent about the true meaning of secularism though he was responsible for firmly advocating it: 'It is perhaps not very easy even to find a good word [presumably in Hindi] for 'secular'. Some people think that it means something opposed to religion. That obviously is not correct. What it means is that it is a state which honours all faiths equally and gives them equal opportunities; that, as a state, it does not allow itself to be attached to one faith or religion, *which then becomes the state religion*.'[7] Banning of cow slaughter is clear proof that Hindu religion is being made into a state religion!

In 1976, when the word 'secular' was included in the Preamble by the Forty-second Amendment, again this question was evaded and no definition was provided. After the massive defeat of the Congress party in the Lok Sabha elections in 1977, the question arose of reconsideration of the highly controversial 42nd amendment, which effectively had rewritten the Constitution on a number of crucial points. The Forty-fourth Constitution Amendment Bill introduced by the Janata government in 1978 contained definition of the word 'secular' as equal respect for all religions. However, this was objected to by the Congress party which still had a majority in the Rajya Sabha (as has been the position in 2014-16) and therefore this clause was dropped. Again, an effort was made in 1993 to include the same definition in the Constitution (Eightieth) Amendment Bill on separation of religion from politics but, as stated earlier, this bill itself fell through. As a result, as of now, there is no definition of this term.

One has to fall back on the diverse ways in which the word has been described. In governmental parlance, it is understood as *sarva dharma samabhava*—treating all religions equally or equal respect for all religions. The Hindi translations of the word, namely, *dharmanirapeksha* or *panthanirapeksha* or *nidharmee* too have been rightly questioned. Another definition put forth is that the government should be equidistant from all religions. Serious questions have been raised about the validity of these definitions. For example, Late Justice R.A. Jahagirdar has, in his erudite articles in *The Radical Humanist*[8] emphasised how these definitions are untenable.

The Supreme Court has been interpreting the word 'secular' in different ways. At one extreme was its interpretation in the *Bommai* case when it declared that there must be a wall between the state and the religion, and a political party must not be linked to any religion, as otherwise, the religion of such a party is perceived as a state religion.

Reference must also be made to the statement of H.R. Gokhale, Law Minister, during the Emergency. While piloting the Forty-second Amendment Bill in the Lok Sabha, Gokhale was highly critical of the concept of 'basic structure' devised by the Supreme Court. He said: 'First of all I do not agree, with much respect to the Supreme Court, that there is something like the basic features which could not be amended...*What is not defined cannot exist and it is incapable of defining it.*'[9] If the same logic is extended to secularism, since the word 'secular' has not been defined, does it mean that India is not secular?

Since secularism has been declared by the Supreme Court as a part of the basic structure of the Constitution, governments, both at the Centre and in the states, must be made accountable for implementing it. But, how can the state be held accountable unless the meaning of the term 'secular' is clear? It is high time a national debate is started on the subject so as to arrive at a political and societal consensus and to include the definition in the Constitution.

Define the word 'minority'

I shall now turn to the word 'minority'. The concept of secularism is based on recognition and protection of minorities. The two cannot be separated. One would have therefore expected that the founding fathers of the Constitution would first define the term minorities. Unfortunately, this was never done. The Constitution merely takes off from where the British had left it, which was in fact the very epitome of the British policy of 'divide and rule'. For want of a clear definition, the Supreme Court has adopted the highly questionable criterion of numerical strength. As a result, a community will be treated as a minority till its population exceeds 50 per cent of the total. This will make a mockery of the concept of minority. In the Indian context, apart from other considerations, this is highly relevant. Muslims are already 14 per cent of the population. According to some estimates, their population is expected to stabilise at about 20 per cent in the next few years. Even if this estimate turns out to be an underestimate, as some would like to believe, it may stabilise at 25-30 per cent of the total. Should it be recognised as a minority? What should be the cut-off? This issue needs to be debated. It is no doubt an extremely sensitive and divisive issue but, as a mature democracy, India must debate it rationally and objectively, keeping the political baggage aside.

Creation of a Commission on Secularism

The Supreme Court has done a great service to the country by declaring that secularism is a part of the basic structure of the Constitution. But this declaration has remained on paper and no steps have been taken so far to translate it into reality, except for it becoming a part of political rhetoric in the country. Some of the other features of basic structure, recognised by the Supreme Court, are parliamentary democracy, independence of judiciary, freedom of press, etc. For each one of these, over the years institutional and legal framework has been established to make sure that they are carefully nurtured and safeguarded. For example, the Election Commission of India has been sufficiently empowered to ensure that there are free and fair elections in the country and electoral malpractices are put down with a heavy hand. Parliament of India is vigilant about safeguarding its independence, privileges and supremacy. The judiciary, after its shocking experience of being undermined during the Emergency in 1975-77, has been vigilant in guarding its turf. In fact, since then, the Indian judiciary has emerged as the world's most powerful judiciary with even matters pertaining to appointments of High Court and Supreme Court judges coming entirely under the Supreme Court. This is the only case of its kind in the world. In 2015, the Supreme Court has declared unconstitutional the law unanimously passed by Parliament to appoint a National Judicial Commission for the purpose. The Supreme Court and the Election Commission have emerged as the most respected institutions in the country, enjoying highest credibility. This is no mean achievement.

Against this background, it is particularly unfortunate that no steps have been taken by the government to ensure proper implementation of secularism and to give it credibility. In fact, secularism has lost all credibility since it has become a plaything in the hands of political parties, irrespective of which hues and colours they belong to. At the same time, it needs to be emphasised that secularism will decide how India would emerge over the years. In the decade of the 1980s, we have seen how fringe and extremist elements in the miniscule religious minority of Sikhs, comprising just about 1.5 per cent of India's total population, held the country to ransom for nearly a decade and led to shocking alienation of common Sikhs, not just in India but also those residing abroad.

By comparison, the Muslim population in India is already a little over 14 per cent. As stated earlier, it is projected to stabilise around 20 per cent in the next few years. Most Muslims in India are highly tolerant and peace-loving, but there are fringe and extremist elements which cannot be overlooked. Particularly with the external forces such as ISIS, Al-Qaeda and ISI, it would be in India's interest to ensure that homegrown terrorist forces are not permitted to emerge. But this is only the negative side of it. It is necessary that the issue should be addressed in a positive manner so as to bring the Muslims in the mainstream of society. In this context, the atmosphere in the country since the beginning of 2015 is of serious concern.

The issues pertaining to secularism emerge in diverse sectors of society. These relate to attempts at rewriting history, communalisation of academic and research institutions, rewriting of textbooks, circumscribing artistic freedom and so on. At present these issues can be agitated primarily before the higher judiciary as Parliament has mostly become dysfunctional. And whatever is raised in Parliament inevitably becomes highly politicised and is looked upon on the basis of party loyalties and strategies.

The experience of agitating issues pertaining to secularism by way of Public Interest Litigation (PIL) has also been far from happy. Strictly speaking, PIL is supposed to be a non-adversarial litigation. It is expected that both parties would look at the issues constructively to find a workable and acceptable solution to the problem at hand. However, experience has been quite the contrary. Practically in every case the government has taken an adversarial position and contested even reasonable proposals put forth by the petitioners. Secondly, as brought out in my book, *The Judiciary and Governance in India* (2008), the process of admission of a PIL itself is somewhat opaque and the outcome can hardly ever be predicted. Thirdly, it takes unduly long time to get the final decision of the court. For example, in the PIL pertaining to appointment of a Lokpal, due to the resistance of successive governments, the case was heard by the Supreme Court on 29 occasions and was finally closed on 12 September 2003 as 'none is ready with the matter to make submissions'. In the case of the PIL pertaining to non-implementation of the recommendations of the National Police Commission regarding modalities for appointments, etc of police officers, it took over 12 years for the Supreme Court to give a final decision. The same was the position in PILs pertaining to Haj subsidy, proliferation of Shariat courts as a parallel judicial system, *Ram Janmabhoomi*-Babri Masjid dispute and so on. In this light, taking recourse to PIL does not appear to be an alternative to setting up of any independent institution for deciding matters pertaining to secularism.

Clearly, the time has come to create a new institution, namely, a Commission on Secularism (COS) for ensuring adherence to the constitutional mandate on secularism. I had propounded this idea while discussing the lessons of Partition in my book *The Holocaust of Indian Partition—An Inquest* (2006). To be effective, such a commission must be appointed by an amendment of the Constitution and should be presided over by a former Chief Justice of India, with five other members drawn from among former judges of the Supreme Court, Chief Justices of the High Courts, eminent jurists, and other public figures of highest integrity and reputation. The term of the members should be five years or attainment of the age of 72 years, whichever is earlier. The commission should be covered by the provisions of the Contempt of Court Act.

The selection of the chairman and members of the COS should be transparently apolitical. The selection committee may comprise the Vice President of India, the Prime Minister, the Speaker, the Chief Justice of India, Union Home Minister and the leaders of opposition in the Lok Sabha and the Rajya Sabha.

Such a commission will be able to take a holistic view on all matters pertaining to secularism and even intervene in matters coming up before the High Courts and the Supreme Court. Reference may be made in this context to the very laudable role played by the National Human Rights Commission (NHRC) which had intervened in the cases pertaining to Godhra pogrom before the Supreme Court and has become an important moral voice to reckon with. At the time when there are only a few national leaders of stature left in the country with any moral authority and credibility who command universal public respect, the commission on secularism will be ideally suited to fill the vacuum.

The COS will be best equipped to create public awareness on secularism. Its open hearings will provide an opportunity to all political parties, intellectuals, religious leaders, non-government organisations, and concerned citizens to argue their points of view, either in person or through an advocate, in a free and fair manner. Keeping in view the basic purpose of setting up the COS, it is suggested that the hearings of the commission should also be televised. It is only through such a public discourse that the values of secularism enshrined in the Constitution can be translated into reality.

The commission should have the responsibility to pronounce judgments on all declarations, actions and programmes of political parties, public institutions, state and central governments, electronic and print media, and others, so far as their impact on secularism is concerned. The commission may take cognisance of such actions *suo motu* or on an application from any individual or organisation. The decision of the commission should be binding on all concerned, unless it is set aside or modified by the Supreme Court. Thus, inevitably the powers and authority of COS will have to be much wider than those of National Human Rights Commission, whose recommendations are not binding on the government. It may be relevant in this context to recall that the often violent agitations for ban on cow slaughter subsided, when the matter went before the High Courts and later the Supreme Court, irrespective of the merits of their decisions. Similarly, the highly emotive and explosive issues pertaining to implementation of secular policies need to be depoliticised by entrusting them to a constitutional commission on secularism. It may be recalled that Turkey's ruling Justice and Development Party (AK Parti) faced a serious battle for survival in 2007 when the country's constitutional court reviewed a case to ban the party for its alleged anti-secular activities in violation of the Turkish Constitution.

The reports of all commissions and bodies set up by the government are required to be submitted by them to the government which in turn submits them to Parliament. Often, there is considerable delay in the process and the government chooses the time politically most convenient and opportune for the purpose. Looking to the special position proposed to be accorded to the COS, it is suggested that the annual or any special reports of the commission may be submitted by the commission directly to Parliament and the government, and released simultaneously to the media and the public.

Secularism is a precious Fundamental Right of each citizen and the COS would ensure that it becomes a reality. I am aware that such a step will be resisted by vested interests, but if pressure of public opinion is built up, its establishment would make a significant difference to the way India is governed. The question which remains is whether there will be statesmanship and political will to support this far-reaching and overdue political reform. A national campaign needs to be launched to prevail upon all political parties to initiate and support steps for a constitutional amendment to set up a commission on secularism.

Separation of Religion from Politics

The serious problem of communalism and communal violence was brought out earlier. It is interesting to see from the fortnightly letter of Nehru to chief ministers as far back as 3 September 1954 that the nature or the intensity of the communal problem has not changed even after passage of 62 years since then, underlining the importance once again of separation of religion from politics. Nehru had written: 'There are some Muslims in some centres who might be prone to mischief. There are one or two Muslim organisations that have been carrying on objectionable activities... The Hindu communal organisations are definitely aggressive and they can play on the religious or other feelings of the majority community... Agitations like the anti-cow slaughter one are also used for this purpose. I have no doubt that many people who participate in this agitation are influenced by political or like motives and not so much by religious ones. The RSS (Rashtriya Swayamsevak Sangh) utilises this for its own purposes.'[10]

Earlier, Jawaharlal Nehru had reiterated in his fortnightly letter to the Chief Ministers on 5 February 1948: 'There is a strong opinion in the country, with which I sympathise, that no political-religious organisation or rather no organisation confined to a particular religious group and aiming at political ends, should be allowed to function. We have suffered enough from this type of communalism whether it is Muslim or Hindu or Sikh...I do not want, of course, to suppress any legitimate political activity. But the combination of political activity with a religious group is a dangerous one as we know from experience. You will have to give thought to this matter as to what should be done.'[11] Unfortunately, these remained only pious wishes and, during his long tenure of 17 years as Prime Minister, Nehru failed to take any further action.

I firmly believe that unless this issue is addressed with sufficient political resolve so as to carry through a suitable constitution amendment, it will be futile to talk about India as a secular nation. On the basis of the past experience and to meet the concerns expressed by some political parties during the debate on the Constitution (Eightieth) Amendment Bill in 1993 regarding the likely misuse of such an enactment, I would suggest that the amendment bill should be confined only to deregistration of a political party which has religious links and restraining such political party from contesting elections at any level in the country. A political consensus needs to be built up among political parties for the purpose. If any political parties are not prepared to join in the consensus, a strong public opinion will have to be created nationally to isolate them and to go ahead with the constitution amendment, disregarding their opposition. Some persons may consider this a tall order but there is no getting away from such a surgical operation, if the nation is to be saved!

Right to Propagation of Religion

Apart from giving freedom of conscience and permitting free profession and practice of religion, Article 25 gives freedom of propagation of religion. There was considerable controversy about giving this right, and that too as a Fundamental Right. Several members in the Constituent Assembly had spoken against giving such a right but their objections were overruled on the specious plea that it was necessary to give this right in accordance with the compromise which was arrived at with the Muslims and the Christians who had argued that propagation was a duty cast on them by their religion. The recommendations of the Niyogi Committee on Activities of the Christian Missionaries on the subject underline how serious has been the problem of conversion, particularly in the tribal areas.[12]

There are a number of decisions of the High Courts and the Supreme Court according to which *the right to propagation is not a right to conversion.* The activities of Muslims and Christian missionaries in some parts of the country have led to serious law and order problems. The *ghar-wapasi* movement undertaken by the Hindu organisations has also led to communal tensions and agitations in various places. It is high time this problem is nipped in the bud by amending Article 25 to delete the word 'propagation' therefrom.

Doing Away with Protection to Minority Educational Institutions

Articles 25 to 29 of the Constitution are really the crux of secularism, except for the word 'propagation' as discussed earlier. Article 30(1) which gives right to minorities to establish and administer educational institutions is, in one sense, an appendage and need not have been there at all. But this too was inserted, particularly at the instance of the Christians and Anglo-Indians who had a number of educational institutions. There was considerable opposition to this article in the Constituent Assembly, but the Congress party wanted to be generous to the minorities, disregarding the likely long-term implications of encouraging separate identities and undermining spread of secular education. There is no justification to continue this right. If at all, it could be retained for the linguistic minorities. But considering the rapid spread of English as a medium of instruction all over the country, including in the rural areas, due to the forces of globalisation and spread of information technology, it is no longer necessary to give this right even to linguistic minorities.

Deleting Provision for Prohibition of Cow Slaughter

Article 48, though a part of the Directive Principles, has now been elevated in public discourse to the level of a Fundamental Right. The marginal note of this article is innocuously worded as 'organisation of agriculture and animal husbandry'. However, the sting is really in the sentence which asks the state to prohibit the slaughter of cows and calves and other milch and draught cattle. The basic question is whether such a total ban on slaughter of cows and their progeny is justified on any grounds at all except that of the religious sentiments of the Hindus. But even in regard to them, there is no universal demand for a total ban by all Hindus. Most importantly, such a ban is not in keeping with secularism. Particularly in the drought-hit areas in a number of states such as Maharashtra, it is causing large-scale distress to farmers. As I have stated earlier, the Indian

Constitution is a mix of several compromises, particularly insofar as its proclaimed secular ideology is concerned.

Particularly after the BJP government came to power at the Centre in 2014, the demand for banning cow slaughter has gained strength. Effectively 'ban the beef' has become the national motto and another potent instrument in the hands of extremist elements to disturb peace, tranquillity and communal harmony in the country. Jawaharlal Nehru had stoutly opposed the demand for banning cow slaughter during his term and had even staked his prime ministership thereon. Thereafter the stand of the Congress party has changed completely and now it seems to be as much in favour of the total ban as the BJP and the Shiv Sena. It is time to consider seriously whether India can sustain its claim as a secular nation by resorting to such populist measures. I am firmly of the view that all well-meaning people in the country should come forward to strongly oppose the present moves on the subject.

Two Basic Electoral Reforms

Making Voting Compulsory

Secularism in India has remained at the margin mainly because people have not looked at it as their Fundamental Right. In fact, it is considered an important ingredient of vote-bank politics. Unless all eligible voters participate in the elections, the accountability of the political parties cannot be established fully. The government of Gujarat had taken the initiative in the matter by enacting a law for making voting compulsory for elections to village panchayats. The Governor had reserved the bill for approval of the President. In many instances in the past, the central government has looked at a number of proposals received from the state governments in a partisan manner. This bill was one of them and was kept pending by the UPA government for a long time. A Private Members' Bill had also been introduced in Parliament during the UPA regime to make voting compulsory, but it was not supported by the government.

Voting has been made compulsory at least in 30 democracies around the world. They include, among others, Argentina, Australia, Austria, Belgium, Bolivia, Brazil, Costa Rica, Cyprus, Fiji, Greece, Luxembourg, Peru, Singapore, Switzerland and Uruguay. Compulsory voting was introduced in Australia in 1924 when the voter turnout was just about 58 per cent in the elections in 1922. Now Australia consistently boasts of a voter turnout of over 90 per cent. Compulsory voting in Belgium dates back to 1893. Currently, the voter turnout in Belgium is over 90 per cent.[13]

As can be seen, the results achieved are quite striking. The objections raised to making voting compulsory are hardly convincing. For example, it is argued that a person cannot be forced to vote if he does not want to. The law can provide that a person would have the option to go to the polling station and mark his preference on the ballot paper in a separate box showing his disinclination to vote. Another objection which has been raised is that it would be administratively impossible to deal with hundreds and thousands of cases where people default and do not vote. Even this objection is not sustainable as such cases can even be dealt with by post by conveying to the person that he would have to pay the prescribed fine for contravention of the law for compulsory voting. Even announcing on a notice board, in the case of village panchayats, and in newspapers, in other cases, the names of persons who have not voted, could serve the purpose of *shaming the persons*. Particularly in a case like India where the day of voting is declared a public holiday, there is no justification to not vote. *In the final analysis, the question is whether absentee democracy is what we are aiming at.* If all minorities, for example, make it a point to go and vote, their political leverage will increase by leaps and bounds, and their voice cannot be ignored by the political parties any longer. When the voting age was reduced by Rajiv Gandhi government from 21 years to 18 years, doubts were raised about its advisability but we have seen what difference it has made to the political life in the country. Similarly, now voting needs to be made compulsory for the elections to the local bodies, state legislatures and Parliament.

Making 50%+1 Vote Necessary to Win

The first-past-the-post system adopted in India since the British times, though simple to administer, suffers from some important deficiencies. It is seen that in most cases the winning candidate gets negligible votes, at times just 20 to 30 per cent of the total, which is a mockery of representative democracy. In the elections to the UP Assembly held in 2007, 96.53 per cent of the winners polled less than 50 per cent of the votes cast. The corresponding figures were 89.71 per cent in Bihar (2005), 88.89 per cent in Bihar (2006), 81.63 per cent in Tamil Nadu (2006), 93.84 per cent in Jharkhand (2005) and so on. In the Lok Sabha elections in 2004 the corresponding percentage was 59.85.[14]

The National Commission to Review the Working of the Constitution (NCRWC) has also invited attention to this matter and has stated:

> The multiplicity of political parties combined with our Westminster based first-past-the-post system results in a majority of legislators and parliamentarians getting elected on a minority vote. In other words, they usually win by obtaining less than 50 per cent of the votes cast, i.e. with more votes cast against them than in their favour. There are states where 85 per cent to 90 per cent of the legislators

> have won on a minority vote. At the national level, the proportion of MPs who have won on a minority vote is over 67 per cent at an average for the last three Lok Sabha elections. In extreme cases, some candidates have won even on the basis of 13 per cent of the votes polled.
>
> But more importantly in this system often the winning candidate confines his propaganda to his own caste, creed, language or religious group. Particularly in a country like India which is a multi-religious, multi-racial, multi-linguistic and multi-ethnic society a system must be devised which would make it as representative of this diverse community as possible. This can be done only by laying down that a winning candidate must get minimum 50 per cent plus 1 vote. To be able to achieve this a candidate would necessarily have to appeal to a broad spectrum of his constituency. This will be specially important for minorities since they are often neglected and overlooked in the present election campaigns.

At times it is argued that this will prolong the election process and would be administratively impossible to implement. However, this is clearly not based on any in-depth understanding of the issues. With the adoption of the electronic voting system it should not be difficult to hold a second round of voting among the two top candidates who had received the maximum votes. The Election Commission has also favoured this suggestion and has said that it sees no difficulty in its implementation. The NCRWC had also recognised 'the beneficial potential of this system for a more representative democracy'. The commission has recommended that the government and the Election Commission of India should examine this issue in all its aspects, consult various political parties and other interests that might consider themselves affected by this change and evaluate the acceptability and benefits of this system. The Commission recommended a careful and full examination of this issue.[15]

If secularism is to be strengthened in the country, I strongly believe that this electoral reform is absolutely necessary and needs to be implemented as soon as possible.[16]

Centre-State Relations and Bogey of Federalism

During the last few years a number of critical issues facing the country have got bogged down due to the fears expressed by the states about the federalism getting adversely affected. This cry for 'federalism in danger' is as dangerous as the cry of 'religion in danger'. This has affected policies in various areas such as enacting a model law for Lokayuktas, enactment of a central legislation for the Central Bureau of Investigation, reorganisation of the Railway Police Protection Force, setting up of a federal police agency and so on. When the Constitution was prepared, the problems of law and order, terrorism, naxalism, organised crime, and crime with international ramifications were not serious enough and therefore the subjects 'public order' and 'police' were put in the State List. Ideally, both these should have been put in the Concurrent List, as is the case in a number of Western democracies. As a result, the states have been objecting to the role of central government in these matters. But this has not prevented the states from relying on the deployment of central para-military forces, when the occasion demanded. But restricting the role of the central government has led to cases such as Ayodhya debacle, Godhra riots and major communal riots in a number of states. Time has therefore come to take a serious view on amendment of the Constitution. Needless to say, federalism will be relevant only if the country survives!

These issues are particularly relevant if communal violence and communal riots are to be dealt with effectively. The experience so far shows that unless the central government is enabled to take an active role in the matter, merely making available to the states central paramilitary forces and intelligence inputs from central agencies will not be adequate.

Restructuring Police Departments

Experience has shown that weaknesses and inadequacies of police have been largely responsible for starting or escalating communal violence. The root cause of this is the politicisation and communalisation of police in various states. Several judicial commissions of inquiry appointed on major communal riots have strongly brought out this point.

Reference must be made in this context to the decision of the Supreme Court in the public interest litigation on non-implementation of the recommendations of the National Police Commission. The final decision of the court came only in September 2006, nearly 12 years after the filing of the PILs. Though inordinately delayed, the Supreme Court laid down guidelines for reorganisation of the police departments in the states and at the Centre. Though nearly a decade has elapsed since the decision of the Supreme Court, most major state governments have not implemented the court orders. For example, the data collected by the Bureau of Police Research and Development (BPR&D) for the year 2013 shows that almost 80 per cent of Superintendents of Police (SPs) in districts across the country got transferred within two years of their tenure in a district. More than 50 per cent got transferred in less than a year. According to the data, UP has been the worst offender in terms of transferring officers before their two-year tenure is complete. Even officers senior to SPs have not been spared. As per the data, in 2013, 114 range DIGs faced transfers within a year of their tenure. As many as 48 were transferred within two years. (*IE*, November 29, 2015: 7) For some strange reason, the Supreme Court has been reluctant to haul up the defaulting states for contempt of court.

Another matter of serious concern is the politicisation and communalisation of police. In this connection special mention must be made of the statements of L. K. Advani who had spearheaded the Babri Masjid agitation. He has written in his autobiography, *My Country My Life*:

> I recall vividly an experience en route from Ayodhya to Lucknow [on December 6, 1992 after demolition of the Babri Masjid]. In spite of strict security all along the 135-kilometre journey, I could see people engaged in celebrations everywhere. Within half an hour of our departure from Ayodhya, our car was stopped by the police. On seeing that the car carried Pramod Mahajan and me, a senior officer of the UP government walked up to us [and] said, 'Advaniji, *kuch bacha to nahin na? Bilkul saaf kar diya na*?' (I hope nothing of the structure is surviving and that it has been totally raised to the ground.) I am recounting this incident only to highlight the general mood of the populace, including employees and officials of the state government, after the tragic development in Ayodhya—that of jubilation.[17]

The National Police Commission in its eighth and concluding report submitted in May 1981 had made one significant recommendation. An officer who has functioned as the DGP /IGP, after his retirement from service, shall not be eligible for any employment under the Government of India or under the state government or in any public undertaking in which GOI or the state government have a financial interest.[18] This is equally relevant for the senior Indian Administrative Service officers. This very critical recommendation ought to have been acted upon expeditiously. There have been any number of instances where senior police [and IAS] officers who had obliged the political party in power during the communal riots have been handsomely rewarded. One can cite dozens of instances to support this. I would suggest that even now it is not too late to accept this recommendation. I would like to suggest only one amplification thereof, namely, such officers will not also be given political party tickets to contest elections during a cooling-off period of three years.

If a sense of confidence is to be created amongst the minorities that they will be treated fairly, justly and their life and property will be safeguarded, all efforts will have to be made to deal with the communal bias in the police. The precepts of secularism, safeguarding the interests of the minorities and importance of human rights are some of the subjects which need to be included in the syllabus of police training institutions. In the refresher courses organised for field police officers and constabulary, actual case studies of communal riots, findings of official inquiries or judicial commissions of inquiries must be placed before them for discussion. Knowledgeable representatives of minority communities could be invited for interaction with the police personnel in the training sessions. Unfortunately, this important aspect has been totally lost sight of.

It is also necessary to give sufficient representation to minorities in the police services. In this context, the example of the Rapid Action Force of the central government which is often deployed during communal riots is noteworthy. Conscious efforts have been made by the central government to give representation to minorities in this force. This example needs to be replicated in the states.

The indication of how the winds are blowing since the coming to power of the BJP government at the Centre in 2014 is the recent instruction issued by the home ministry to the National Crime Records Bureau (NCRB) not to publish the data on Muslims in police. The publication of such data first began 16 years ago. It is for the first time that such a ban has been imposed. (*Indian Express*, 30 November 2015: 1) Such efforts are counter-productive for the success of secularism. It is interesting to see that the NCRB report for 2013 showed that there were 1.08 lakh Muslim police personnel who accounted for 6.27 per cent of the total strength of 17.31 lakh police in the country, as compared to their percentage of 7.55 in 2007. Public pressure must be brought on the government to revise this decision to ensure that data on Muslims in police will be published each year.

Rule of Law and Reality

Even if police departments are restructured as above and other changes suggested herein are effected, unless rule of law is established in the country, nothing substantial can be achieved. This is particularly true in dealing with an important and sensitive subject like secularism.

Reference must be made to the important provisions of Sections 153-A and 153-B of Indian Penal Code (IPC) which have largely remained on paper. The 'majesty of law' about which a common citizen hears time and again is supposed to have laid down that 'howsoever high you may be, the law is above you'. This is certainly not true so far as the high and mighty in public life are concerned.

Full powers need to be given to the senior police officers to directly prosecute persons infringing these provisions, without the necessity of obtaining the approval of the state government. Experience has shown that the state governments look at this question entirely from a political point of view and withhold the approval for prosecution or even reject the proposal altogether. It is seen that cases filed under these Sections are often withdrawn later at the behest of the government for political ends. If secularism is to be translated into reality, communalism will have to be put down with a firm hand. And this would be possible only by ensuring that the above provisions of IPC are made effective. The National Commission to Review the Working of the Constitution has also said that 'effective implementation of laws is lacking. This deserves the highest degree of attention.' (p. 87)

Towards this end, as recommended by the Second Administrative Reforms Commission (SARC), the provision contained in Section 196 CrPC requiring prior sanction of Union or state governments or the district magistrate for initiating prosecution for offences under Sections 153A, 153B, 295A[19] and 505[20] of IPC, be deleted. It has also rightly suggested that the punishment for communal offences be enhanced, and special courts should be set up for speedy disposal of the cases. I fully agree with the recommendation of SARC that a separate law to deal with communal violence is not required. The UPA government's proposal in this regard had led to bitter confrontation between the states and the Centre and also the political parties which were in opposition then. Strengthening of the provisions of the IPC and CrPC will be adequate to deal with the situation.

Last 69 years since Independence have seen not only repeated incidents of communal violence, as brought out above, but regrettably some of these riots had literally turned into massacres. To recall, a few of these were: Jabalpur riot in 1961, Ahmedabad riot in 1969, anti-Sikh riots in Delhi in 1984, Mumbai riots in 1992-93 and Godhra riots in 2002. Against this background, it is necessary to make a special provision to deal with genocides such as these. The law should provide to make such offences cognisable and non-bailable and much stricter punishment extending up to life imprisonment. Fear of law must be inculcated unambiguously, and anti-social elements which generally take advantage of these situations and the government functionaries who either connive with them or even support them must also be dealt with severely.

Unusual times call for unusual solutions. Experience has shown that hardly any worthwhile action has been taken so far against government functionaries who were handling these situations and had failed miserably. Time has come to examine whether the provisions of the law of torts should be extended to all those remiss in handling the genocides. Class action suits need to be initiated in such cases as it would be impossible for the individual victims to file cases against the concerned powerful politicians and police functionaries. It is only by applying the provisions of the law of torts that they would become seriously aware of their responsibilities.

Another legislation which has wholly remained on paper is the Religious Institutions (Prevention of Misuse) Act, 1988. Rajiv Gandhi government must be given credit for enacting this legislation but it has remained only as a showpiece. It was seen during the Punjab agitation that there was a large-scale misuse of Gurudwaras by the terrorists for preaching their ideology. In Jammu and Kashmir the separatists have been using Friday Namaz gatherings to launch their ideological offensive against the central government and its organisations. Hardly any action has been taken in these cases. Same is true of the Places of Worship (Special Provisions) Act, 1991 which too has not been acted upon.

It is equally frustrating to see that communal speeches made by candidates have not been adequately dealt with under the provisions of the Representation of People Act, 1951. In this context, the observation of the Supreme Court in one of the cases is significant. The Court had said: So long as communal political parties are not banned from participating in political life of the country, there is very little that the courts can do to restrain. Reference must also be made to the recommendation of the National Commission to Review the Working of the Constitution in this regard. The commission has recommended: 'Any election campaigning on the basis of caste or religion and any attempt to spread caste and communal hatred during elections should be punishable with *mandatory imprisonment*. If such acts are done at the instance of the candidate or his election agents, these *would be punishable with disqualification*.' (p. 87) Unfortunately, no action has been taken by the government on this recommendation.

Adoption of Inquisitorial System

The experience of investigation of crimes in communal riots has raised serious questions, whether it be anti-Sikh riots in Delhi or riots in Mumbai or Godhra or any other major communal riots in the country. There is a widely prevalent view that such cases are not investigated vigorously or objectively and the police often act under political pressure or in a communal manner favouring one community or the other. It would be recalled that in some cases even a plea was made to the high courts and Supreme Court that a special investigation team (SIT) may be appointed by the court and the investigation may also be carried out under the supervision of the court. Such petitions were agreed to by the Supreme Court in Godhra cases but obviously this cannot be done in every case considering the workload of the High Courts and the Supreme Court. It is therefore time to consider whether in cases involving serious communal riots, the French model of 'police judiciare' should be adopted.

Justice Malimath committee on reforms of criminal justice system has noted that:

> *The inquisitorial system is certainly efficient in the sense that the investigation is supervised by the judicial magistrate which results in a high rate of conviction.* The committee on balance felt that a fair trial and, in particular, fairness to the accused, are better protected in

> the adversarial system. However, the committee felt that some of the good features of the inquisitorial system can be adopted to strengthen the adversarial system and to make it more effective. This includes the duty of the court to search for truth, to assign a pro-active role to the judges, to give directions to the investigating officers and prosecution agencies in the matter of investigation and leading evidence with the object of seeking the truth and focusing on justice to victims.[21]

B. K. Nehru, former civil servant, diplomat and Governor, in his book *Thoughts On Our Present Discontents* has invited attention to the fact that:

> In a country where telling lies in a court of law is not regarded as immoral, and where the police is unfortunately not always above manufacturing evidence and extorting confession, a system of this kind [inquisitorial] would, ... be definitely more suitable to our needs than our present procedures. As a result of a thorough magisterial investigation already made, the onus to prove his innocence lies heavily on the accused. This will shock our lawyers who have inherited Anglo-Saxon prejudices along with their system, but there is reason to believe that there are fewer miscarriages of justice under the continental system and much greater enforcement of the law than is prevalent in India today.[22]

The Law Commission in its seventy-seventh report submitted in 1978, had recommended that 'Although we have adopted the accusatorial system the trial judge should not play an altogether passive role, but must take greater interest and elicit such information as may be helpful in finding the truth'.[23]

In spite of these valid arguments there are many legal luminaries who are strongly opposed to any change-over from the existing system. I had in my book *The Judiciary and Governance in India* (2008) examined these facets in the light of experience in a number of cases. I had stated: '*This touching faith in the present state of Indian criminal justice system is difficult to understand.* Even a cursory look at the data regarding the conviction rate should be instructive in this regard. In 1968 the conviction rate was 70 per cent. In 1999 it came down to below 40 per cent and in 2003 it was 35 per cent. In 2006 it was estimated to be below 30 per cent. According to the then Chief Justice of Bombay High Court Justice M. B. Shah, the conviction rate was just 5 per cent. I had suggested that a trial should be given to the inquisitorial system on a pilot basis in selected districts. (Godbole 2008: 440-4) This has assumed new urgency in the context of increasing threats to secularism. In all major cases with a bearing on secularism in recent years, it has come to light that the police investigations and convictions leave much to be desired. This has created a great sense of insecurity among the victims of these riots who mostly belonged to minorities. I therefore believe that the time has come to take a decision that at least in cases of serious communal riots, to begin with, inquisitorial system should be adopted. This one single step will go a long way in reassuring the minorities that the government is serious about making a reality of secularism.

To Sum Up

The above analysis shows that a great deal remains to be done if secularism is to become a way of life in India. This will be possible only if there is a real political, social and intellectual commitment to it and, the state and central governments, the political parties, the civil society and the media strive for it.

Notes

1. Some portions of the speech have been italicized for emphasis.
2. Gopal S. and Iyengar Uma, eds., *The Essential Writings of Jawaharlal Nehru*, vol. I, Oxford University Press, New Delhi, 2003, p. 186.
3. Government of India, Ministry of Information and Broadcasting, *Independence and After—A Collection of the More Important Speeches of Jawaharlal Nehru from September 1946 to May 1949*, New Delhi, 1949, pp. 47-51.
4. Madhav Godbole, *Unfinished Innings—Recollections and Reflections of a Civil Servant*, Orient Longman, New Delhi, 1996.
5. Madhav Godbole, 'Ayodhya and India's Mahabharat: Constitutional Issues and Proprieties', *Economic and Political Weekly*, 27 May 2006.
6. Madhav Godbole, *The Judiciary and Governance in India*, Rupa & Co., New Delhi, 2008, p. 69.
7. Gopal S., *Jawaharlal Nehru—An Anthology*, Oxford University Press, Delhi, 1980, p. 330.
8. Jahagirdar R.A., 'Secularism Revisited', *The Radical Humanist*, February 2015 (p. 24) and March 2015 (pp. 35-6).
9. Kashyap Subhash C., *History of the Parliament of India*, vol. 4, Shipra Publications, Delhi, 1997, p. 91.
10. Gopal S. and Iyengar Uma, ed., *The Essential Writings of Jawaharlal Nehru*, vol. I, Oxford University Press, New Delhi, 2003, pp. 190-1.
11. Parthasarathy G., ed., *Jawaharlal Nehru—Letters to Chief Ministers 1947-1964*, Jawaharlal Nehru Memorial Fund, New Delhi, 1985, p. 60.
12. Niyogi Committee Report on Christian Missionary Activities, 1956, *http://en. wikipedia.org/wiki.*
13. Godbole Madhav, *Good Governance Never on India's Radar*, Rupa & Co., New Delhi, 2014, pp. 174-5, 248-9.
14. Gopalaswami N., Political Parties and Elections: Some Issues, *Journal of Constitutional and Parliamentary Studies*, vol. 41, Nos. 3-4, New Delhi, July-December 2007, p. 196.

15. Government of India, *Review of the Working of the Constitution, Report of the National Commission to Review the Working of the Constitution*, vol. II, Book 1, New Delhi, 2002, pp. 91-2.
16. According to the Nepal's Ambassador to India, Deep Kumar Upadyay, Nepal's newly promulgated Constitution is the most progressive in South Asia with its provisions of 33 per cent reservation for women. It also has both first-past-the-post system as well as proportional representation. This combination of the two ensures that minorities' representation is taken care of. (*Indian Express*, September 24, 2015: 1)
17. Advani L.K., *My Country, My Life*, Rupa & Co., New Delhi, 2008, p. 402.
18. Government of India, Ministry of Home Affairs, *Eighth and Concluding Report of the National Police Commission*, New Delhi, 1981, p. 52.
19. (Deliberate and malicious acts, intended to outrage religious feelings of any class by insulting its religion or religious beliefs).
20. (Statements conducing to public mischief) Sub-sections (1)(c) (with intent to incite, or which is likely to incite, any class or community of persons to commit any offence against any other class or community), (2) (statements creating or promoting enmity, hatred or ill-will between classes) and (3) (offences under Sub-section (2) committed in place of worship, etc.)
21. Government of India, Ministry of Home Affairs, *Report of the Committee on Reforms of Criminal Justice System (Justice V.S. Malimath Committee)*, vol. I, New Delhi, 2003, pp. 265-6.
22. Nehru B.K., *Thoughts on Our Present Discontents*, Allied Publishers, Delhi, 1986, pp. 111-2.
23. Government of India, Ministry of Law and Justice, *Law Commission of India, Seventy-seventh Report on Delays and Arrears in Trial Courts*, New Delhi, 1978, p. 157.

3

'THESE COMMUNAL RIOTS GO ON HAPPENING. HAVE WE ADDRESSED THAT PROBLEM?'

The B.G. Deshmukh Memorial lecture scheduled to be delivered this month by Madhav Godbole, *former Union home secretary, was cancelled at the last minute, presumably because it questions several decisions of the BJP government. The lecture—Is India a Secular Nation?—has now been circulated widely.* Godbole, *who was pursued by the organisers (led by the Maharashtra Chief Secretary) to deliver the lecture for the third time, was told about the cancellation over a phone call with a terse email the following day confirming it. He remains firm on the need to separate politics and religion through a constitutional process.* Prachi Pinglay-Plumber *caught up with him at his home in Pune. Excerpts from the interview:*

Outlook magazine, 15 April 2016.

What's the reaction to your address?

Some people felt that this needed to be said. Unfortunately, few speak out these days. That's why they were quite pleasantly surprised that it was a blunt, open speech.

What is your definition of secularism?

As I have said before, there is no authentic definition of the word so far, which is the main stumbling block in its implementation. There is a need for a national debate on this. As I see it, secularism does not mean irreligiousness. A synthesis of the ethical and moral precepts of all religions should be the guiding force of governance of the country. But religion should strictly be a personal matter and it should have nothing to do with the affairs of the state or the politics of the country. The state must be equidistant from all religions.

You say secularism has lost credibility.

This has been my impression, having seen it through the years. The earliest was Emergency and the whole family planning campaign, which created quite a stir. It was clearly a blow to secularism. Then came the 1984 riots. I was home secretary in 1991 when these cases against the officers came up because many of them were due for promotions and deputation. I took the position that until cases were decided, no one would be given promotion. I also lived through the demolition of the Babri Masjid.

Can you tell us what happened then?

It was shocking. We were convinced that Kalyan Singh could not be believed, that the state government could not be relied upon to take any action. The only way the structure could be saved was by imposing President's rule and to guard the structure. We were requesting the Prime Minister for several weeks to take the decision. We had specifically mentioned this decision must be taken before *kar sevaks* arrived at the site because then your options would be closed once the monument was surrounded by a lakh or two lakh people.

That decision was never taken then?

The proposal to impose President's rule was to be preceded by taking action under Section 355, which would have enabled the government to deploy forces without the state government's consent. I wanted the forces to move in the middle of the night to take over that structure; then the proposal could be put to the cabinet at midnight, without circulating the note earlier (because in Delhi nothing remains a secret). After the forces had taken charge at the monument, during the night the President could be asked to sign the ordinance.

We had 20,000 central paramilitary forces deployed at a distance of 10 km from Ayodhya—doing nothing because without President's rule the Centre cannot act. They were just waiting for an order to deploy them. When the demolition started, I telephoned the Home Secretary in UP, the Home Minister spoke to the CM requesting him to call for forces. He never did. The interesting bit was that he had given instructions to police saying no firing should be carried out. That's the prerogative of a state government. As a result, the Masjid was demolished and we all know what happened after.

You talk about provisions that sought to set the secular tone in the country.

In fact, the first item I talk about is the separation of religion from politics. If you see the Constituent Assembly debates, this was the first resolution of substance (1948). This was the first major legislative initiative by the Constituent Assembly to pass a resolution. There was practically unanimous support for it. Ananthasayanam Ayyangar moved it. Nehru supported it. He continued to write to Chief Ministers in his fortnightly letters about how important it was but during the 17 years of his tenure as PM he took no action. We need a major constitutional amendment for this. Then came the 80th Constitution Amendment Bill, which was moved by P.V. Narasimha Rao after the demolition of the Babri Masjid. I have sat in the official gallery in Parliament for years. But I have never seen a bill piloted the way the 80th Constitution Amendment Bill was. There was hardly any consultation. The BJP was naturally opposed to it, but I have never seen an important bill being sent to the select committee with only seven days to report back. The Congress was not really serious. It was just window dressing.

Do you feel that past reluctance of Congress has done more damage than the present right-wing propaganda?

Yes. Who gave this much latitude to right-wing forces to operate in politics? All these people did. During the Emergency and after, when the Leftists were so close to the Congress, they never prevailed upon them to bring this bill. They could have.

Did all political parties tacitly accept or openly support religious politics?

The main concerns of the founding fathers were two: Firstly, to remove communal electorates, and secondly, to remove the reservation of seats on the basis of population strength for particular religious groups. They were eminently successful in persuading the minorities but then they had to compromise. So, the right to propagation of religion (as desired by Muslims and Christians) was agreed to. And it was given constitutional sanctity by making it a fundamental right despite severe resistance. In any case, we cannot hold them accountable to contemporary standards.

How was cow slaughter discussed then?

There was no real debate. Two or three staunch Hindus spoke on the subject and it was passed. Nehru was opposed to banning the cow slaughter. In the pre-independence days, Nehru had said 'cow is like a horse to me' and people wanted to haul him before the court of law. But the same Congress party is now supporting the ban.

That brings us to communalisation.

Reluctance to separate religion and politics is the biggest issue that India faces, and no one is prepared to address it. Look at the demolition of the Babri Masjid. However sacred the place may have been, one cannot rewrite history. At that time Rao said that the Masjid would be built. Nothing happened. Communalisation of the polity is the antithesis of secularism. Year after year, communal riots go on happening. Have we addressed that problem? Is there a rule of law in the country? If there were, we'd not have this situation.

You made several recommendations...

Take the case of Sections 153A and 153B pertaining to communal hate speeches. Very few cases are filed compared to the number of speeches made. The cases are also mostly withdrawn. All powers are with the government. So, I am suggesting these powers should be given to senior police officers. Take away these powers from the government and give them to senior police officers so they will be accountable to court for implementation of these provisions. Then, there is need to increase representation of minorities in the police. It has come to the stage when even data is not being released. We have to ensure the data is released and have representation of minorities in the police.

Tell us about the inquisitorial system you recommend.

The inquisitorial system (as opposed to accusatorial) operates in a number of places in Europe. Under this, the police investigate under the supervision of a magistrate. At every stage the magistrate considers the evidence and decides its merit and if the investigation should go on. It does not stop till the magistrate is satisfied that it's a fit case to reach the court. This is why acquittals are rare in Europe.

Is there any acceptance for this?

There is opposition from lawyers who say this would compromise the main principle that a person is presumed to be innocent until proven guilty. But I disagree. The police, of course, will have a problem. It's a major debate but it should at least be made applicable in the case of communal riots. This one step will create a sense of confidence in the minorities—assure them we are serious about implementing secularism.

4

'SECULARISM WAS MEANT TO INTEGRATE US, BUT HAS TORN US APART'

'At no time since Independence the issue of whether we are a secular country or whether we are a Hindu Rashtra has come up in this manner.'

'This is the most important issue which is going to decide whether we remain together as one country or not.'

'We can't hold together until you stick to the principle of secularism.'

'It is not a choice,' former home secretary Dr Madhav Godbole tells Rediff.com's Archana Masih.

'FOR A COUNTRY to be secular, it is not enough that its Constitution and government are secular. It is equally necessary that its society and individual citizens are secular,' Dr Madhav Godbole writes in his just released book, *Secularism — India at a Crossroads.*

Rediff.com, 2 September 2016.

Dr Godbole served as a bureaucrat for 33 years before resigning as Union Home Secretary after the Babri Masjid demolition in 1992. The author of over 15 books, a lecture he was to deliver on secularism at the Maharashtra secretariat in Mumbai was mysteriously cancelled.

In a two-part interview with *Rediff.com*'s Archana Masih at his home in Pune, Dr Godbole says there should be an agreed definition of secularism and minorities, the need for a commission on secularism and wonders whether India is a secular country today.

What are your concerns about India in its 70th year?

We need to take a stock of where we are; some aspects of the Constitution need to be re-examined seriously. The slogan of federalism being in danger is as disturbing as religion being in danger.

The Goods and Services Tax (GST) bill has taken 13 years. It shows the manner in which we function in the country.

In the twenty-first century, the world is going in a different direction and we are going at snail's pace. Are we going to function in the same manner or are we going to take stock of how we are going to function in the coming years?

Let us take some examples: When the Lokpal Bill was being discussed, there was a proposal to have such a model law in the states for Lokayuktas. It was vehemently opposed by states likes Tamil Nadu and West Bengal, saying that it goes beyond federalism.

All the law was proposing was to lay down principles on the basis of which states should formulate their own laws.

This recommendation for Lokayuktas has been there for 20–25 years and we have still not been able to act on it—and that proposal was given up.

In another case, a continental-sized country like India does require a federal police. This is the only Western style democracy of this size which has no federal police. This proposal has been opposed on the ground of federalism.

A central law for the Central Bureau of Investigation (CBI) has been opposed on the ground of federalism. A simple thing like having one police for the railways has also been objected to.

When the Constitution was framed, there were no concerns of major crimes with international ramifications. That is why the founding fathers put the subjects of 'police' and 'public order' in the States List. Isn't it time to take a fresh look at it?

But we are so engrossed in petty politics that these larger issues relevant to the country in the coming years are not being looked at.

Are our political parties unable to rise above politics to address the larger issues?

It is interesting that at one time or the other in the last 60-65 years, almost all political parties have now been in power. They have seen it from inside and outside. In spite of that, it has made no difference to their thinking.

I would have expected half a dozen people from various political parties to at least raise these issues and to press for them politically, but they haven't.

Take the case of the Delhi anti-Sikh riots, Bombay riots, or Gujarat riots—there is a proposal that the Centre must have power in extreme cases to deploy central forces in the state and be responsible for managing the situation till it comes back to normal. What is wrong with this?

What is important is how we are going to address issues that are going to be relevant for the next 15-25 years. This bothers me and there is no thought and preparedness in the political system to look at these issues.

Apart from federalism, what are the other issues that concern you?

Secularism. We are really at crossroads.

At no time since Independence has this issue of whether we are a secular country or whether we are a Hindu Rashtra come up in this manner on the streets and in public discourse as it has now.

This is the most important issue which is going to decide whether we remain together as one country or not.

According to me, this is the one single proposition which holds the country together.

Twenty per cent of the population consists of minorities. 14.5 per cent are Muslims. In the next 15-20 years the minorities will be 30 to 35 per cent.

The country can't hold together until you stick to the principle of secularism. It is not a choice before the country.

The composition of the country makes it incumbent on you to adhere to and make a success, but there are very serious problems.

Therefore, in my book I have proposed major constitutional amendments. Are we prepared to take a look at the concept of secularism itself?

You have also mentioned there is no definition of secularism.

When the Constitution was made, there was no agreement among the members of the Constituent Assembly for calling it secular.

Some thought it would be interpreted as secularism in the Western concept and would mean the total negation of religion which will never be accepted in India.

Secondly, when Pakistan has declared itself a Muslim state, do we have to declare ourselves as a secular state was the other question.

If at all, we should declare ourselves a Hindu state was the demand by some at that time. Finally, the idea of declaring it a secular state was given up.

It (secularism) was introduced by Indira Gandhi during the Emergency. There was no discussion on this because almost all the Opposition leaders were in jail and the press was under censorship.

Therefore, you can't really say that it has become part of the Constitution in the real sense because there was no debate and acceptance.

Then an effort was made to introduce a Constitution amendment bill after the Babri Masjid was demolished for the separation of religion from politics. It fell through because the Congress did not bother to consult all political parties.

What is the definition of 'secular'?

When you say the country should be secular, people should know what secularism is. There should be an agreed definition of secularism.

The whole concept of secularism is based on minorities and there is no definition of minorities in the Constitution.

What the Constitution did was take whatever definition of minorities was adopted by the Britishers and the same categories were continued without any discussion.

The time has come to examine who all are minorities. For example, Muslims are already 14.5 per cent, we are the second largest Muslim country. According to estimates, by 2050, India will be the largest Muslim country in the world.

This kind of a huge population, is it a minority?

Unfortunately, people don't read these days, including the much-publicised social media. For example, in the debates on the adoption bill during the Janata period, one of the prominent Muslim members said, 'We are a minority, but we are not a such a small minority that you can do whatever you want with it, we have a leverage and we will exercise that leverage.'

For example, when the Education Bill in Kerala went before the Supreme Court in the 1960s, the Supreme Court in that context defined minorities as a community less than 50 per cent. If that definition is carried to the logical conclusion, does it mean that till Muslims exceed more than 50 per cent of the Indian population they continue to be minorities?

In Jammu and Kashmir, Hindus in Jammu call themselves a minority, but they are in a majority. Hindus in Punjab call themselves a minority because in certain parts they are in a minority.

These issues are important in the Indian context and cannot be pushed under the carpet any longer.

It is a difficult problem, therefore, no political party wants to talk about it.

In spite of our differences we Indians have a secular ethos. Are we, as a people, secular?

No, I don't agree. It is a myth that has been created.

What has kept us together if we are not secular?

It is true that several religions were absorbed, but it doesn't mean that because it happened in the past, it is happening today.

The question is whether we are a secular country today. We are not. The religious divides are becoming wider every day.

Did this division begin with the demolition of the Babri Masjid? When did our secular ethos start wavering?

The demolition happened because of the manner in which we worked our secularism.

Secularism was one idea which was meant to integrate this country. It is a tragedy that this one idea has torn us apart.

Hindus believe there is a pampering of the minorities and therefore don't want secularism.

Muslims believe they have got nothing out of secularism and don't want it and want a separate identity.

When Sikh militancy was acute, the same thing was happening and the same is happening today in Jammu and Kashmir.

Therefore, I propose that there should be a commission on secularism to whom any member of the public can raise any matter which can have an adverse implication on secularism.

There should be a televised public hearing and it will give a speaking order which will be binding on the government.

If anybody is unhappy, she/he can file a petition in the Supreme Court and that decision will be final.

Then this will be an enforceable right, today it is an entrenched right

So, is it a myth that we are secular?

Look around and ask yourself if we are a secular country. There are extreme communal pronouncements by Muslims and by Hindus.

Every few years there are major communal riots in the country.

I feel ordinary Indians, at the people-to-people level, are secular.

The amity at the people-to-people level gets submerged when you bring in politics. Therefore, you need to separate religion from politics.

This is something our founding fathers were acutely aware of and in 1947 a resolution was moved that there should be a complete separation of religion from politics.

That resolution was passed almost unanimously except for one Muslim member who opposed it and we are in 2016 and it has still not been implemented.

There were occasions when the Congress was in power during Nehru, Indira, and Rajiv's governments when there was a two-thirds majority, so the Congress cannot proclaim itself as a secular party if it has not taken action on this basic issue that governs secularism.

Now it is going to be increasingly difficult with a rightist party at the Centre, but even now an effort must be made to build up a societal agreement.

Addressing a question that you raised, a common man has no problem with dealing with a Muslim, Christian or Sikh, but why is it that politically there is a problem?

That is something which can be dealt with only if we remove religion from politics.

5

INDIA IN SEARCH OF SECULARISM

DEMONETISATION SHOCK THERAPY has had some unexpected fallouts, some of which are distinctly in national interest. One of them is that the clamour for making India a *Hindu Rashtra* has, at least for the time being, fallen off from the national agenda of the ruling dispensation at the Centre. Since the coming to power of the BJP government headed by Narendra Modi in May 2014, for the first time since independence, serious questions have been raised about whether it would not be more appropriate for India to declare itself a Hindu Nation. Any such major change in the Constitution would require two-thirds majority in both houses of Parliament and approval by half the state legislatures. The BJP and its supporting parties do not have such a mandate. But this should not make us complacent. For, the basic issue raised in this debate is important for the very survival of India as a country.

The precepts of secularism are firmly entrenched in Indian Constitution as Fundamental Rights. India's is one of the

---

The Week, 25 December 2016.

very few constitutions in the world which has made such an unequivocal commitment to secularism. The Supreme Court of India has declared that secularism is a part of the basic structure of the Constitution and Parliament has no power to dilute or erode it in any way.

However, when Constitution was being framed, due to political compulsions of the time, several compromises had to be made to arrive at a consensus on its adoption. It would be useful to recapitulate some of them. Since India had firm grounding in and commitment to the teachings of various major religions, declaring India a secular state, in the western sense of the term, which would have made it an atheist nation, was clearly not acceptable to the Constituent Assembly, though all basic precepts of secularism such as freedom of religion and conscience etc. were firmly grounded in the Constitution. For the same reasons, there was no agreement on defining the term secular in the Constitution. Further, unreasonable demands put forth by the majority and the minority communities had to be accommodated in the larger interest of getting unanimity on adoption of the Constitution. This led to adoption of two very significant provisions which have come to haunt the polity even after a lapse of over six decades. The first pertains to the provision regarding ban on cow slaughter. Such a provision could not be justified on any reasonable definition of secularism. However, it was included in Article 48 of the Constitution as a part of the Directive Principles of State Policy. All that could be said to the credit of the Constitution-makers was that, in spite of persistent demands by a section of the majority community, this provision was not included as a Fundamental Right. Jawaharlal Nehru was totally opposed to this provision and he resisted its implementation during his term as Prime Minister by even offering to resign on this issue. Times have changed so completely that the Congress party is now strongly in favour of an all-India ban on cow slaughter.

The second important compromise pertained to enactment of a uniform civil code for all citizens. There was extensive, erudite and animated discussion on this subject in the Constituent Assembly. One of the finest speeches was by B. R. Ambedkar, Chairman of the Drafting Committee. In his speech, Ambedkar had brought out the fallacy of the argument put forth by Muslim members that Muslims were governed by the Shariat law since ages. Ambedkar had shown that in several provinces, including the Bombay Province, the United Province and the Frontier Province, Muslims were governed by the Hindu law. It was only when the British, in keeping with their policy of divide and rule, enacted Shariat law that, over a period of time, Muslims came to be governed by it. Even at that time choice was given to Muslims to decide if and when to opt for Shariat law. In spite of this very clear enunciation, the Muslim members were strongly opposed to any provision being made for a uniform civil code. The members of the majority community, on the other hand, wanted this provision to be included as a Fundamental Right. As a matter of compromise, this provision too was finally included in Article 44 as a Directive Principle of State Policy.

Yet another contentious issue pertained to permitting propagation of religion as a Fundamental Right. Overriding vociferous objections of several sections of the Constituent Assembly, as a compromise, and in deference to the wishes of the Muslim and Christian members, who pleaded that propagation of religion was an obligation cast on them by their religions, right to propagation became a Fundamental Right. India must be the only country in the world which has gone this far to meet the demands of its minorities.

Yet another provision made as a Fundamental Right, which has become controversial, is the right given to minorities to establish and administer educational institutions. Over the years this has created such a severe sense of injustice that, particularly after the persecution by the Communist government in West Bengal, even leading Hindu educational and cultural institutions such as Ramakrishna Mission claimed that they were minority institutions and should have the same freedom and right to establish and administer their educational institutions. These cases were fought by them right up to the Supreme Court. As expected, their claims were negatived. But it raises an important question whether in a secular society, minority educational institutions ought to be given such a preferential treatment.

India, being a multi-religious, multi-lingual, multi-racial and multi-cultural country, has no real option but to be secular. Even at present, nearly 20 per cent of India's population comprises religious minorities. By 2050, this figure is likely to cross 30 per cent. By that time India would also be the country with the largest Muslim population in the world. Sustaining a homogeneous society consisting of such diverse elements is a challenge, but it will not be new to India. India has assimilated various religions and cultures since times immemorial and has prospered culturally, socially and in every other sense of the term. Religious conflicts and animosities, fundamentalist rigidities are of recent origin and with a spirit of accommodation on all sides it should not be difficult to deal with them effectively.

When the founding fathers made secularism a basic feature of the Constitution, it was expected that this would become a cementing force among all religious communities. However, experience over the last 70 years has shown that secularism has become a bone of contention, among all communities whether belonging to the majority community or the minorities. It is difficult to believe that none of the communities is satisfied with the manner in which secularism has been practised. While the Hindus believe that minority communities are being unduly appeased as vote banks, the minority communities feel that injustice has been done to them in all matters of development and their welfare. It is important to underline that this compartmentalisation has led to serious feeling of neglect and alienation among minorities. The walls of separation have been raised so high that Parliament did not think it important to spare any time to discuss important findings of the Sachar Committee Report on the welfare of Muslims. The Justice Ranganath Mishra Commission Report on minorities met with the same fate.

The adverse effects of majoritarianism have become starkly evident in recent years. The series of Constitution amendments undertaken by Indira Gandhi government during the Emergency in 1975-77, which effectively rewrote the Constitution and demolished its basic structure, was an eye-opener of what majoritarianism can do. These trends are again becoming evident since coming to power of the BJP government on its own strength in 2014. Democracy can function only with its empowered institutions and the mechanisms of checks and balances. Increasingly both of these are getting compromised and raising serious fears about creeping democratic deficit.

Against this background, it is imperative that secularism is not permitted to be eroded in any way. Time has come to create an institutional mechanism by which the precepts of secularism entrenched in the Constitution are translated in the governance of the country. I have therefore been advocating the setting up of a Constitutional Commission on Secularism which would adjudicate on the functioning of not just the government but all institutions and sections of society to ensure that their policies, programmes and actions do not jeopardise secularism. This commission will have to be somewhat different than other commissions such as the National Human Rights Commission or the National Commission on Scheduled Castes, and its decisions will have to be not just recommendatory but binding on the government and other concerned agencies and institutions such as the political parties and the media. If anyone is dissatisfied with the decision of the commission, he would have the freedom to approach the Supreme Court, whose decision will be final.

For success of secularism, while the Constitution and what it prescribes is important, this, by itself, is not enough. India cannot ever hope to be or even claim to be a secular nation unless its society as a whole is secular and each citizen has a secular outlook. Looked at from this larger perspective, India has a long way to go. Recurrent communal violence and riots such as in Godhra, communalisation of law enforcement agencies, wanton demolition of Babri Masjid, and vandalisation of churches in several states are disconcerting reminders that we have miles to go. India is yet to accept the proposition that religion should not be the deciding factor in the public life and governance of the country. Separation of religion from politics has remained a distant dream though the Constituent Assembly had passed a resolution to this effect way back in 1948. Though the Congress party enjoyed a two-thirds majority in Parliament for nearly three decades during the prime ministerships of Jawaharlal Nehru, Indira Gandhi and Rajiv Gandhi, it failed to take any action on this issue for want of political will and foresight. In a sense, India's token search for secularism has begun, for the first time since independence, with the reference made by the government to the Law Commission of India for advice on enactment of a uniform civil code. The reactions of Muslim fundamentalists and other conservative elements to the questionnaire issued by the commission for ascertaining public opinion is unnerving. Some of them have even refused to take cognisance of the questionnaire, leave aside responding to it. Reaching the objective of a truly secular society is not a challenge. But what is at stake is seeing the emergence of a resurgent India at peace with itself.

6

SUPREME COURT VERDICT: BACK TO SQUARE ONE, IF NOT MINUS ONE

THE SUPREME COURT decision on 2 January on the interpretation of Section 123 (3) of the Representation of the People Act (RP Act) forbidding seeking of votes in the name of religion, race, caste, community or language has made a candidate liable to the risk of being guilty of electoral corrupt practice.

Several political parties such as the Bharatiya Janata Party (BJP) and the Congress have welcomed it. But, looking to the experience so far, the question is whether the judgment is going to make any real difference to the political life of the country.

Though the Supreme Court has declared secularism a part of the basic structure of the Constitution, it has continued to languish in terms of its operationalisation.

No other feature of the basic structure has been neglected so blatantly.

Rediff.com, 11 January 2017.

To give just one example, not even a show cause notice has been issued by the Election Commission of India to any political party for contravening the commitment to abide by the tenets of secularism, leave aside taking steps for cancellation of its registration.

It is important to note that the judgment is not unanimous and is based on a slender majority of 4:3.

Attention needs to be invited to the very weighty points raised in the dissenting judgment. The issues raised therein cannot be brushed aside and are bound to come up whenever Parliament decides to go for the revision of the RP Act and attempts suitable constitutional amendments.

The question of separation of religion from politics was identified as a critical issue for the political life of the country way back in 1948, even before the Constitution was promulgated.

The resolution on the subject moved by Ananthsayanam Ayyangar was nearly unanimously adopted by the Constituent Assembly (Legislative), barring the single dissenting vote by Ishaq Seth.

It is a travesty that though nearly 70 years have elapsed, India is still struggling with the question of translating it into a reality.

During this period, repeated observations of the Supreme Court have highlighted how it is helpless in doing justice in the appeals in election cases filed before it as there is no law separating religion from politics.

P. B. Gajendragadkar, the then Chief Justice, speaking for the Supreme Court in *Kultar Singh vs. Mukhtiar Singh* (AIR 1980, SC 354) had, *inter alia*, observed that 'there are several [political] parties in this country which subscribe to different political and economic ideologies, but their membership is confined to, or predominantly held by, members of particular communities or religions. So long as the law does not prohibit the formation of such parties and in fact recognises them for the purpose of election and parliamentary life, it would be necessary to remember that an appeal made by such candidates of such parties for votes may, if successful, lead to their election and in an indirect way, may conceivably be influenced by considerations of religion, race, caste, community or language.'

'This infirmity cannot perhaps be avoided so long as parties are allowed to function and are recognised, though their composition may be predominantly based on membership of particular communities or religions.'

In *Dr Ramesh Yeshwant Prabhoo vs. Prabhakar Kashinath Kunte* (AIR 1996, SC 1113), which is known as the Hindutva case, the court held that the term 'Hindutva' is related more to the way of life of the people in the sub-continent.

> 'It is difficult to say that the term 'Hindutva' or Hinduism, per se, in the abstract, can be assumed to mean and be equated with narrow fundamentalist Hindu religious bigotry or be construed to fall within the prohibition in Sub-section (3) and/or (3A) of Section 123 of the RP Act...'
>
> 'The word Hindutva is used and understood as a synonym of "Indianisation" i.e. development of uniform culture by obliterating the differences between all cultures co-existing in the country.'

I had highlighted in my book, *Good Governance Never on India's Radar* (Rupa & Co, 2014, p.158) that this will evoke fears of obliterating the religious and cultural identities of the minorities in the country.

Equally difficult to understand is the logic of the court in its assertion that a mere statement that the first Hindu state will be established in Maharashtra is by itself not an appeal for votes on the ground of his religion, but the expression, at best, of such a hope.

The fact that all these election petitions were based on the speeches made by leaders of the Shiv Sena and the BJP, whose political ideology is based on the furtherance of Hindu religion at any cost, also has an important bearing on the issues at hand.

Rajeev Dhawan, senior advocate, has recalled how he had appealed the 1995 order the same year, but the court had refused to reopen the judgment except for any problems in technical matters, in case they existed.

'So that judgment hangs over our heads as Hindutva hangs on our head, as it is a political platform.'

Dhawan has also stated that 'Justice J.S. Verma (*who had delivered the 1995 judgment*) too was apologetic about that judgment and said it had been misunderstood.' (*The Indian Express*, 3 January 2017). It was way back in 1996 that a three-member bench of the Supreme Court in the *Abhiram Singh* case had directed that the issues arising out of the Hindutva case be placed before a larger bench of five judges at an early date so that all questions could be decided authoritatively and expeditiously.

Later, in January 2014, a five-judge bench referred this question to a larger seven-judge bench.

It is unfortunate that this issue has still remained undecided though the Hindutva judgment goes to the very crux of the problem of separation of religion and politics.

Unfortunately, the Supreme Court judgment in January also sidestepped this issue.

The inordinate delay in the decision on the Hindutva case underlines the need to ensure that the Supreme Court deals with crucial Constitutional questions expeditiously.

This was also underlined by the question pertaining to the rampant misuse of the Ninth Schedule of the Constitution, which was nothing less than a fraud on the Constitution but was decided by the Court only in January 2007.

The Swaran Singh Committee on Constitutional Reforms, whose recommendations led to the highly controversial 42nd Amendment of the Constitution during the Emergency, had highlighted the Supreme Court's importance as a Constitutional court.

However, as it often happens, the baby was thrown out with the bath water and the question of ensuring that the Supreme Court discharges its functions as a Constitutional court speedily and effectively still remains to be addressed.

Disturbingly, the dissenting judgment of the Supreme Court has raised doubts whether religion, race, caste, community, language, etc. can be separated from politics at all.

It has rightly underlined that this question should be addressed by Parliament rather than the Supreme Court.

Due to the unnerving memories of the Partition of the country and the poison of communalism which has continued to afflict the country to this day, separation of religion from politics is a matter of serious and urgent concern.

Such an effort was made in 1993 after the demolition of the Babri Masjid by frenzied mobs. But the Constitution Amendment bill and the bill to amend the RP Act failed to get support in Parliament.

This was largely due to the failure of the government in building a political consensus on the subject before introduction of the bills.

It was also due to the fact that the scope of the bills included not just the separation of religion from politics, but also to bring in their ambit race, caste community, language, etc.

The government should have desisted from excessively widening the field of legislation, as many of the concerns pertaining to race, community, caste, and language are already addressed in the Unlawful Activities (Prevention) Act.

If necessary, that Act could have been amended suitably.

The thrust of the 1993 amendments ought to have been restricted to eliminating the association between religion and politics.

Other concerns could also be partly dealt with by amending the election law and laying down that a candidate would have to get minimum 50 per cent plus one vote to win an election to a legislature or Parliament.

This would impel the candidates to make an appeal to broader segments of their constituencies.

The issues involved are highly controversial and emotive. Any legislative and other steps taken by the government are likely to be challenged in the court leading to endless litigation. Considerable precious time has already been lost. I would therefore suggest that the President of India (central government) should seek an advisory opinion of the Supreme Court under Article 143 of the Constitution without any loss of time.

7

BJP'S RESPONSE TO RAM MANDIR WILL DECIDE COURSE OF INDIA'S HISTORY

NEVER BEFORE HAD the Bharatiya Janata Party (BJP) won such a massive mandate in Uttar Pradesh (UP). Its performance in the three other states, and particularly in Uttarakhand, has been impressive.

Nearly two-thirds of India's population now lives in BJP-ruled states. This opens a new chapter not only in the history of the BJP, but also of India. Hereafter, all major national and regional issues will have to be considered with this new perspective.

The foremost among these is the construction of the Ram temple in Ayodhya at the site where the demolished Babri Masjid stood.

Though not even a day had elapsed since the declaration of the results in UP, hot-heads in the Rashtriya Swayamsevak Sangh (RSS), the BJP, and its 'so-called' ally, the Shiv Sena, were already demanding that expeditious steps must now

---

Rediff.com, 16 March 2017.

be taken for the construction of the Ram temple at the disputed site.

The BJP's response to this single issue will decide the course of India's history.

Public memory is phenomenally short. It would therefore be pertinent to recall the BJP's stint in power in Uttar Pradesh in 1992 under chief minister Kalyan Singh which actively promoted the demolition of the Babri Masjid by its actions and inactions.

Kalyan Singh had given a commitment to the central government, the National Integration Council and the Supreme Court that all steps would be taken to protect the Babri Masjid.

Shockingly, none of these was fulfilled.

When the central government decided to station 20,000 paramilitary forces at a distance of about 10 kilometres from Ayodhya, Kalyan Singh had furiously objected to it.

Repeated suggestions of the central government to deploy the central paramilitary forces in the first protective ring around the Babri Masjid were turned down by the state government.

Kalyan Singh had also given instructions that under no circumstances should the state police guarding the structure open fire on the *kar sevak*s.

Kalyan Singh had also warned the central government that if any pre-emptive action was taken by it to impose President's rule or to take over the structure, no guarantee could be given for its protection.

Unfortunately, P.V. Narasimha Rao, the then Prime Minister, was reluctant to act on the home ministry's advice to dismiss the Kalyan Singh government and to impose President's rule under Article 356 of the Constitution.

As a result, ultimately, the Babri Masjid was wantonly demolished by the *kar sevak*s under the watch of the Kalyan

Singh government and in full view of the massive strength of the state police and senior BJP leadership.

It was only after the demolition of the Masjid was nearly complete that the state government called for the assistance of the central paramilitary forces.

But since magistrates were not made available by the state government for quite some time in spite of repeated requests by the paramilitary forces, they were unable to enter Ayodhya which had lakhs of *kar sevak*s milling around.

When Kalyan Singh was hauled up for contempt of court for having failed to abide by the commitment given to the court, he got away only with imprisonment till the rising of the court!

After the BJP came to power at the Centre in 2014, Kalyan Singh was rewarded with governorship of a major state.

The Liberhan Commission of inquiry, even after toiling for 17 years, failed to bring out the enormity of the crime and identify those who should be held responsible.

The criminal cases against the guilty have not made any headway though over 20 years have elapsed.

It is only on 7 March 2017 that the Supreme Court has held that the discharge of senior BJP leaders on a technical ground was inappropriate and has given directions to reopen the cases.

The court has also expressed concern at the delay in conducting the trial.

This is an eloquent commentary on the total failure of governance on this highly emotive and sensitive issue.

I have deliberately invited attention to these shocking developments during the BJP regime in UP in 1992.

It must be underlined that the massive mandate received by the BJP in the elections this year was entirely due to Modi Magic and his slogan *Sabka saath, Sabka vikas*. This has galvanised people belonging to all religions, castes, creeds and communities.

This new social engineering needs to be strengthened and carried forward consciously in a responsible manner.

Mayawati has pertinently observed that even in Muslim majority areas in UP the BJP has received a clear mandate. This is a very welcome development from a national perspective as it clearly shows that Muslims and scheduled castes, scheduled tribes and other weaker sections have reposed their faith in Modi's appeal for inclusive growth.

Nothing must be done to let down these widely held expectations.

The BJP has been harping on a Congress-*mukt* Bharat. In their turn, the so-called secular parties are calling for a BJP-*mukt* Bharat. This has split the Indian polity, like the Republicans and Democrats in the USA.

In spite of the BJP's massive win in the recent elections, it needs to be stated that the BJP is considered an untouchable by most other political parties in the country.

It may be considered a travesty, but it shows that even the BJP needs to be brought into the mainstream of political thinking in the country.

The moves which the BJP makes for construction of the Ram temple at the disputed site will be a litmus test for this purpose.

The construction of the temple in Ayodhya is an emotive issue for large sections of Hindus. All efforts made during the last two decades to arrive at an amicable solution in consultation with Muslim groups have failed. The matter is now before the Supreme Court.

It will be best if all stake-holders, including the state and central governments, and the Hindu and Muslim groups make an appeal to the Supreme Court to take up this case for a very early decision.

Attention needs to be invited in this context to the suggestion made by some BJP activists that if the court decision goes against the Hindus, a law should be passed by the state government to take up the construction of the temple at the disputed site.

These are dangerous portents.

It is imperative that all parties categorically make a commitment that they shall abide by the final decision of the Supreme Court.

This will be the best way to bring a closure to the issue.

It is time India moves on to face several other multifarious challenges before it.

8

INDIA AS LYNCHISTAN, FRIGHTENING AND DISHEARTENING

MOB LYNCHING HAS emerged as a formidable threat to the image of India as a civilised country. India has truly become Lynchistan, rather than Hindustan, as some protagonists of the Hindutva cause would like it to be.

Suspected cow smugglers, child lifters, black magic practitioners, and innocent, law-abiding people have become the victims of this mindless violence. It is mobocracy in action.

This changeover of India in recent months has been frightening. But the institutional and societal response so far to this grave challenge is disheartening.

The Twitter war between the Congress and the BJP showed the extent to which public life has been muddied. The Congress party has asked for an inquiry into mob lynchings by a sitting judge of the Supreme Court. The government has responded the way it is used to, wherever states are concerned, by appointing a committee under the union home

---

The Citizen, 16 August 2018.

secretary and appointing a group of ministers to deliberate on the issues.

It has refreshed the country's memory by reiterating that 'police' and 'public order' are state subjects, and that the central government's role is restricted to issuing advisories to state governments, which it has done. Appeals to the nation's conscience could have been made by the Prime Minister speaking authoritatively on the subject at the earliest opportunity.

But Prime Minister Modi, so eloquent otherwise, did not find it necessary to condemn the repeated incidents of lynching until several weeks had elapsed, giving the wrong impression about where the Government of India stood on the subject. It was equally shocking to see a central minister felicitating the accused in a lynching case by garlanding them when they were granted bail by the court.

The response of the state governments concerned has been equally casual and lackadaisical. The Supreme Court has condemned the spate of lynchings as 'horrendous acts of mobocracy', lamenting also the apathy of bystanders, mute spectators, police inertia and grandstanding on social media by the perpetrators of these crimes.

The Supreme Court has suggested that the central government issue a directive to state governments under Article 256 of the Constitution. The Court also suggests that a separate law be enacted to create a deterrent against the tendency to take the law into one's hand.

Let us deal first with the question of issuing a directive to state governments under Article 256. This article which deals with the obligations of states and the Union lays down that 'the executive power of every state shall be so exercised as to ensure compliance with the laws made by Parliament and any existing laws which apply in that state, and the executive power of the Union shall extend to the giving of such directions to a state as may appear to the Government of India to be necessary for that purpose.'

I seriously doubt whether the central government is competent to give any directive under this article to the states, on a subject which clearly falls in the 'state list' in the Constitution. The states will consider it as going against the principles of federalism, which is now a favourite hobby-horse of all opposition parties.

It is also important to note that a directive can be effective only when its breach can lead to stringent penal action. The only action which can be taken against a state government is to treat this as a failure of the Constitutional machinery and to impose President's rule. But, considering the composition of Parliament, this is clearly not feasible as such action is unlikely to be approved by Parliament.

Considering the fact that almost all states, except for a few such as Punjab, Karnataka, Kerala, Tamil Nadu and West Bengal are ruled by the same party which is in power at the Centre, it is most unlikely that the central government will be prepared to impose President's rule in any of these states for breach of the directive. Any such action against state governments ruled by the opposition parties is bound to be branded as political vendetta. Further, any such action is bound to be challenged in the Supreme Court and I have grave doubts that it will be upheld by the court.

Is a new law an answer to the problem? Let us await the recommendations of the Ministry of Home Affairs – but what is our experience so far? There are literally hundreds of laws on the statute books. The question is one of making use of the laws and taking action.

The main instrument for this purpose is the police, which has become totally ineffective by its blatant politicisation and communalisation. This is evident from the fact that even the directions issued by the highest court in the land in 2006 on restructuring police organisations at the Centre and in the states have remained unimplemented, though over a decade has elapsed.

It has made no difference which political party has been in power. There is no political will to reform the police. On taking the reins in 2014, Prime Minister Narendra Modi declared that his government would strive for 'less government and more governance.' I had expected police reforms to be of the highest priority in any such programme. But, these hopes have been belied.

The response of Rajasthan police in the recent lynching episode is a case in point. As I brought out in my book, *Secularism – India at a Crossroads*, the Uttar Pradesh Provincial Armed Constabulary is known to have been communally oriented for a long time, and it had also come under adverse notice during the demolition of the Babri Masjid.

The observations of L.K. Advani in his autobiography, *My Country, My Life*, are also highly disturbing. He has written that when he was returning to Lucknow on 6 December 1992, after the demolition of the Masjid, a senior UP police officer walked up to him and said, '*Advaniji, kuch bacha to nahin na? Bilkul saaf kar diya na?*' (I hope nothing is surviving and that it has been totally razed to the ground?)

Advani has cited this as evidence of public enthusiasm for demolition of the Masjid, but to me it conveys the pernicious communal mindset of the police. The Muzaffarpur riots in the 1980s and the police's role therein is still keeping horrific memories alive. In cases of mob lynching, another disturbing aspect of police functioning can hardly be overlooked. Demands for entrusting the investigation of cases to the police of other states are a significant pointer to the steeply declining credibility and dented image of the police.

There are also matters such as misuse of state governments' power to withdraw of cases, which has diluted the deterrent effects of the penal provisions of law. Such provisions need to be amended to curtail the discretion of state governments.

During the hearing of the question of dealing with the lynching cases, it was stated on behalf of the government that responsibility needs to be fixed on district officers for any lapses in such cases. There is nothing new in this suggestion. The main question is how to deal with the political aspects of these cases. It is time some out-of-the-box thinking was done to deal with this aspect.

MLAs and MPs are public servants and derive concomitant benefits such as frequent upward revision of salaries, allowances, pension, medical facilities and so on. There is no reason why they should not be held responsible and accountable for any acts of mob lynching in their constituencies.

For, as seen since Independence, there are severe limits on what officers can do when politics enters the picture. It is only by holding the elected representatives responsible, as public servants, that major issues in public life can be addressed.

Finally, the nefarious role of social media in spreading fake news, propagating rumours and creating panic has been primarily responsible for mob violence and lynching. But there is a reluctance to address these issues due to misplaced concerns about safeguarding individuals' right to privacy.

Reasonable restrictions on such rights are inevitable in the larger public interest and must be enforced. A surveillance machinery for this purpose must be put in place by the government without delay. All efforts must be made to eradicate the blot of mob lynchings on India's image.

9

'THE CENTRE WOULD BE JUST AS HELPLESS IN SUCH A CRISIS TODAY'

MADHAV GODBOLE, WHO was the Union home secretary at the time of the Babri Masjid demolition, Prachi Pinglay-Plumber talks to Outlook about what happened during those days and in the aftermath. Taking a stand, Godbole resigned from his job and has since advocated a more robust understanding and implementation of the Indian Constitution.

What were the circumstances and factors that led you to believe that the mosque would be demolished, unleashing nationwide violence?

It was clear that this was a place of worship for one religion, and any attack on it and any possibility of its demolition would be a catastrophe. That's why we were keen that the state government should take steps for its protection. But from what we could make out of their intentions, that was not going

---

Outlook magazine, 30 November 2017.

to happen. For example, one suggestion we made was to keep the central police in the close first ring of protection of the monument, so they could take over if any untoward incident occurred. The state government was reluctant to do it—they only wanted the state police. This was the first warning sign. We also had some information which led us to believe the *kar seva* would not be peaceful, although there was no concrete evidence of a conspiracy. That's why the contingency plan to establish President's rule and take over the state administration was made—but that did not happen.

Did you anticipate the situation going out of control?

When violence erupts in the country, under the Constitution, the central government's power to intervene is limited, as policing and public order are in the State List. All we can do is assist the state by providing paramilitary forces or intelligence inputs or placing the army at their disposal. In this case, paramilitary forces were kept on alert near sensitive states and the army was informed to keep their units ready to move if the states asked for assistance. Actual intervention is not possible beyond that.

The demolition led to riots in Mumbai and then the serial blasts. It changed the city's social fabric permanently.

Even then, we knew Maharashtra was likely to have serious problems. But the decision to impose President's rule is essentially political and depends on which party is in power in which state. When matters went to Parliament regarding President's rule in the BJP-ruled states of Rajasthan, Himachal, UP and MP, the Home Ministry had indicated that it should also be imposed in Maharashtra, Gujarat and Karnataka. But this was unacceptable, and so it was imposed only in BJP-ruled states. Therefore, we saw what happened in Maharashtra.

Effectively no government was functioning in the state—the Shiv Sena had practically taken over.

The Sena also came to power afterwards, and not much was achieved despite the report of the Srikrishna Commission.

You speak of the Srikrishna Commission. Take the case of the Liberhan Commission, which created a world record by taking 17 years to report. One reason for this was the number of times matters went before the courts, resulting in stays being granted. I have been saying for over a decade now that the Commission of Inquiry Act needs to be amended to preclude intervention by the courts. Currently, a commission authorised by an Act of Parliament, may be stymied by a court-granted stay that continues indefinitely.

Public memory is too short. If you go back to the Emergency, what did Indira Gandhi do when the Shah Commission was appointed? She simply refused to appear. The commission says, 'I have no power of contempt and therefore I cannot take any action. At the most I can go to court.' In this case, the magisterial court took its time and she got away without any action. All such commissions have recommended that they should be given powers for contempt of court in order to be effective, but no political party wants to do anything about it.

What do you see as the demolition's lasting impact? Have any processes improved?

As I look back on the past 25 years, nothing has changed and all our problems are the same. We should learn some lessons from such a catastrophe, where all our constitutional institutions came under serious attack. Let us start with the state government, which was responsible for protecting the monument, which had given all assurances to the Supreme

Court and the National Integration Council, failed in its duty. What action was taken? President's rule afterwards was too little, too late.

Second, the Supreme Court. It was monitoring the case and what happened? The CM of the state got away in the case of the contempt petition. The final case is that of the Government of India. The common man may not understand the intricacies of the Constitution. But he asked, 'What was the Government of India doing?' He saw it with folded hands doing nothing.

And we have done nothing to ensure that if a similar situation arises, the Centre will have the powers to intervene on its own through a constitutional amendment, which would mean carrying all the states with us. What happened in Gujarat in 2002? The central government could not intervene.

Today if another catastrophic event of this nature should occur, you will find the government of India as helpless as it was at that time. We have learnt no lesson.

PART TWO

Good Governance Must Be A Fundamental Right

THE CHALLENGE OF GOOD GOVERNANCE

SEVERAL PROVISIONS OF the Indian Constitution such as Fundamental Rights, Directive Principles of State Policy, protection of interests of minorities, remedies for enforcement of fundamental rights, and powers given to the High Courts and the Supreme Court to issue writs clearly underline the importance of good governance. However, when the Constitution was written, the term 'good governance' was not prevalent and therefore it does not find a mention in the Constitution. But the Supreme Court has recognised a number of rights as fundamental rights even though they do not find an explicit mention in the Constitution. These include, among others, freedom of press, right to privacy, right to clean environment, right to speedy trial and so on. Based on this logic, in my Public Interest Litigation (PIL) filed in the Supreme Court in 2004, I had pleaded that good governance should be recognised as a fundamental right and the higher civil services as one of the instruments for translation of this right into reality. Towards this end, I had suggested a number of institutional and other safeguards for more effective, responsive and accountable functioning of the civil services.

I had hoped that a decision by the Supreme Court would go a long way in strengthening the hands of common persons in asking for fulfilment of this fundamental right. Unfortunately, the court dismissed the PIL at the admission stage itself as 'not necessary'! Maybe I was ahead of time. This section brings out the pros and cons of the issues.

My book, *Good Governance Never on India's Radar* (2014), had brought out how, right since Independence, emphasis on good governance had been neglected. It was therefore a pleasant surprise when Prime Minister Narendra Modi, while taking over charge in 2014, made an important announcement that his government would strive for less government and more governance. I was struck with its sheer audacity as this is easier said than done. Some salutary steps have no doubt been taken towards this end by the government and they have also been recognised by multi-lateral institutions such as the World Bank and the International Monetary Fund (IMF). The steep climb of India's ranking in the 'Ease of Doing Business Index' during the last three years is a welcome proof. But a great deal still remains to be done, particularly at the cutting edge of administration.

My open letter to the Prime Minister on huge arrears of court cases and the need for adopting a time-bound programme to bring down the arrears draws attention to an important facet of the problem. The outdated criminal justice system in the country continues to be neglected. Reforms of the criminal justice system are proceeding at a snail's pace. Provisions such as of anticipatory bail, which are taken advantage of by the rich and powerful to avoid arrest, have shaken the confidence of the people in the supremacy of the rule of law and the tenet of equality before law.

The constitutional protection given to the civil services has remained on paper. The services have become politicised and lost their independence and freedom to give frank and objective advice to the political executive. Administrative reforms have no takers either among the senior civil servants or their political masters. The Second Administrative Reforms Commission had done commendable work and had produced 15 voluminous reports. Hardly any action has been taken thereon. There is no evidence of any perceptible improvement in administration. There has been no downsizing of government or shedding of responsibilities by the government. Not a very happy, cheerful or hopeful note on which to end this brief introduction, but it should vet the interest of the readers to go through the articles and debate the issues.

10

ADMINISTRATIVE REFORMS: MIRAGE, RHETORIC AND REALITY

WITH EVERY NEW government coming to power, whether in the states or at the Centre, pronouncements are made of radical changes which would be made in administration, to improve governance and to give to the people a friendly, responsive, transparent and accountable government. The phrases such as zero tolerance for corruption, supremacy of rule of law, the law taking its own course, and howsoever high you may be, the law is above you, are routinely bandied about. Ushering in good governance has become yet another popular slogan. Narendra Modi government at the Centre, which has just completed its first year in office, is no exception.

As one looks back, there is a feeling of *déjà vu* among the usually well-informed persons. For example, the Expenditure Commission appointed by the Centre over a decade ago had made a number of recommendations for pruning the government machinery and restructuring the ministries. Hardly any action was taken on them. The Second Administrative

---

Governance Now, June 2015.

Reforms Commission (SARC) had in 2012 and 2013 made a series of recommendations on the whole gamut of issues for improving governance but there is no information in public domain on actions taken thereon. It was over a decade ago that the National Commission to Review the Working of the Constitution (NCRWC), set up by the Vajpayee government under former Chief Justice of India, M.N. Venkatachaliah, had submitted its recommendations but these have been put in cold storage. I have illustratively cited only a few instances of shocking inaction on the recommendations of some of the recent important commissions. This speaks volumes of the political parties which have been in power at the Centre.

Reports of the judicial inquiry commissions appointed by the Centre and the states during the last few decades bring out the rapid deterioration in administration and how serious is the problem of minister-civil servant relationship. The Shah Commission on the Emergency excesses during 1975-77 had, in its last report, summarised the anguish of the preceding commissions on this matter and had underlined how the state governments and the Centre had failed to take any remedial action thereon. There has been no change in position in this regard. In fact, the situation has worsened perceptibly. The memoirs written by senior officers over the years have brought out this aspect. But there is no inclination on the part of the political leadership to address this issue. It is not even on the radar of political leadership.

It is often said, somewhat derisively, that officers become enthusiastic about enforcing the rule of law only when they are appointed in constitutional posts such as the Election Commission, the Central Vigilance Commission, the Information Commission and so on. But this is a pointer to what needs to be done to change the administration in the real sense of the term. If constitutional protection is given to senior civil servants, there will be a sea change in the face and functioning of administration. It is with this end in view that my former colleague from Andhra Pradesh cadre of the Indian Administrative Service (IAS), Dr E.A.S. Sarma and I had filed a public interest litigation (PIL) in the Supreme Court in 2004. We had prayed that just as the Supreme Court had recognised the right to privacy, freedom of press, right to information, etc. as fundamental rights, good governance too should be recognised as a fundamental right of every citizen and civil services should be declared as instruments for translating it into reality. The petition had suggested an exhaustive list of steps that could be taken to empower civil servants and at the same time to make them fully accountable for their actions. If these submissions had been upheld by the Supreme Court, the series of serious scams during the 10-year regime of the UPA (United Progressive Alliance) could have been largely avoided. However, clearly, we were ahead of times and the Supreme Court in its wisdom decided not to admit the PIL. If the question of improving the governance in the country is to be addressed seriously and with a sense of purpose, there is no alternative to declaring good governance as a fundamental right.

Attention must be invited to a highly disturbing development of the central and state governments neglecting the implementation of the decisions of the highest court in the land. It would be recalled that the Supreme Court gave a decision in 2006 on PILs pertaining to police reforms which had been filed to urge very early action on the recommendations made by the National Police Commission under Dharma Vira as far back as in 1978. The Supreme Court had, in principle, accepted the thrust of the main recommendations of the commission and had laid down a time-bound action plan for the purpose. It included setting up of establishment boards of senior police officers for dealing with personnel matters, doing away with political interference in transfers and personnel matters of police, setting up of a machinery for addressing public grievances relating to the police and so on. A minimum term of 2-3 years was also laid down for officers working at various levels so as to prevent their frequent transfers. Even partial implementation of these directives would have improved the functioning of the police. One comes across shocking accounts of police encounters and atrocities, increasing indiscipline in police, their criminalisation and communalisation, and shocking high-handedness. It will not be possible to bring about even a semblance of good governance unless the functioning of the police department is improved. Unfortunately, though nearly a decade has elapsed since the pronouncement of the Supreme Court decision, most state governments have not implemented the decision. With the judgment of the Supreme Court being treated in such a cavalier fashion, there can be hardly any hope for the better.

Maximum governance with minimum government is a good objective but it is by no means easy to implement. It is often believed that economic reforms mean 'free for all' and government withdrawing itself from its responsibilities. This is far from true. Logically, minimum government should imply maximum regulatory supervision, not by government agencies, but independent statutory regulatory commissions. These commissions must be empowered to regulate the actions of the concerned agencies in the larger public interest in keeping with the framework of rules and regulations on the subject. These bodies must be given full autonomy and their working must be made completely transparent. All decisions must be taken by the regulatory bodies after holding open hearings and issuing 'speaking orders'. Any interested person, who is dissatisfied with the order of the commission should have the freedom to approach the High Court and/or the Supreme Court. The decision of the court would be final and binding on all concerned. It is imperative that the government must remain aloof from the functioning of these regulatory bodies. The appointment of the chairperson and members of the commission must be recommended by independent statutory selection committees on which, apart from the Prime Minister and concerned Minister, the leaders of opposition in both Houses of the legislature and a representative of the Chief Justice of India/High Court is represented. If the objection of any member of the selection committee is to be over-ruled, the reasons therefor must be recorded in writing and placed before the legislature. Unfortunately, as seen in the regime of the National Democratic Alliance (NDA) as also the UPA, no political party is really committed to give such autonomy to the regulatory commissions. Unless there is a national consensus in this regard and public pressure is built up, the ideal of maximum governance and minimum government would remain only on paper. The Modi government has not taken any credible steps in this matter so far.

The lack of commitment of the Modi government to the cause of the Right to Information (RTI) is seen from the fact that the post of Chief Information Commissioner has been lying vacant for months together. Enactment of the Right to Information Act was the only decisive action taken by the UPA government to bring about good governance in the country. But the initial enthusiasm of even the UPA government was seen to be wavering in the last few years with actions such as granting blanket exemption to the Central Bureau of Investigation (CBI), challenging the decision of the Information Commission to bring the main political parties under the RTI Act, etc. The Modi government seems to be equally disinterested in empowerment of citizens. This was evident from decisions such as non-release of the Henderson-Brooks-Bhagat Report on the 1962 China war and refusal to make public the papers relating to Subhash Chandra Bose's disappearance. The Modi government could have improved its credentials by taking more proactive steps in the implementation of the RTI Act.

It is high time the role and functions of the Prime Minister's Office (PMO) are examined afresh. It would be recalled that during the regime of Jawaharlal Nehru, in spite of his pre- eminent position and towering personality, there was a strong opposition in the cabinet to a strong PMO. It was for the first time in the history of independent India that the PMO was permitted to become far too powerful by Indira Gandhi, over- riding the cabinet secretariat and the ministries. In the NDA and UPA governments, this trend continued. The Modi government is following in the same footsteps. Needless to say, any democracy is only as strong as its institutions. Undermining institutions of governance in this manner has long-term deleterious effects. It is imperative that the institution of PMO is subjected to close scrutiny by a high-level committee and its recommendations are used to help evolve a national consensus on the subject.

Finally, reference may be made to lack of action on some important points which have caught the imagination of the people. Positive action on these could have established the Modi government's commitment to ushering in the good governance. First, taking speedy steps to establish the Lokpal. Unfortunately, even the first step to appoint a search committee for selection of the chairperson and members of Lokpal is yet to be taken. Second, to give a constitutional status to Lokpal, and Lokayuktas. The latter has been recommended by the All India Lokayukta Conferences for over 25 years. Third, enactment of a model law on Lokayuktas to bring about uniformity in their powers and functions. This recommendation of the all India conference of Lokayuktas too is pending for over 25 years. Fourth, abolishing the privileges available to MPs and MLAs under Articles 105(2) and 194(2) of the Constitution, respectively, in cases involving corruption.

This was suggested by the Supreme Court in the *Jharkhand Mukti Morcha case* in 1998, by the NCRWC in 2002 and the SARC in 2013. Apathy by the successive governments in this behalf is an eloquent commentary on their real commitment to cleanse public life. Fifth, amendment of Article 311 of the Constitution to take away the protection provided therein to public servants in cases involving corruption. This recommendation was made by the Santhanam Committee in early 1960s, the National Police Commission in 1978 and has been repeated by the SARC in 2013. Sixth, action on a number of other points can establish the credentials of the government on eradication of corruption. These include holding bribe-givers (along with bribe-takers) responsible for offences of corruption, substantially increasing the punishments for various corruption offences, making 'collusive corruption' a serious offence, as recommended by the SARC, setting up of additional CBI courts for speedy disposal of corruption cases and laying down a time limit of six months for disposal of such cases, attachment and confiscation of properties found to have been acquired in disproportionate assets cases, and so on. This is only an illustrative list of actions which could be taken to establish the credentials of the government and change the perceptions of the people at large that corruption will not be permitted to continue as a way of life in India.

11

NARENDRA MODI'S LEGACY SHOULD BE BRINGING DOWN THE ARREARS OF COURT CASES IN INDIA

DEAR PRIME MINISTER Narendra Modi, The Supreme Court, in its annual reports released in January 2017 on judicial administration 2015-16 and the lower courts in the country, has brought out once again the enormous pendency in the courts. But this is not new. It is only restatement of the fact. Increasing arrears of court cases have continued to cause anxiety since early years after Independence. Addressing a conference of state law ministers in 1959, the then Prime Minister Nehru had expressed alarm at the slow pace of the wheels of justice. Justice K. Subba Rao had observed in 1970 that 'law's delays are not a new problem. The basic problem is as old as the English wig'. On 30 July 1978 the then law minister, Shanti Bhushan, had expressed the hope that 'the backlog of cases would be cleared in 5 years so that no case took more than a year to be decided in the high courts'. He

---

Firstpost, 16 January 2017.

had further stated that 'the government is determined to create a situation where a case from trial court to final appellate court would take one year to be completed.' All these have remained *Mungerilal ke sapne* (just the pipe dreams). Eminent jurist and senior advocate the late Nani Palkhivala had rightly said, 'I am not aware of any country in the world where litigation goes on for as long a period as in India... The law may or may not be an ass, but in India it is certainly a snail and our cases proceed at a pace which would be regarded unduly slow in a community of snails.' The National Commission to Review the Working of the Constitution (2002) had referred to the formidable arrears of court cases at various levels and stated: 'Particularly disturbing has been the chronic and recurrent theme of the near collapse of the judicial trial system, its delays and the mounting costs. The glorious uncertainties of the law have frustrated the aspirations for an equal, predictable and affordable justice.' With the pendency of nearly three crore cases in courts, there has been no improvement in the situation over the years. In fact, the situation has sharply deteriorated.

In a democracy, peoples' grievances are expected to receive timely attention from their elected representatives. However, this subject has continued to be neglected irrespective of which political party was in power at the centre and in the states. This is primarily because millions of harassed and dejected litigants are effectively faceless and unorganised and are not considered important as a vote bank. For the first time in the history of the country, former Chief Justice of India, T.S. Thakur, was moved to tears, more than once, signifying his utter helplessness to deal with the problem. India must be the only democracy which saw such a shocking spectacle.

Ushering in good governance has become a favourite slogan of all political parties. Any well accepted definition of good governance includes institutional, procedural and legal guarantees for speedy dispensation of justice. This concept has been incorporated into the Virginia Declaration of Rights of 1776 and later into the Sixth Amendment of the Constitution of the United States of America. There is also a Federal Act of 1974 called 'Speedy Trial Act' which establishes a set of time limits for carrying out the major stages of the trial. The right to speedy trial is recognised as a common law right flowing from Magna Carta. This is the accepted view in the United Kingdom, Canada and New Zealand. Under Article 14 of the International Convention of Civil and Political Rights, 1966, the right to a speedy trial is recognised. Article 3 of the European Convention of Human Rights also provides for it. The scope of Article 21 of the Constitution of India pertaining to protection of life and personal liberty has been interpreted widely by the Supreme Court to provide against delays in bringing the accused to trial and ensure speedy trial. The Court has also declared that a procedural law is void if it does not provide for speedy trial and that speedy trial is a component of personal liberty. In spite of this enunciation, this right has continued to be neglected.

Sir, you have brought home the power of tremendous personal political clout and popular support enjoyed by a Leader of a non-Congress party, for the first time in the country. In fact, your coming to power has seen the very unusual combination of presidential and parliamentary systems operating together. However, there are legitimate apprehensions that, as in the Indira Gandhi regime, forces of majoritarianism may come into play, leading to weakening of institutions vital for strengthening and sustaining democracy. In such a situation, the institution of judiciary must not be weakened in any way. Success of democracy lies in institutionalised system of checks and balances. In this context, it will be pertinent to recall some significant judgments of the Supreme Court of India which were responsible for the survival of not just the democracy but of the Constitution itself during the notorious Emergency (1975-77). These included, among others, *Kesavananda Bharati* case, *Bank Nationalisation* case, *Privy Purses* case and *Minerva Mills* case. In spite of the shocking majority judgment of the Supreme Court upholding the suspension of rights under Articles 19 and 21 of the Constitution, the dissenting judgment of Justice H.R. Khanna in *ADM Jabalpur vs Shukla* case, helped in sustaining the confidence of the beleaguered nation. Justice Khanna had underlined: 'The State has got no power to deprive a person of his life or personal liberty without the authority of law. That is the essential postulate and basic assumption of the rule of law in every civilised society.' The concept of basic structure of the Constitution enunciated by the Supreme Court during the period has been invaluable for sustenance of democracy, secularism and the rule of law in the country. The Supreme Court has also laid down that a procedure prescribed by any law must be reasonable, fair and just. In *Bommai* and other cases, the Court has declared that even orders of the President of India must conform to the tenets of the Constitution and are liable to be scrutinised by the Court.

It must be underlined that the relationship between the judiciary and the executive, as visualised by the scheme of the Constitution of India, has to be inevitably adversarial. As well-known Justice Frankfurter of the United States Supreme Court had stated: 'The court has no reason for existence if it merely reflects the pressures of the day.' It will be foolhardy to try to convert the judiciary into a 'committed judiciary', as was attempted during the Indira Gandhi regime. If there is one lesson of the dreadful years of Emergency which must never be forgotten it is that judiciary's independence must not be compromised in any way.

It appears that the tussle between the government and the judiciary on this critical issue has been largely responsible for the delays in appointments of judges of the High Courts and the Supreme Court, transfers of High Court judges, and the central government turning a deaf ear to the plea of the judiciary for larger budgetary provisions to meet its requirements.

The problem of arrears has been examined by a number of committees and commissions, including parliamentary committees, over the years. They have unanimously recommended appointment of more judges, depending on the period which is to be specified for clearance of arrears and disposal of new cases. All that is wanting is the political will to announce a time-bound programme to address the issues. Whatever rigorous tests are applied, cost benefit analysis of additional expenditure on judiciary would bring out that this expenditure would give handsome returns.

Sir, some of the initiatives taken by you have become unduly, and often undeservedly, controversial and divisive. But, taking time-bound steps for eradication of the huge arrears in court cases will, I am sure, receive unanimous support in the country from all well-meaning and informed sections of society and the political parties. I would earnestly urge you to announce that the arrears of court cases would be wiped out in a period of three years and for this purpose all necessary infrastructure and manpower will be provided. I would further suggest that the central government should bear the entire cost of providing requisite infrastructure to the courts all over the country. The recurring revenue expenditure by way of appointment of judges and staff etc. could be shared by the central and state governments with the central government bearing, for a period of 10 years, larger share in poor states.

Sir, you have laid down the eminent goal of less government and better governance. Your other commitment of *sabka saath, sabka vikas* (taking everyone along and inclusive development) is evocative and has caught the imagination of the people. If these pledges are to be translated in reality, I would urge that an announcement as above be made, and steps taken to bring down the arrears of court cases in a period of three years. There can be no better gift to the citizens of India than such an announcement. This can be your lasting legacy.

With best regards,
Madhav Godbole,
A concerned citizen

12

INDIAN CIVIL SERVICES REPLETE WITH CONSTITUTIONAL ANOMALIES AS REFORMS CONTINUE TO BE ANATHEMA

RECENT DECISION OF the central government compulsorily retiring some officers needs to be welcomed as a step in the right direction. But the other recent decisions of giving extension to selected secretaries to Government of India, in some cases well beyond the age of retirement, is disconcerting.

When there is no dearth of meritorious and deserving officers, this cannot be justified on any ground. This has understandably led to considerable demoralisation among officers, giving mixed signals about Modi government's commitment to undertaking civil service reforms, which have been neglected all these years. It needs to be appreciated that economic reforms aimed at globalisation and achieving double-digit economic growth will be incomplete without adequate emphasis on civil service reforms.

Firstpost, 27 January 2017.

It may be recalled that in spite of Jawaharlal Nehru's reluctance, it was only due to the insistence of Vallabhbhai Patel that specific provisions were made in the Constitution of India to create the two all India services to serve the centre and the states and give protection to service matters of all civil services. Patel was of the firm view that independent, apolitical civil services, which can provide objective and fearless advice to the ministers were necessary for India's future. Their importance was also underlined by Justice R.S. Sarkaria Commission Report (1988) on Centre-state relations.

Unfortunately, like several other provisions of the Constitution, these constitutional safeguards too have remained on paper.

When Dr Rajendra Prasad, President of the Constituent Assembly, rose to move the motion for adoption of the Constitution in 1949, with great foresight, he had said, 'Whatever the Constitution may or may not provide, the welfare of the country will depend upon the way in which the country is administered. This will depend upon the men who administer it.' Similar sentiments were expressed by B.R. Ambedkar, Chairman of the Drafting Committee of the Constitution, in his closing speech in the Constituent Assembly in November 1949, 'However good a Constitution may be, it is sure to turn out bad because those who are called to work it, happen to be a bad lot. However bad a Constitution may be, it may turn out to be good if those who are called to work it, happen to be a good lot. The working of the Constitution does not depend wholly upon the nature of the Constitution. The Constitution can provide only the organs of state such as the legislature, the executive and the judiciary.'

The experience of the working of the Constitution during the last 67 years has shown how true these observations are. Rapid decline in standards of governance have also been commented upon by a number of committees and commissions.

After summarising the observations of a number of commissions of inquiry held earlier, the Shah Commission on Emergency excesses, had, in its last report (1978), noted: 'One cannot but be struck by the near unanimity in the observations of several commissions on the unhealthy factors governing the relationship between the ministers and the civil servants. Yet nothing seems to have been done, at any rate effectively, to set right such of the aspects of these relationships which, prior to the Emergency, had contributed to the several developments which came in for indictments by the commissions. In the light of this, it may be easy to conclude that what happened during the Emergency is merely a tragic culmination of the particular trend that has been identified and condemned from time to time by the commissions of the past.'

The National Commission to Review the Working of the Constitution had, in its report (2002) stated, 'The present situation is characterised by a pervasive disenchantment with the way things have worked out. It is futile to debate whether it is the institutions provided by the Constitution that have failed or whether the men who work those institutions have failed.'

It is disappointing to see that such a high-powered commission comprising legal luminaries and eminent public figures failed to go into the relevant issues and remained satisfied with such a bland conclusion, which does not make anyone any wiser.

Good governance has now become a globally accepted concept. All political parties in India are seen to be vying with each other in making promises to voters to provide good governance. There is a recognition that good governance can be an effective antidote to the dreaded phenomenon of anti-incumbency. This is borne out by some chief ministers enjoying three or even more terms in office. However, the essential pre-requisites for good governance have been deliberately neglected. Prominent among them are civil service reforms.

Unfortunately, even the judiciary, which is the last bastion for upholding the Constitution, has, till recently, been reluctant to take on the political executive, when it came to management of civil services. Repeated pleas made to the Supreme Court against arbitrary mass transfers, undeserved supersessions in promotions, favouritism and suspension of all India service officers failed to elicit worthwhile response. Prominent among these was the writ petition filed by me in the Supreme Court (C) No. 69 of 2004.

It was submitted to the court that the words 'governance of the country' appear only in Article 37 of the Constitution in Part IV on Directive Principles of State Policy but good governance is writ large and implicit in several provisions of the Constitution. In this light, it was urged that time had come to declare right to good governance as a Fundamental Right.

This would be in keeping with the Supreme Court declaring a number of other rights such as right to privacy, right to information, freedom of press and environmental protection as fundamental rights, though they did not find explicit mention in the Constitution.

All political parties in India are seen to be vying with each other in making promises to voters to provide good governance. There is a recognition that good governance can be an effective antidote to the dreaded phenomenon of anti-incumbency. Prominent among them are civil service reforms.

The Supreme Court itself had observed in *Maneka Gandhi* case (AIR 1978 SC 597) that 'The attempt of the court should be to expand the reach and the ambit of fundamental rights rather than to attenuate their meaning and content by a process of judicial construction.' I had urged that civil services should be recognised as the instruments for translating the fundamental right of good governance into a reality.

For this purpose, they should be given independence and autonomy. Simultaneously, I had also proposed a number of civil service reforms such as:

- Pre-mature retirement of officers whose work is assessed to be unsatisfactory
- An officer, who is not empanelled for the post of joint secretary in Government of India or secretary in the state government, and for each stage of promotion thereafter, should be retired
- There should be a cooling-off period of two years after retirement, before a public servant can join a political party.
- There should be a total ban on grant of extension in service or re-employment.

Unfortunately, the Supreme Court decided not to admit the writ petition. If it had been heard and pleas therein accepted, the series of major scams which rocked the country after 2004 could have been avoided.

Fortunately, the trend of non-interventionist attitude of the Supreme Court was reversed with the decision of the Supreme Court in *Prakash Singh and others v. Union of India* ((2006) 8 SCC 1) pertaining to the recommendations of the National Police Commission which had remained unimplemented since 1980.

The Supreme Court has given comprehensive directions for reorganisation and management of police departments of the state governments and the central police organisations. This was followed by the decision of the Supreme Court in writ petition (civil) No. 82 of 2011 filed by T.S.R. Subramanian pertaining to transfers and promotions etc. of All India Services and other central civil services. By its decision dated 31 October 2013 the Supreme Court has laid down some broad guidelines for management of service matters of these services.

However, now a very disturbing trend is evident. Shockingly, the orders of the highest court are being blatantly flouted by several states. The petitioners are left with no other alternative than filing contempt petitions in court. This is not easy for individual officers to do, considering the time, money and effort required for the purpose. Regrettably, the Supreme Court also appears to be reluctant to haul up the defaulting states, which it can do, *suo motu*, if it so desires. As for Parliament and the state legislatures, less said the better. They have no time to spare for these 'mundane' matters.

We have ostensibly adopted the British model of civil service. But this is only in name. The basic principles, values, rules, procedures, conventions or the esprit de core of the British civil services are nowhere to be seen.

In fact, the Indian civil services are the unholy mix of British, feudal and American systems, with a unique Indian touch and flavour. It is therefore no wonder we have such highly politicised and arbitrary management of civil services.

Well-known cartoonist Sudhir Telang had memorably depicted in one of his cartoons in 1990, two IAS officers introducing themselves as belonging to Rajiv Gandhi and V.P. Singh batches. Nothing has changed since then. They would now be of Manmohan Singh or rather Sonia Gandhi batch, or Modi batch!

13

'TINKERING WITH THE CIVIL SERVICE IS NOT ADVISABLE'

MADHAV GODBOLE SERVED the country for 33 years as an IAS officer before resigning as India's home secretary after the demolition of the Babri Masjid in 1992.

The author of several books and an important voice on the India of today, he discussed his latest book *Indira Gandhi, An Era of Constitutional Dictatorship*—which he (Dr Godbole) presented to Prime Minister Narendra Damodardas Modi on June 22—and Indira Gandhi's similarities and differences with **Rediff.com's Archana Masih.**

In this concluding segment of the interview, Dr Godbole, one of the finest bureaucrats to serve the nation, discusses the government's proposed changes in the Indian civil services.

As a former bureaucrat, what do you think of the proposed change in the Indian Administrative Service (IAS) of allocating services to selected civil service recruits only after adding to their scores their

---

Rediff.com, 27 July 2018.

assessments during the Foundation Course? How will this impact the civil service?

The pros and cons of this proposal are far from clear. It is not clear if it means allotment of candidates to various services.

This is done today according to the merit of the candidates in the competitive examination and their individual preferences. There is no reason to change this.

Short foundation training period can hardly provide an opportunity to judge the aptitudes of candidates. Neither is the training content designed for the purpose.

As for allotment of IAS, IPS (Indian Police Service) and IFS (Indian Forest Service) candidates to state cadres, the present method seems to work quite satisfactorily.

It is designed to ensure that all states get meritorious candidates by turn and the interests of ushering in good governance all over the country are served.

Tinkering with the civil service matters without adequate thought and public discourse would hardly be advisable.

How will inviting professionals from outside the IAS at the Joint Secretary level change the existing way of functioning? Is this a good move?

I have serious reservations. A number of reforms are necessary in the civil services, but this certainly is not one of them.

There is no dearth of highly qualified persons in the civil services.

The question is of permitting them to give their best which is lacking due to the environment in which they have to function.

Lateral entrants from the private sector will be faced with the same situation.

Further, inducting persons at such a senior level directly will lead to demoralisation among regular officers as their chances of promotion and advancement will be adversely affected.

The tendency to consider the other side of the fence greener and more attractive has been evident in the past too.

When Rajiv Gandhi was Prime Minister, he had initiated a scheme of deputation of officers of the rank of joint and additional secretaries from government to the private sector in the hope of improving the functioning of the government. This scheme failed miserably. I had criticised it in the past.

Functioning of the private sector has its own pluses and minuses and by no stretch of imagination the functioning of the government sector can or should be brought in line with it.

Are these the reforms civil services need? Or reforms should include some other initiatives?

I have written extensively on the subject over the years. My books *Public Accountability and Transparency: The Imperatives of Good Governance* (2003), and *Good Governance: Never on India's Radar* (2014) are a case in point.

I had also filed a Public Interest Litigation in the Supreme Court in 2004 with a plea that, like freedom of press, right to information, right to privacy, etc, which are not explicitly mentioned in the Constitution as fundamental rights, but have been recognised as such by the Supreme Court, good governance should also be recognised as a fundamental right of every citizen.

Unfortunately, I was ahead of time and the court did not admit the petition.

I have been advocating a number of Constitutional and statutory changes to improve the functioning of the civil services which include, among others, amendment of Article 311 of the Constitution to take away the protection to persons who are charged in corruption cases, taking away powers of suspension of all India service officers from the state governments, weeding out officers at levels of joint secretary onwards if they are not found fit for promotion to the next level, doing away with extensions and re-employment after retirement, filling positions in statutory and Constitutional bodies by an open and transparent process in which the selection committees will include the Leader of the Opposition, the Speaker of the Lok Sabha and so on, and providing for a cooling-off period of two years for officers to join politics or take up employment in the private sector.

A few months ago, 48 retired bureaucrats sent a letter to Prime Minister Modi expressing concern at the decline in the secular, democratic, and liberal values enshrined in our Constitution.

I entirely share these concerns. I had commented on these issues at length in my book, *Secularism: India At A Crossroads* (2016). I have urged therein that India's future is inexorably tied to making a success of secularism.

I have suggested a number of Constitutional changes towards this end which include, among others, defining the words 'secular' and 'minorities', deleting the provision pertaining to 'prohibiting the slaughter of cows and calves' in Article 48 of the Constitution, and setting up of a commission on secularism to closely monitor policies and programmes not just of the government but also the private sector, media, educational institutions, political parties and all other sections of society, which may detract from secular precepts.

India cannot be called a secular country unless its whole society becomes secular.

Do you think our institutions are failing and bureaucrats are not discharging duties fairly?

Empowering institutions and ensuring their proper functioning must be accepted as a national challenge.

People often wonder how officers appointed as Election Commissioners function so well and why their counterparts in other positions in the government are so ineffective.

The answer is to be found in the Constitutional office which they occupy and the powers and independence which they enjoy.

Are we prepared to give the same autonomy and independence to other officers?

My Public Interest Litigation in 2004, referred to earlier, had raised precisely this and other related issues.

Gross political interference in the working of officers in the states and at the Centre and politicisation of services shows how the situation has steeply deteriorated over the years.

Even the directions of the Supreme Court regarding restructuring of police departments in the states and at the Centre, given in 2006, have hardly been implemented.

A series of contempt petitions had to be filed and the Supreme Court which has in July 2018 reiterated its directions on the subject.

The wheel does not need to be reinvented. The question is whether we are prepared to put our shoulder to it to make it turn.

14

A CASE FOR GOOD GOVERNANCE AS A RIGHT

THERE IS NEVER a dull moment in India. One does not have to go to a movie theatre or sit in front of the idiot box to watch a thriller. When one sees the chaos around, one wonders why nothing can be done about it. Prime Minister Narendra Modi had declared, on assuming office in 2014, he would strive for less government and more governance. Effectively, this meant providing good governance, or *Ram Rajya*, according to the idiom of Hindutva.

The Constitution contains all ingredients of good governance: Fundamental Rights, Directive Principles of State Policy and provisions of checks and balances. But when it was framed, the term good governance was not current and, therefore, did not find mention in it. Subsequently, the Supreme Court has inferred a number of rights, which are not explicitly recognised as such in the Constitution, as Fundamental Rights. These include the freedom of press, right to information, right to privacy, right to speedy trial and right to clean environment.

The Tribune, 27 November 2018.

PIL on good governance

Against this background, I had filed a Public Interest Litigation (PIL) in the Supreme Court in 2004, urging that good governance be recognised as a Fundamental Right, and the higher civil services, which are the instruments for translating this right into reality, be given freedom and autonomy for the purpose. It was pleaded that the protection given by the Constitution to the civil services, which had been grossly eroded, should be restored. The PIL had also suggested a number of steps to make the civil services more sensitive, accountable and answerable. The SC's directions would have made a perceptible difference to governance. However, it dismissed the PIL at the admission stage itself, saying it was unnecessary.

After Prime Minister Modi's announcement as above, I had hoped that the government would take the initiative and propose an amendment of the Constitution to declare good governance as a Fundamental Right. This would have helped bring about a number of institutional and systemic changes to make a qualitative difference in public life. Even a private member moving a Constitution Amendment Bill could have helped the cause. At least the position of the government and of other political parties on the subject would have become clear. But this too has not happened though 14 years have elapsed since the filing of the PIL. Unless public pressure is built, the situation will not change.

RTI Act not fully implemented

Reference must be made to another important debilitating subterfuge which is so often adopted to undercut the rights conferred by law. Such disempowerment was seen when the Benami Transactions Act was made into a dead letter by the United Progressive Alliance (UPA) government by not formulating rules under the Act for over a decade. The same is being done by the National Democratic Alliance (NDA) government by undercutting the implementation of the Right to Information (RTI) Act by keeping the posts of Information Commissioner vacant for months, exempting institutions like the Central Bureau of Investigation (CBI) from the purview of the Act and attempting to keep out file notings from disclosure. In several states, the position of the implementation of the RTI Act is pathetic. Now that over a decade has elapsed since the Act came into force, a high-level expert committee must be appointed to examine how the law can be made more effective.

Lokpal yet to come to being

Another example of making a mockery of the legislation is the non-implementation of the Lokpal Act. Though over four years have elapsed since the passage of the law, the Lokpal is yet to come into being for one reason or the other. For a long time, the search committee was not constituted on the specious excuse that there was no Leader of the Opposition in the Lok Sabha after the 2014 elections. The deficiency could have been made good by promulgating an ordinance to replace the words 'Leader of the Opposition' by 'Leader of the largest Opposition party' in the Lok Sabha.

Clearly, the Modi government is not interested in appointing a Lokpal. One would have to wait for the 2019 Lok Sabha elections for that. By comparison, laws pertaining to the revision of the salaries and allowances of MLAs and MPs are passed without discussion on the very day the bill for the purpose is introduced and they come into effect even before the ink on the enactment gets dry!

PILs remain on paper

Article 32 of the Constitution has been acclaimed for the right conferred on a citizen to approach even the Supreme

Court for enforcement of his/her Fundamental Rights. But in this wondrous land, decisions of the High Courts and the Supreme Court in PILs have not been implemented for years. I had highlighted this shocking state of affairs in my book, *The Judiciary and Governance in India* (2008). Literally, hundreds of decisions in PILs have remained on paper.

An outstanding example of this is the non-implementation of the directions of the Supreme Court given in 2006 on police reforms. I had suggested that the High Courts and the Supreme Court should set up a mechanism for monitoring the implementation of their decisions. Unless this is done, the confidence of the people in getting expeditious redress of their grievances will be eroded. That would be one more proof of disempowerment of the common man.

This litany of woes is unending. Sadly, no political party is prepared to take notice, even with the impending General Elections next year.

PART THREE

PUBLIC LIFE - A DOWNHILL JOURNEY

PUBLIC LIFE – GROWING CONCERNS

PUBLIC LIFE IS expected to be the eternal reservoir from which democracy draws its sustenance. One would expect that in India, which proclaims itself as the world's largest democracy, public life would be a treasure trove. Unfortunately, the reality is quite the opposite.

The strength of democracy lies in its institutions. And the institutions in turn draw their strength and resilience from the public life of the country. Any wayward behaviour of any institution must come in for a public chastisement. There can be no better, more effective, self-sustaining and self-correcting system of checks and balances. On this criterion, public life in India leaves a great deal to be desired.

The foremost prerequisite for a vibrant public life is the spirit of tolerance, capacity to give and take ideas, constructive debate and discussion, and the willingness to understand, appreciate and evaluate the viewpoint of the opposite party before coming to any conclusion. As one looks around in India today, all these attributes are wanting.

The erosion in the credibility and image of Parliament, which is the prime mover of democracy, is the most troublesome of them all. The steep fall in the glorious traditions and the highest standards for parliamentary behaviour and norms, laid down by Jawaharlal Nehru and Sardar Vallabhbhai Patel, is unbelievable. It has literally left Parliament in ruins. Even on critical national issues such as demonetisation, Goods and Services Tax, Rafael deal, CBI conundrum and so on, Parliament has become irrelevant. It has remained only as a forum for scoring political points over adversaries and not for any serious, constructive debate and discussion. Walk-outs from and boycott of Parliament have become the norm, session after session. Important instruments for ensuring accountability of and fixing responsibility for government's actions and inactions, namely, Public Accounts Committee (PAC) and Joint Parliamentary Committee (JPC), which were held in awe once upon a time, have lost their credibility. I had analysed this phenomenon extensively in my book, *India's Parliamentary Democracy on Trial* (2011). As I had underlined therein, Parliament needs to take itself seriously if it is to regain public esteem.

A related subject pertains to electoral reforms. No political party is interested in seriously debating the issues, far from agreeing on any time-bound programme of action. Almost all electoral reforms, which have come about in the recent past, have been at the instance of the Supreme Court, in spite of almost unanimous opposition of all political parties! There cannot be a more eloquent commentary on India's democracy. Two urgent reforms which I have been advocating for quite some time are to make voting compulsory and to make a minimum 50 per cent+1 vote mandatory for a candidate to win. But they have no takers.

The position of Indian judiciary as the world's most powerful judiciary is unique. As compared to any other country, the judiciary in India has taken an important hand in the governance of the country. Its activist role has come in for a lot of criticism though I have been its strong supporter. But, as I have brought out in my book, *The Judiciary and Governance in India* (2008), some important changes are necessary to ensure that the instrument of Public Interest Litigation (PIL) becomes more effective and the judiciary too becomes more transparent and accountable. It was against this background that the press conference held by the four senior-most judges of the Supreme Court to agitate some of their grievances came as a public shock and raised a number of questions of institutional integrity and dependability. The most unusual step taken by the Supreme Court to invite senior Air Force officers to seek information on some features of Rafael aircraft has raised disturbing questions about how far the activism of the judiciary should go and will need to be debated extensively.

The country was rocked by a number of major scams during the ten-year United Progressive Alliance (UPA) regime. These included, among others, the 2G scam, and the coal scam, to name just a few. The Court decisions in these cases raise important points of policy and handling of corruption cases by the investigating agencies and the government itself. Unless lessons are learnt and remedial actions taken, same disastrous mistakes will get repeated in future.

15

'IN KASHMIR, WE'RE IN A TUNNEL WITH NO LIGHT AT THE END'

'It is good we are trying to create an image for India on the world stage but it hasn't taken us far enough—whether in Pathankot or Jammu and Kashmir (J&K), world opinion hasn't come out strongly in favour of India,'

Former Union home secretary Dr **Madhav Godbole** tells *Rediff.com*'s **Archana Masih.**

What does the government need to do urgently in Kashmir?

IN KASHMIR FOR the first time we are in a tunnel and there is no light at the end of it. And we don't even know we are in a tunnel.

At one stage, it was believed that a PDP-BJP coalition will bring the extreme thinking parties together and enable a new beginning, but it hasn't happened.

Rediff.com, 8 September 2016.

The Kashmir problem cannot be addressed unless you address Pakistan. It has to be accepted that the Pakistan military establishment's one-point objective is to disintegrate India.

It has been a failure of our foreign policy that we have not been able to convince world opinion that something needs to be done about Pakistan.

This is not something that can only be addressed bilaterally unless there is pressure of world opinion brought on Pakistan.

Irrespective of all the strategic dialogues, successive US governments have continued to help Pakistan including with the latest batch of F-16s.

It is good we are trying to create an image for India on the world stage, but it hasn't taken us far enough—whether in Pathankot or J&K, world opinion hasn't come out strongly in favour of India.

That is the biggest failure of foreign policy and we don't seem to be concerned.

How do you assess the Kashmir situation?

Pakistan and the Kashmir issue cannot be segregated. Our refusing to talk to Pakistan is something that is problematic.

Even in India, we have made no effort in recent years to build a national opinion on this subject amongst political parties. At least we should speak as one country.

There is a unanimous resolution of Parliament to say that Kashmir is an integral part of this country and under no circumstances will it be ceded.

Therefore, there is need to arrive at a consensus—even that effort is not being made.

There also needs to be talks with the people of Kashmir.

Yes, you cannot afford to take an antagonistic position.

A three-member panel selected by the Centre comprising Dilip Padgaonkar, Radha Kumar and M.M. Ansari submitted a report on Kashmir (in 2011) but no one has bothered to read it. I am surprised that the report hasn't been placed in Parliament.

Let the issues come out in the open. We are a democracy. Major national issues cannot be decided behind closed doors in North Block and South Block but in Parliament.

In fact, the government should have said we would like a day or two to be set aside to discuss this subject in both Houses of Parliament.

Therefore, people outside the country feel that India doesn't want to deal with this issue at all.

It wants to deal with it only as a law and order problem. Keeping such a large contingent of armed forces in J&K after 60–65 years of Independence is untenable.

Whether it is the North East or J&K, the country can't be governed in this manner.

My problem with the Armed Forces Special Powers Act (AFSPA) is not the Act, but keeping the army there which is a political decision.

The army does not need to be in the whole state, it can be deployed in troublesome districts and withdrawn from other districts as we go along, but now it will be even more difficult.

Public opinion must be created and people told that it is up to you now; if you want to give up violence, we are prepared to go one step ahead and withdraw the army from these areas.

Let there be some experimentation on these issues. After all, there are no simple solutions.

Apart from secularism and federalism, your recently launched book *Secularism: India at a Crossroads* proposes some other concepts of the Constitution that need a relook.

Another issue to be looked at as a Constitutional amendment is the propagation of religion. It was agreed upon at the time the Constitution was framed as a compromise with minorities.

The time has come to take a serious look about the right to propagation be given to Muslims and Christians because it is their religious precept.

If you are a real secular country, religion is your own personal family matter and has nothing to do with the public. Therefore, the propagation right should be done away with.

Let's take the instance of *gau rakshaks*. The concept of abolishing cow slaughter does not go with secularism. This is the programme of one particular religion.

If a religious programme has to be accepted, then it should be accepted of all religions which cannot be in a secular State.

Therefore, there is an inherent contradiction having this kind of Directive Principle in the Constitution and proclaiming that you are a secular State.

Nowhere in the Hindu religion does it say that you should not eat cow's meat. I have quoted from various people who have written over a period of time, including strong adherents of Rightist ideology like (*Vinayak Damodar 'Veer'*) Savarkar had said there is no sense in this, leave aside Nehru who was, of course, totally opposed to it.

India is a noisy democracy. The rightists and secularists are out there in the open public space — how do you see this duel panning out?

Today it has become a curse word if you say you belong to the secular lobby. That must go. The true meaning of secularism has not been defined by the people.

Let there be an agreement on what is meant by secularism. For example, treat all religions equally.

This also has a problem in the manner in the way we have dealt with religion in last 60–70 years. Rightly, a point is made that all attention of Parliament has concentrated on reforming the Hindu religion, what about other religions? We have no answer.

The other suggestion is let the state be equidistant from all religions. We need to work on these definitions.

Secularism and communalism are topics that are debated vigorously in the country.

You cannot have a secular state and communalism going together.

This country is the most communal country apart from a country like Pakistan which is a theocratic state.

We have addressed communalism administratively, never politically.

Every political party takes recourse to it one time or the other when it suits them.

Therefore, there are provisions in law which need to be amended.

According to Articles 153A and 153B, if you say anything that goes against anyone's religious sentiments or inflames religious sentiments, you can be hauled up before the courts.

If you take stock of how many people have been punished under these sections, you will be able to count on the fingertips of a single hand. Why? Because cases are not put up in the court because these are politically powerful people.

If a case is registered, it is withdrawn at a later stage as a compromise as it happened during the Bombay riots.

Therefore, there's a proposal to say that these powers that are with the state government and district magistrate should be taken away and given entirely to the police at the senior level.

Then the police will be responsible to the courts and not be responsible to a political executive.

How can the law be more powerful in this matter?

(*We need to think*) Whether there should be a separate law for genocide.

Unless you make people aware that this is a serious crime which will call for even life imprisonment.

There should be provisions to file lawsuits together by a group of people like it happens in the US and elsewhere because individuals cannot really pursue cases particularly in communal riots.

In the 1984 anti-Sikh riots, hardly any individuals were prepared to come forward because of worries that they will be targeted.

I have also argued that the European system of prosecution should be adopted for communal cases in which the investigation is supervised by a magistrate. Only after s/he is satisfied should the case be put up before the court.

There is resistance to this idea because we are wedded to the old British principle that everybody is innocent till it is proved otherwise.

This is contrary to the British principle of punishing a person by proper investigation under independent supervision of a magistrate which has been resisted here all these years.

We should at least make a beginning in communal riot cases so that the minorities will get a feeling that their cases will be pursued.

In the Gujarat riots, there was a demand that the Supreme Court should supervise the cases. It cannot because of its workload, neither can the High Courts.

There has to be an institutionalised system for supervising the investigation.

Your book has proposed some other changes in the way we function as a country, what are they?

I have proposed two changes in the electoral laws—voting must be made compulsory. This is the only country perhaps which gives a public holiday (*on election day*). Compulsory voting will empower the minorities.

The minorities are taken for granted because they do not always exercise their vote. There is NOTA (None of the Above), so no one is forcing you to vote, but you should exercise your vote as a voter.

There is such fossilised political thinking on this subject. Gujarat passed a law to make voting compulsory at the panchayat level. The Governor sent it for approval, it was not approved because the government at the Centre was of a different party from that in the state.

Legislation can't be looked at with such a partisan angle. That legislation was only cleared after the Modi government came to power at the Centre. These issues must be looked at apolitically.

Secondly, for anybody to be elected, a candidate should get 50 per cent + 1vote. Then the candidate will appeal to all sections.

This is the only way the concerns of the minorities can be brought forward.

MLAs/MPs get elected with 10 to 15 per cent of the vote and hence are not really representatives of the constituencies.

So, what happens to the big issues that political parties do not want to tackle?

Every year or every alternate year some election comes up. All attention is on winning that election. Now it is UP, Gujarat.

Last year there were elections in 3-4 states, therefore the suggestion that the new government has been toying with is to hold simultaneous elections for Parliament and states.

Then at least for 5 years everyone can go back to the business of governing. Otherwise governing becomes secondary to electioneering.

If you see the historical record, in the first 3-4 general elections all elections were held simultaneously.

When Indira Gandhi realised that her hold over the country was weakening, she came up with the idea of separating parliamentary elections from state elections and we are stuck with it.

The sedition law is another law that has come under criticism.

According to me, a sedition law in a democracy doesn't make sense.

Hardik Patel had every right to carry on an agitation. If he had broken any law, he can be hauled up for breaking that law.

Somebody writes a poem against prohibition or against Amma, you prosecute under this law; somebody who supports Naxalites in Maharashtra gets prosecuted under this law and on one side we say more governance and less government, but here the government seems all pervading.

16

THE TRAVESTY OF JUSTICE IN 2G, COALGATE SCAMS SHOWS WHY WE BADLY NEED A LOKPAL AND AN AUTONOMOUS CBI

THESE WERE SCAMS that became a definitive byword for corruption in recent times—common people heard earth-shaking figures like 'lakh crores' for the first time. The recent decisions by the Central Bureau of Investigation (CBI) courts in 2G and Coalgate are, therefore, disconcerting and raise a number of questions.

In the 2G case, the court has come to the shocking conclusion that there was no scam at all, and no case had been made out against any of the accused. They have all been acquitted. The role of the CBI has come in for severe indictment. In the coal scam, the court has convicted almost all accused, including the former Chief Minister of Jharkhand and the then Union Coal Secretary. However, this judgment too raises a number of serious questions.

Outlookindia.com, 27 February 2018.

The two judgments bear out the well-known adage that, often, courts are courts of law and not courts of justice. While pursuing these criminal cases is important, equally crucial is to address the larger questions of accountability. Several key institutions were found wanting and were devalued and eroded irreparably. Even if this sounds more abstract than black-and-white cases of crime, there is very good reason why these concerns must be addressed expeditiously.

Did the PM Know?

Former Telecom Minister A. Raja's book, *2G Saga Unfolds*, has added fuel to the fire. He has reiterated that he had kept the then Prime Minister Manmohan Singh fully informed of the steps he was taking and at no stage had the PM objected.

Raja is also very strident in his criticism of the then Comptroller and Auditor General (CA&G) Vinod Rai. 'The possibility of a "conspiracy-nexus" cannot be ruled out...I am certain that reports of auditors like Vinod Rai which I will show to be mere trash shall be unanimously deemed fit for the dustbin,' he writes. Also: 'It is my contention that the sanctity of the C&AG was severely compromised by its then head Vinod Rai. Rai clearly had ulterior motives in overreaching the bounds of his constitutional function.'

Raja has challenged Rai for a public debate. Some political parties too have been fishing in troubled waters. I am glad Rai has maintained a dignified silence befitting the office he once occupied.

Despite Raja's strident, self-righteous tone, I am not persuaded by his arguments. The 2G case brings out the worst of our public life—an unbelievable, total failure of governance, a shocking collapse of ethics.

Crony capitalism was brazenly at work from the beginning, via the assignment of cabinet portfolios. The Niira Radia tapes showed the extent of corporate influence exerted to ensure Raja was given this portfolio. Even a person of the stature of Ratan Tata had no qualms in urging the Supreme Court that his conversations with Radia not be made public and his right to privacy be protected! The apex court had found the Radia tapes 'mind-boggling' but the CBI decided to close the case as no crime could be established!

The JPC Farce

Parliament, the highest forum of inquisition in a democracy, hardly lived up to expectations. The Public Accounts Committee (PAC) and the Joint Parliamentary Committee (JPC) are key parliamentary instruments expected to function as non-partisan forums. Unfortunately, this has hardly ever happened. In the past, JPCs on Bofors and the bank scam were divided along party lines. The same thing happened in 2G.

Initially, the UPA opposed the demand for a JPC. When it finally came into being, it functioned entirely on party lines. The government made strenuous efforts to protect Finance Minister P. Chidambaram and the then PM and the demands to call them before the committee were turned down. Even officers from the PMO were not called to give evidence. Raja's request to appear before the committee was rejected.

Sitaram Yechuri, CPI(M) general secretary, rightly stated in his dissenting note, 'The role of the JPC is to assign political responsibility and to check if decisions are taken according to the policy.' The JPC clearly failed to do so.

Its final report elicited many stinging notes of dissent from opposition members. One went to the extent of describing the report as 'perverse'. Another said, 'It will go down in history as a complete farce.... Parties will have to think twice before demanding a JPC in future.' It was shocking to see certain portions of the dissenting notes being expunged by the JPC

Chairman with the approval of the Speaker. What an example to set in the age of freedom of information!

The role of the government's highest law officers, the Attorney General and Solicitor General, was also controversial. The A-G's advice during the Vajpayee Government years that 'public revenue is not synonymous with public interest' was conveniently misinterpreted to give undeserving concessions to the telecom industry and change over to a revenue-sharing regime. The only saving grace was that it was a cabinet decision.

This decision was used as a pretext by the UPA to continue the first-come-first-serve policy, non-auction of spectrum, freezing of entry fee, etc. The role of Goolam Vahanvati, the then Solicitor General (S-G), left much to be desired. His endorsement—'What is proposed is fair and reasonable. The press release makes for transparency. This seems to be in order'—was all the fig leaf they needed. When questioned in the JPC, his defence was ludicrous.

Coalition Karma

It is often accepted that India is now in the coalition era, but even after over two decades, no norms have been evolved to fix and distribute accountability for coalition regimes. The phrase 'coalition dharma', enunciated by A.B. Vajpayee, signifies, in reality, unprincipled and blatant compromises to hold on to power.

The PM's position was weakened to such an extent during the UPA regime that Manmohan was clearly too diffident to assert his position while the 2G affair unfolded. Neither he nor his senior ministers Pranab Mukherjee and P. Chidambaram were prepared to insist on the rules of transaction of business being observed.

The government was certainly competent to decide if revenue should be foregone by fixing a lower entry fee or not insisting on auction of spectrum to ascertain its market-determined price, but such hidden subsidy had to be approved by the Finance Ministry and thereafter by the Cabinet. In this case, the then Telecom Minister Dayanidhi Maran insisted that spectrum pricing be taken out of the purview of the Group of Ministers and left to be decided by his Ministry. The PM meekly agreed, though this was against the Cabinet decision taken in 2003.

Whenever any points were raised by officers against actions proposed to be taken by Raja, his response was that the points were 'out of context'. What context he meant only Raja knew! Shockingly, not even the Prime Minister dared to question him.

The most disturbing aspect of the two scams is the complete erosion of the Prime Minister's Office. In the 2G case, the PM wanted his office to be kept 'at arm's length' (or out of harm's way?). What kind of democratic governance was that? Raja is right when he says he had kept the PM informed from time to time and his letters were routinely acknowledged by the PM. Rules of business were virtually waived—as if, under coalition arrangements, the Telecom Ministry was a DMK plaything.

Soot Boots

P.C. Parakh, former Coal Secretary, has in his book *Crusader or Conspirator? Coalgate and Other Truths* brought out how his efforts in 2004 to have a policy for auctioning coal blocks were stymied repeatedly by Coal Minister Shibu Soren and Minister of State (MoS) Dasari Narayana Rao, and even the PMO. Parakh wrote: 'Neither the industry nor the political system wanted a transparent and objective procedure. Every possible effort was made to delay the introduction of open bidding until all the fully explored good blocks had been allocated.' When Manmohan Singh held charge as Coal

Minister, the proposal was indeed approved for being put up to the Cabinet. But, as soon as Soren returned to the Ministry, it was rejected and shelved.

Specific proposals for allotment of coal mines, recommended by the screening committee presided over by the Coal Secretary, were put up for approval and PM Manmohan, who then held the coal portfolio, approved them without demur. The CBI took the position that he was misled by the then Coal Secretary, Harish Gupta. This makes no sense. Manmohan Singh is not a run-of-the-mill politician. He is a technocrat with a doctorate in economics, who has held highly coveted posts like Chief Economic Adviser, Planning Commission Deputy Chairman and RBI Governor, and later ushered in liberalisation as Finance Minister. To suggest that such an erudite personage was misled by the Secretary, Coal, is ludicrous.

The CBI had filed an FIR against Parakh that was later quashed. Parakh has written that if the CBI Director 'was convinced that the Hindalco allocation was a conspiracy and had he the courage of conviction, he ought to have named the Prime Minister in the FIR.'

The CBI court has observed that due to pressures of work, the PM cannot be expected to have time to read all files closely. But the PM has a full-fledged Secretariat to assist him, manned by a Cabinet Secretary-level officer, with two or three officers of the rank of secretaries, besides scores of senior officers. What were these officers doing when the files were put up for approval? Anyway, as Parakh's book shows, when matters pertaining to open bidding were put up to the PM, they were scrutinised closely. In the pyramid of authority, the Minister is highest. How can the Minister (the PM holding additional charge in this case) not be held responsible?

The Lokpal Question

If we already had a Lokpal, and if the PM's office had been brought under its jurisdiction, as I firmly believe it should be, perhaps these scams would not have taken place. Or at least responsibility would have been fixed for the grave lapses.

The way the Modi government has stonewalled and delayed the setting up of this vital institution is most distressing. Public opinion needs to be built up to force the government for early action on this front.

The million-dollar question of how to reform the CBI also lingers. The 'caged parrot' is still firmly under the Centre's control and the state governments remain as suspicious as ever of its misuse. The Supreme Court had sought suggestions on ways to grant it autonomy. All it got was deafening silence from both the UPA and now the NDA. No political party wants to let go of an instrument that allows it to wield 'police powers'.

Depressingly, there seems no possibility in the near future of a free CBI. In the interim, I would suggest at least three urgent reforms:

- After retirement, the CBI Director be made ineligible for any employment or office of profit under the central government.
- The CBI be brought under the RTI, with a stipulation that information pertaining to an ongoing investigation cannot be asked for and made available.
- The CBI be placed under the Central Vigilance Commission.

The coal scam has another disturbing feature. The then Coal Secretary Harish Chandra Gupta has been convicted for three years of rigorous imprisonment and a fine of Rs 1 lakh. He has been similarly charged in 10 other cases—all cases where he had presided over inter-ministerial screening committee meetings whose recommendations were then placed before the Coal Minister for approval. If the logic of conviction in the first case becomes the standard, Gupta will be in jail for the next 20-25 years. This is when, in spite of vigorous efforts, the CBI has not been able to bring any evidence against Gupta's integrity.

Looking at this case, several senior civil servants have pleaded that Section 13 of the Prevention of Corruption Act (PCA) should be amended. It is argued that Section 13(1)(d), envisaging punishment even without *mens rea* and any personal gain, is fundamentally flawed and makes all public servants liable to criminal prosecution.

While I sympathise with the sentiment, any such amendment may be counter-productive and may weaken the war against corruption. The facts and circumstances relating to Gupta's case, I believe, are exceptional. Coal mine allotments came out of unanimous recommendation of an inter-ministerial committee in which the state government representatives were also present. The CBI should not have included Gupta's name in the FIR. In fact, in some cases, his name was excluded but the court insisted on it being reinstated. I am sure the higher courts will intervene and overturn Gupta's conviction and lay down appropriate law on the subject—perhaps departmental action for erroneous decisions, rather than criminal action.

Recall the scam involving the arbitrary allotment of petrol pumps during the Vajpayee regime. The anomaly: All allotments were cancelled but the chairpersons of committees that recommended them were not held responsible in any way. Incidentally, all were retired High Court judges.

Similarly, the Chairman of the Foreign Investment Promotion Board, who is ex-officio finance secretary, was never personally held responsible though the Board had made favourable recommendations in highly controversial cases such as the Enron power project and Maxis-Aircel. The arc of culpability must always be wide enough to cover the highest responsible authority.

17

COMMISSIONS OF INQUIRY HAVE BECOME WEAK, BLUNTED

DEMOCRACY AND VIBRANT public life need the support of a number of institutions such as Parliament, the media, the judiciary and other specially authorised Constitutional and statutory bodies.

One of them is the mechanism of the commission of inquiry appointed to look into definite matters of public importance. But it becomes frustrating if these institutions start functioning at cross-purposes, as has often been the case with the commissions of inquiry and the judiciary.

The latest example of this is of the judicial commission of inquiry into the land deals of Robert Vadra, Congress leader Sonia Gandhi's son-in-law.

The report submitted by Justice S.N. Dhingra to the Haryana government in August 2016 has been languishing since then as the state government had given an undertaking in the High Court that the report of the commission would not be published till the petition challenging the appointment

---

Rediff.com, 18 September 2018.

of the commission filed by former state Chief Minister Bhupendra Singh Hooda is decided by the court.

Reportedly, there have been 26 hearings in the High Court so far. In March 2018, the Supreme Court had urged the High Court to decide the matter within two months. We are now in September 2018 and the case is still pending. (*The Indian Express*, 5 September 2018)

Several questions arise from the plain reading of the news report. Knowing how matters can be dragged in the courts, should the state government have given an undertaking that the report of the commission will not be released till the matter is decided by the court?

Why did the state government not request the court to permit it to release the report pending the court's decision in the matter?

Why could the High Court itself not have taken up *suo motu* the question of releasing the report, pending the decision in the case, since the Commission of Inquiry Act itself lays down that the report of the commission is to be made public within six months of its submission.

This is not the first time that judicial proceedings have led to frustrating the very purpose of setting up of a commission of inquiry. I had dealt with these issues at length in my book, *The Judiciary and Governance in India* (2008).

At the outset, the distinctive features of an inquiry by a commission must be noted. In such an inquiry, there is no plaintiff or prosecutor and there is no defendant or accused.

The commission is not expected to act as a judge but has to make every effort to arrive at the truth. Strict rules of evidence do not apply, and the commission does not pass any order which is binding on the government.

It merely makes recommendations based on its findings. It is left to the government to decide whether to accept the recommendations or to overlook them altogether.

The main idea is to bring all facts to the notice of the people at large in open hearings, unless the matter pertains to state secrets or are such that the commission feels that they may not be made public till they are fully inquired into, as was the case in the inquiry regarding the assassination of Indira Gandhi.

Looking at the above, it is difficult to understand why anyone should object to an inquiry by a commission. And even if such an objection is raised, the courts must lay down the strictest possible requirements before entertaining such pleas.

The most scandalous case of challenge to the appointment of a commission of inquiry was by Indira Gandhi to the appointment of the Justice J. C. Shah Commission to look into the excesses committed during the Emergency.

She not only refused to take an oath and depose before the commission but went to the extent of casting aspersions on Justice Shah, a former Chief Justice of India.

When she was proceeded against in a criminal prosecution, as Arun Shourie had written in his book, *Institutions in the Janata Phase* (1980), the Delhi High Court, going out of its way, knocked the bottom out of the Commissions of Inquiry Act and effectively provided a blanket cover for malfeasance and abuse of power.

In another case pertaining to the commission of inquiry appointed by the government of Maharashtra, on the Enron power project, under the chairmanship of a retired judge of the Supreme Court, the objection to the setting up of the commission was raised by the central government and Sharad Pawar, former Chief Minister of Maharashtra, who had approved the project.

In this case, the Supreme Court gave *ex parte* stay, without giving a hearing to the state government. The stay continued for such a long time that the state government, which had reluctantly appointed the commission under intense public pressure, conveniently decided to wind up the commission!

The issues, which were considered to be of public importance according to the state government's own notification, ceased to be so due to the injudicious intervention of the apex court.

Another striking case is that of the Liberhan Commission of Inquiry in respect of the Babri Masjid demolition. The Government of India appointed the commission within two weeks of the demolition of the masjid in December 1992.

It took 17 years for the commission to submit its report. This was the longest time ever taken by a commission of inquiry so far. But, a substantial part of the delays was accounted for by the stays granted by the Allahabad and Delhi High Courts from time to time, when approached by concerned parties.

I have been advocating over the years that the Supreme Court must lay down a guideline that any stay granted to the proceedings of a commission of inquiry should not be operative for more than three months and should automatically lapse at the end of such a period.

Unfortunately, the apex court has not taken cognisance of this major hurdle in the working of the commissions of inquiry.

Successive commissions of inquiry have highlighted yet another handicap which they had encountered, and this was of the lack of contempt of court powers.

As a result, the commissions had become weak and ineffective. Almost all such commissions are judicial commissions appointed under retired High Court and Supreme Court judges.

It was therefore disappointing to see that the National Commission to review the working of the Constitution took a very restrictive view and recommended that no other court, tribunal or authority should have, or be conferred with, the power to punish for contempt of itself.

I am of the view that it will be in the larger public interest if powers under the Contempt of Courts Act are given to the commissions of inquiry.

It is unfortunate that most of the institutions of oversight of India's robust democracy have fallen in disuse. The most prominent among these are Parliament and state legislatures. A number of statutory bodies such as Lokayuktas have become paper tigers.

Commissions of inquiry are potentially powerful instruments to fix responsibility on public functionaries but everything possible has been done to blunt this instrument as well.

Successive governments at the Centre have failed to take any remedial action. Though over four years have elapsed since assuming power, the Modi government's slogan of 'less government and more governance' has remained on paper as the Commission of Inquiry Act has not been amended in the light of experience so far.

Unlike in most other democracies, the judiciary in India holds the reins of governance in the country. Let us hope that the judiciary will not continue to contribute to undercutting the potency of commissions of inquiry.

18

THE MARATHA RESERVATION CONUNDRUM WILL OPEN A PANDORA'S BOX. HERE'S WHY

MAHARASHTRA IS PRESENTLY in a volatile state. The state-wide agitation for Maratha reservation is spreading like wildfire and is both unpredictable and frightening. It is completely leaderless. No one knows whom to talk to, to resolve the impasse.

The Maratha Kranti Morcha has organised 58 massive silent rallies throughout the state over two years. There is a legitimate grievance that no action has been taken by the state government so far. Now, *jail bharo* (fill the jails) and other agitations are on all over the state. There has also been considerable violence and large-scale destruction of public and private property. A number of suicides by agitators have raised serious concerns.

Leaders of all political parties have supported the demands of Marathas and have stressed that these ought to have been conceded right away. Chief Minister Devendra Fadnavis being

---

The Wire, 3 August 2018.

a Brahmin, is under attack, though he has announced more than once that the demand of 16 per cent reservation for Marathas is reasonable and it is only a matter of time before formal orders are issued.

His minister, Pankaja Munde, went to the extent of saying that if she was made the chief minister she would sign the relevant file the day it is put in front of her! A former Chief Minister of Maharashtra, Narayan Rane, who has joined the BJP, in an interview on television asserted that there were no constitutional difficulties and as soon as the report of the National Commission for Backward Classes is received, a special session of the legislature can be called, and further action taken to announce the reservation. Fadnavis himself has stated that irrespective of the recommendations of the Commission, as soon as the report is received, the state government will take steps to announce the reservation.

But the question is whether an important and complex public policy issue should have been handled in such a casual, and cavalier manner.

What the Constitution says

The Constitution of India contains specific provisions for dealing with welfare of Scheduled Castes (SCs), Scheduled Tribes (STs), and the backward classes. Article 46 of the Directive Principles of State Policy casts an obligation on the state to promote, with special care the educational and economic interests of the weaker sections. Also important are the provisions in the Fundamental Rights. Article 14 states that 'The State shall not deny to any person equality before the law or the equal protection of the laws within the territory of India.' Article 15 prohibits discrimination on grounds of religion, race, caste, sex or place of birth.

Sub-section 4 thereof clarifies that the State can make any special provision for the advancement of any 'socially and educationally backward classes of citizens' apart from SCs and STs. Article 16 also must not be lost sight of. It states that there shall be equality of opportunity for all citizens in matters relating to employment or appointment to any office under the state. Clause 4 of this Article enables the state to make any provision for the reservation of appointments or posts in favour of any backward class of citizens which, in the opinion of the state, is not adequately represented in the services under the state.

By the Constitution (77th Amendment) Act, 1995, this enabling provision has also been extended to making reservation in matters of promotion. Reference must also be made to Article 335 which, inter alia, lays down that claims of SCs and STs shall be taken into consideration, 'consistently with the maintenance of efficiency of administration.'

Thus, the whole scheme of the Constitution is to maintain a fine balance between the various competing interests in society. It also mandates that various provisions of the Constitution must be borne in mind. Thus, the Supreme Court has held that the element of efficiency of administration is a limit on Article 16 (4). As a result, so far, reservation in excess of 50 per cent has been regarded as discriminatory. The only exception has been the case of Tamil Nadu in which reservation of 69 per cent has been sanctified by Parliament through the Constitution (Seventy-sixth Amendment) Act, 1994.

When this large reservation was struck down by the Madras High Court and the Supreme Court passed an interim order reiterating that reservation should not exceed 50 per cent in the matter of admission to educational institutions, the Tamil Nadu Assembly, in a special session held on November 9, 1993, unanimously resolved to call upon the Union government to take steps to amend the Constitution. An all-party meeting called by the central government endorsed the proposal. As was to be expected, the Constitution Amendment

Bill was passed the day of its introduction in both the Rajya Sabha and the Lok Sabha. The Tamil Nadu Act was also included in the Ninth Schedule to ensure its protection from judicial challenge.

The situation was, however, quite different in the early years after the adoption of the Constitution. Jawaharlal Nehru, as Prime Minister, was very firm that administrative efficiency should not be permitted to be compromised. While considering the Appleby Report, the Union Cabinet had, inter alia, directed that greater emphasis should be placed on merit as a criterion for promotion in order to encourage really competent persons and seniority should only be a secondary consideration. In his letter to Chief Ministers dated 18 May 1952, Nehru had written:

'I have pointed out repeatedly to our army people and to others that while we should honour seniority, merit must be the most important criterion in every high appointment.' (*Letters for a Nation: From Jawaharlal Nehru to His Chief Ministers 1947-1963)*

It is often suggested that an alternate criteria of economic backwardness may be adopted to get over the controversies pertaining to caste reservations. However, the Constitution permits reservations only for SCs, STs (which, because of historical injustices and deprivations fall in a special category) and socially and educationally backward classes of citizens. The case of any sections, other than SCs and STs, has to be justified on the basis of their social and economic backwardness.

It was therefore wrong on the part of the Chief Minister and other politicians to say that irrespective of what the Commission for Backward Classes says, the decision on reservations for Marathas will be announced as soon as the report is received. Recent data show that Marathas have a 14 per cent share in state government employment. Any decision on reservation is bound to be challenged in the High Court and the Supreme Court and the courts will deeply examine the question—whether there is quantifiable data showing social and educational backwardness of the community.

The Shiv Sena and some other parties are advocating that all demands for reservations should be considered and settled at the same time. At present, such demands are mainly from Marathas, Muslims and Dhangars. There may be some others as well. Presently, there are 52 per cent reservations in Maharashtra. To this will have to be added 16 per cent for Marathas, and 5 per cent for Muslims, which was announced earlier but has been stayed by the court. All available studies bring out the social and educational backwardness of the Muslims. Even if Dhangars are given a nominal reservation of 2 per cent, the grand total will work out to 75 per cent. This will be even in excess of Tamil Nadu's highly questionable example. The remedy of including the legislation in the Ninth Schedule will also not be easy any longer after the Supreme Court decision in 2007 mandating close scrutiny by the court of each such new entry in the Ninth Schedule. One of the tests laid down is whether the concerned law violates any fundamental right. Any legislation prescribing more than 50 per cent reservation will certainly not satisfy this test and cannot be included in the Ninth Schedule.

Maratha reservation is a Pandora's box. Once it is opened, India will have to be ready to face a number of unpalatable, unsavoury questions, not just in Maharashtra but all over the country. At least four dominant castes—Gujjars, Patidars, Jats and Marathas—are insisting on reservations. The ensuing caste wars will raise existential questions for India which is already faced with drummed up opposition to the National Register for Citizens in Assam, the spectre of Lynchistan that India has become and the perceptibly widening communal divide. Is India ready for it?

19

'MODI HAS BEEN SCRUPULOUSLY HONEST. INDIRA GANDHI INSTITUTIONALISED CORRUPTION'

A STORMY INTERLUDE COULD perhaps be among the most dramatic titles for a book written on Indira Gandhi so far.

Former Union Home Secretary **Dr Madhav Godbole** wrote a book in Marathi on Indira Gandhi to commemorate her birth centenary in 2017.

It was published under the title *Indira Gandhi: Ek Wadali Parva* (A Stormy Interlude) last year.

Its more comprehensive study in English, *Indira Gandhi: An Era of Constitutional Dictatorship*, was published last month to coincide with the declaration of the Emergency in June 1975.

Dr Godbole presented a copy of the book to Prime Minister Narendra Modi on June 22.

Rediff.com, 21 July 2018.

The book brings out how Indira Gandhi—who served as Prime Minister for 16 years—would be judged by history in terms of her impact on the social, political and economic life of the country.

Dr Godbole served the country for 33 years as an IAS officer before resigning as Home Secretary after the demolition of the Babri Masjid in December 1992.

The author of several books and an important voice on the India of today, he discussed the decisions made by Mrs Gandhi that continue to affect the nation to this day, the stormy interlude of the Emergency imposed by her and the similarities and differences with Narendra Modi in an e-mail interview with **Rediff.com**'s **Archana Masih.**

Why did you want to write a book on Indira Gandhi?

Dilip Majgaonkar of Rajhans Prakashan, Pune, a well-known Marathi publishing house, had requested me to write a book on Indira Gandhi to commemorate her birth centenary in 2017.

The book brings out the positives and negatives of her long years in office and what it has meant for the public life in the country.

In a sense, it is the first draft of history.

Do you remember your first meeting with her?

I did not work with her directly and had no occasion to interact with her, but I worked for three-and-a-half years on the personal staff of Y.B. Chavan who was Home and Finance Minister in her government.

I also worked as Secretary to the Chief Minister of Maharashtra during the Emergency when S.B. Chavan was Chief Minister.

I negotiated a loan from the World Bank for fertiliser projects, which were mired in controversy because of the (*Ottavio*) Quattrochi angle, when I was working in the Department of Economic Affairs.

I had interacted closely with several officers and public figures who worked for Indira Gandhi. These impressions and recollections form critical inputs in the book.

What was it like for bureaucrats who worked under her?

Her close advisers, among officers, were all Kashmiri Pandits, often known as '*Panch Pandavas*'—P.N. Haksar, D.P. Dhar, P.N. Dhar, T.N. Kaul and R.N. Kao.

Others like I. G. Patel who saw her at close quarters have often written critically about her style of working.

So has P. N. Dhar who was Secretary to Prime Minister. She was a strong advocate of 'committed bureaucracy' and expected intense personal loyalty.

She frowned on the concept of an independent, apolitical, civil service.

The present woes of the civil service are largely her legacy.

What kind of a leader was she?

She was a ruthless, authoritarian and inscrutable leader who was suspicious of everyone around her.

She demolished the internal democracy within her own party. Even state chief ministers used to be chosen by her. She reshuffled her Cabinet any number of times.

It was one-woman rule. She established family dynasty, without any scruples.

First, it was Sanjay who was declared as her heir. After his death, it was Rajiv.

The highlights of her prime ministership were bank nationalisation, the victory in 1971, the Emergency, Operation Blue Star—which of these has affected India most? The impact adversely or positively that is continued to be felt today?

Each one of these events has left its their scars behind which have become more pronounced over the years.

As she herself told I. G. Patel, who was Secretary, Economic Affairs, bank nationalisation was a purely political decision.

The politicisation of the banking structure and the crony capitalism it has generated has transformed India into a 'banana republic'.

Successive bank scams and huge recurring burden of non-performing assets are bleeding the budgets year after year.

After defeating Pakistan in the Bangladesh war in 1971, an excellent opportunity was squandered away during the Simla talks with Pakistan by not settling the Kashmir dispute.

Operation Blue Star was totally avoidable and showed how several opportunities for settling the Punjab problem were lost.

The Emergency was the climax of her regime in which all democratic institutions were devalued and the rule of law was trampled.

The worst part was that Indira Gandhi refused to take any responsibility for all the misdeeds, injustices and excesses.

After she came back to power in 1980, she ordered the withdrawal of the Shah Commission Report on Emergency excesses and had its copies destroyed.

Series of reports of other commissions of inquiry appointed by the Janata (Party) government which had indicted her regime were consigned to the archives.

The million-dollar question of how to punish Indira Gandhi for her wrongdoings in the Emergency remained unanswered.

As I have argued in the book, the only way she could have been punished was to disfranchise her from contesting and voting in elections for a period of 12 years, by passing a special legislation for the purpose.

If she had not ridden roughshod over the higher judiciary, India's Constitution would have been quite different today.

For example, the powers of selection of High Court and Supreme Court judges would not have been taken over by the Supreme Court to itself.

The court would not have laid down the *Laxman Rekha* of basic structure for delimiting the powers of Parliament to amend the Constitution.

Strength of democracy lies in its institutions. Indira Gandhi weakened and devalued all of them.

This is her devastating legacy.

Many say there are similarities between Mrs Gandhi and Mr Modi, how are they similar?

They are unmistakably alike in their style of functioning. Both being leaders with mass appeal, charisma and all India following.

It needs to be noted that in most Western democracies, it is seen that there is effectively prime ministerial form of government in which the lead in all matters is given by the Prime Minister.

The cabinet form is only in name. And so has it been in India. But the similarity between Indira Gandhi and Modi ends there.

Modi has been scrupulously honest. His personal integrity is beyond doubt, while Indira Gandhi institutionalised corruption.

She had laid the foundations of family dynasty. Modi has no family at all!

As I have brought out in my book, though Indira Gandhi had two-thirds majority not only in Parliament but most state legislatures which would have enabled her to get the

Constitution amended as required, she deliberately did not take any action on five major issues confronting the country at the time, namely electoral reforms, giving a decisive blow to the politics of defections, appointment of Lokpal, dealing with black money, and separation of religion from politics.

The manner in which a series of ill thought out Constitutional amendments were carried out showed that it was purely majoritarianism at work.

Modi, on the other hand, has shown political courage by instituting several economic reforms which include demonetisation, ushering in of Goods and Services Tax, increasing the pace of divestment from public sector enterprises, eradication of *benami* transactions, enacting a code of bankruptcy, making a beginning of privatisation of coal mines, and so on.

20

JUDICIARY CANNOT BE A LAW UNTO ITSELF

ON A POSTSCRIPT to the Introduction of the reprint of the book, *The Judiciary and Governance in India*, former home secretary MADHAV GODBOLE talks about recent developments and decisions of the Supreme Court which raise serious forebodings. Extract from the book:

It has been a decade since I wrote the above mentioned Introduction. This has been a significant decade which, for the first time, has given rise to serious forebodings about the role of the judiciary. This is particularly worrisome considering the unique position which the judiciary occupies in India's national life.

Of the three organs of the state, the judiciary continues to be the most trusted, enjoying the highest public credibility. The Supreme Court has been the court of first, rather than the last, resort. Since Parliament has become irrelevant for resolving any major issues, the Supreme Court had to step in even in matters such as electoral reforms.

India Legal, 23 December 2018.

In a politically fragmented polity, Constitutional bodies like the National Development Council and the Inter-State Council have become irrelevant and remained inactive. As a result, issues of Centre-state relations have had to be agitated in the Supreme Court.

It is unbelievable but matters such as infighting in the CBI had to be taken to the Supreme Court, instead of being dealt with by the government administratively. Normally, a controversy such as the Rafael contract should have been debated in Parliament. If necessary, a parliamentary committee could have been appointed to look into allegations of irregularities and corruption. But since these instruments of democratic governance and accountability have become non-functional and have lost all credibility, the issue had to be raised in the Supreme Court. In no other country, the judiciary has been asked to take a hand in the governance of the country to this extent.

It is for this reason that some recent developments, stances and decisions of the Supreme Court raise serious concerns and forebodings.

The press conference held by the four senior-most judges of the Supreme Court on 12 January 2018 was most disconcerting and unsettling for common stake-holders. It was more shocking to see that the concerned judges did not see anything wrong in having taken the step. No one was surprised at the internal dissensions among the judges of the Supreme Court. This is not uncommon in any institution, particularly one in which there is so much talent and scholarship under one roof.

In his press conference after his retirement, Justice Kurian Joseph has dilated on a number of issues which led to the holding of the press conference. These included roster and the manner in which it was decided upon, even granting that the Chief Justice is the master of the roster; systems and practices which were considered necessary but were not being introduced; and the need to set up an administrative committee in the Supreme Court as in the High Courts. (IE, 1 December 2018, p 10)

Though systemic issues and troubling practices have been there all along, it is for the first time that they were aired publicly in such a shocking manner. Why had the demand for a collective leadership become so important only now? By contrast, there were times when the Supreme Court exhibited exemplary unity and all judges offered to resign when the senior-most judge was proposed to be superseded in the appointment of the Chief Justice. The esprit de corps has been lost since a long time, with each judge acting for himself. This has permanently damaged the image and public esteem of the highest court of the country and it will take a long time before this unsavoury memory is erased from public mind.

Administrative decision-making in the Supreme Court has always been considered to be opaque by the stake-holders. For example, there are no 'speaking orders' on why and for how long hearing in important cases is put off. The *Ram Janmabhoomi*-Babri Masjid matter is a case in point. There is reason to believe that if the decision in this long pending case had not been put off, the Babri Masjid could have been saved from demolition by mob violence in 1992. The sudden postponement of the hearing in this case from November 2018 to January 2019, and that too not for a substantive hearing but only for deciding procedural and other issues, has led to a dangerous and virulent politicisation of the issue. It will be counter-productive to trivialise the importance of this case by treating it as just a land dispute. It is of utmost satisfaction that even on such an emotive and politically explosive issue, both sides, Hindus and Muslims, have been patiently waiting for the decision of the apex court. It is in national interest that this respect for the judiciary is not permitted to be undermined, consciously or unconsciously.

The same thing can be said about several other important matters which have been pending for decades together. One such case pertains to reservation of 69 per cent granted in Tamil Nadu, which is way beyond the limit of 50 per cent laid down by the Supreme Court. This issue is of utmost national importance considering the agitation for reservations by dominant communities such as Jats and Patels in some states. The government of Maharashtra has recently given 16 per cent reservations to Marathas taking the total reservations in the state to 68 per cent, even without placing the report of the Backward Classes Commission before the state legislature. The state government is also likely to announce reservations for Muslims and the Dhangar community soon. Another important case pertains to review of the Supreme Court decision in the Hindutva case. The importance of this case needs no special emphasis in the current context of clamour for declaring India a Hindu *Rashtra*. The same thing is true of the case pertaining to constitutional validity of Article 35A of the J&K Constitution in which the hearing was postponed by the Supreme Court recently. The case of constitutional validity of the resettlement law of J&K has reportedly been pending for over three decades.

Some time ago, the then Chief Justice of India had talked about how difficult it was to spare judges for deciding constitutional issues. If this is so, should the Supreme Court not be split up and a separate apex court established only for deciding constitutional matters? After all, the issues involved therein are of national importance and keeping them pending for years together is not in the public interest. The Law Commission of India may be asked to examine the subject in depth and prepare a paper for national debate and discussion.

Judicial reforms have been talked about by every incoming and outgoing CJI in recent years. The number of pending cases at all levels continues to be as staggering as ever. Some judges of the Supreme Court and Chief Justices of High Courts, on retirement, have talked eloquently on the subject. One of them is Justice Kurian Joseph (*The Indian Express*, 9 December 2018, p 7). One of the past CJIs had even shed tears on the plight of court litigants. In spite of this acute awareness of the seriousness of the problem, there has been no perceptible change in the situation. I have discussed this matter at length in the book. On taking over charge, CJI Ranjan Gogoi has assured that this subject will receive his close attention. Justice Kurian has stated in the 'Idea Exchange' referred to above that 'the present CJI is going to have regular dialogue with the head of nation'. This is reassuring. Let us hope the long-pending and complex issues pertaining to judicial reforms will be addressed in the dialogue.

Speaking at the second J. Dadachanji memorial debate in December 2018, K.K. Venugopal, Attorney General of India, has invited attention to two important aspects of the working of the judiciary. He has rightly asserted that the Supreme Court has taken over more powers than any other apex court in any other country. Venugopal has also hoped that the concept of Constitutional morality newly invented by the Supreme Court dies soon. Both these concerns are valid and need to be debated nationally. I am particularly worried about the first concern. Such fears were also expressed by Jawaharlal Nehru who had asserted that the apex court should not be permitted to be the third chamber of Parliament. As I have brought out in the book, we have come a long way since then. And I have no quarrel with it as the judiciary has come to occupy the legislative space which had remained vacant for too long a period. Thus, for example, the subject of electoral reforms was being deliberately soft-pedalled by political parties and by whichever government came to power. Even after the Supreme Court decision directing introduction of some reforms, all political parties ganged up to oppose them.

Another case was of resistance to legislate a law for the Lokpal. Finally, it was because of Anna Hazare's agitation and the mass upsurge that the UPA government relented, but the BJP government which came to power in 2014 has been reluctant to give effect to it. The people were left with no alternative but to request for the intervention of the Supreme Court. Enacting a separate law for the Central Bureau of Investigation (CBI) is another case where even the Supreme Court has been helpless. The question has been under discussion for over 50 years but has not impelled the government to enact a law. Dozens of such instances can be given to bring out why the activist role of the Supreme Court is inevitable in India. There is no alternative to the Supreme Court taking a hand in the governance of the country. India is destined to have a guided democracy, democracy guided by the Supreme Court.

But for the same reason, the judiciary has to be accountable and transparent. It cannot be a law unto itself. The selection of judges has to be above board. The process must be transparent and such that it evokes confidence about the fairness, integrity and judiciousness of the system.

Looked at from this point of view, the resistance of the Supreme Court to the setting up of a National Judicial Appointments Commission is totally unjustified. This law was passed unanimously by Parliament and still was declared unconstitutional by the Court. It is difficult to countenance the situation in which the selection of judges will not be open and transparent or that the collegium of judges will not be answerable to anyone. Justice V.R. Krishna Iyer, former judge of the Supreme Court, had minced no words when he called this an incestuous relationship. As for the Memorandum of

Procedure concerning matters pertaining to the appointments, transfers, etc. of the judges of the higher judiciary too, there has not been agreement yet between the Government of India and the Supreme Court. Here also, the Supreme Court is stone-walling the issue and is not prepared for any give and take with the government. Justice Kurian Joseph, who was a member of the collegium till his retirement, has in his interview to *The Indian Express*, said, 'As far as the Memorandum of Procedure is concerned, the Supreme Court is of the view that it is final because it has approved it.' (*The Indian Express*, 1 December 2018, p 10).

This stance of the Supreme Court would have been understandable if India did not have a written Constitution. But the Indian Constitution is an elaborate, bulky, well-conceived and well-drafted document. The Supreme Court has the authority to interpret it, but it is questionable whether it has the powers to rewrite the Constitution as it has done by its decisions on the basic structure, appointments of judges and so on. As for the basic structure doctrine, I have argued in this book that it was invoked by the Supreme Court only due to the Constitution demolition brigade which was active under the then Prime Minister Indira Gandhi and its origin was in the 'argument of fear'. However, due to the political situation in the country, over a period of time, the logic of basic structure has been accepted by all political parties. But matters pertaining to appointments of judges are not in the same category.

If the Supreme Court continues to take a unilateral position on the subject and refuses to accept any open, transparent system, there will be no other alternative than to convene a new Constituent Assembly to deliberate on the issues. To me, this will be opening a Pandora's box. The whole Constitution will then come up for review and with the fractious polity that we have now, one does not know what all compromises may have to be made to arrive at an acceptable new Constitution. Even the basic structure doctrine will come for reconsideration. As far as I can see, even the precept of secularism will be examined anew. The consequences may be horrendous and even unthinkable.

The time has come for even the Supreme Court, which is the world's most powerful judicial institution, to realise that in a democracy, there are limits to each institution's powers and authority. There is no getting away from checks and balances. Let us hope the Supreme Court will see the reason and step back from the precipice.

21

CONCURRENT LIST: THE NATION COMES FIRST

CHIEF MINISTER OF Telangana, K. Chandrashekar Rao who won a second term with a comfortable majority in the recent elections and who has ambitions to play a major role in national politics, has stressed the importance of giving more autonomy to states. He has suggested that the Concurrent List in the Seventh Schedule of the Constitution should be done away with. He believes that state governments should be free to decide what is in their best interest. 'I am going to give a new definition to the political scenario in this country,' he proclaimed recently (*The Indian Express*, 17 December 2018, p. 10). Such half-baked, ill-considered pronouncements by someone who has prime-ministerial ambitions are worrying.

At the outset, it needs to be stated that the Concurrent List includes, among others, items of common concern for states and the Centre such as civil and criminal laws and procedures, education, administration of justice and electricity. The importance of having a nation-wide common approach on a number of such subjects can be readily appreciated. Pooling

---

India Legal, 6 January 2019.

the resources of states and the Centre can go a long way in meeting the ever-rising expectations of people. This is amply brought out by the sizeable investments made by the central government in the electricity sector to supplement the efforts of states. To leave all these subjects entirely to states will retard the progress of the country.

It may be pertinent to note that when the eternal question of powers of the Dominion government to legislate on matters falling in the state's concerns was raised by the State of Ontario in Canada, the Privy Council applying the test of 'national concerns' had held that if the subject matter of the legislation goes beyond local or provincial concerns or interests...it must be treated as affecting the peace, order and good governance of Canada [*Ontario (AG) vs Canada Temperance Federation*]. Thus, universally, the tendency is to look at issues in the larger national perspective. In the case of India too, in the light of experience so far, the Concurrent List needs to be enlarged, rather than curtailed, leave aside abolishing it.

The Indian Constitution is one of the more successful constitutions adopted by any country in recent years. It has been flexible enough to incorporate over 120 amendments considered necessary from time to time in the last 68 years. Except for some highly controversial amendments effected during the term of Indira Gandhi as Prime Minister, most of the others were well conceived and largely welcomed. Significantly, a few of these led to the transfer of some subjects from the State List to the Concurrent List. These included administration of justice; constitution and organisation of all courts (except the Supreme Court and High Courts which were always in the Union List); education, including technical education, medical education and universities; trade and commerce; forests, protection of wild animals and birds; and weights and measures.

In a number of countries, the trend is towards greater centralisation of powers, rather than decentralisation. The decisions of the highest courts in these countries, too, have contributed to this development. The forces of globalisation and the compulsions of increasing international competition, too, have underlined the importance of adopting national policies on a number of subjects. An article by Dr K.K. Aggarwal titled 'One India-One Health Policy?' in the *India Legal* issue of 24 December 2018, for example, makes a plea for adoption of a national health policy on the lines of the national eligibility-cum-entrance test. It has been gratifying to see that the initial resistance of some states such as Tamil Nadu to the entrance test for admission to medical colleges in the country has disappeared completely. There are indications of greater acceptance of the proposal for setting up more all-India services such as for the subordinate judicial service. Laying down all-India standards for various subjects, institutions and services is the only way in which the productivity, efficiency and quality of life can be improved.

After non-Congress governments came to power in a number of states, the overbearing attitude adopted by the Union government from the time of Indira Gandhi's prime ministership led to strained relations between the central government and states and these have become even more acrimonious. As a result, the term 'confidence-building measures', which is generally used in the context of improving relations between countries, is equally apt for mending relations between the Union government and states.

The concept of federalism is being increasingly bandied about by political parties and states in the context of the Lok Sabha elections this year. At the outset, it needs to be underlined that India is not a federation. The Constitution clearly states that India is a union of states. But, for ensuring a smooth working relationship between the Union and states, the founding fathers of the Constitution had consciously included several features of federalism in it. The Constitution can, therefore, rightly be described as quasi-federal. It has also been variously described as a union of federal states, pragmatic federalism, asymmetrical federalism, and amphibian federalism.

The political rhetoric of federalism is being increasingly used by states to oppose even some worthwhile proposals made by the Union government. Two recent examples bring this out. Railway police is a state subject. This police, belonging to the Railway Ministry, is responsible only for watch and ward duties. As has been seen, in the case of offences during travel, the victim has to run from pillar to post to register the offence in the relevant police jurisdiction. It is imperative that the railway police is given powers under the Police Act. Such a proposal made by the ministry of railways was strongly opposed by some states on the ground that it would dilute their powers!

Another issue was that of Lokayuktas who had been repeatedly urging in their annual conferences that a uniform all-India law should be enacted to increase their powers and make their offices more effective. Such a proposal was opposed by some states on the specious ground that it would militate against the federal spirit of the Constitution, whatever it means!

One is unable to see why there should not be an all-India law for police, but this too has been opposed on the ground that police is a state subject. Each state can enact special provisions in the said law to suit its requirements, but there is every justification to have an all-India law on police with common features such as recruitment, training, representation to minorities, women and weaker sections, emphasis on human rights, redressal of public grievances, upholding the rule of law, uniform policy on transfers, fixation of tenure and so on. Why should there not be a national policy on eradication of corruption? Why should autonomy of states intrude into these matters?

When the Constitution was framed, the menace of terrorism was not as prevalent or as acute as at present. Several crimes are now seen to have not only an all-India spread but have international ramifications. Serious and widespread communal violence in places such as Godhra, Mumbai and Ahmedabad, to name a few, had national repercussions. The demolition of the Babri Masjid by frenzied mobs with active connivance of the state government was a new experience which was not foreseen by the framers of the Constitution. It is shocking that in a continental-size country with so many diversities, India cannot have a federal civil police. In this light, it is imperative that the entries 'police and public order' are shifted from the State List to the Concurrent List.

It is necessary that these concerns are looked at in the larger national perspective rather than from the narrow confines of autonomy of states. It is also necessary that they are considered keeping in mind India's emergence as a regional power. The role of the state has to be that of a facilitator in every way. Towards this end, some subjects must not be dealt with even at the state level. Some must be entrusted at the municipal or even the lower level of a village panchayat. But there are a large number of subjects on which a national perspective is necessary.

India has set an outstanding example of co-operative federalism by enacting the Goods and Services Tax. All political parties have come together in achieving this. The UPA government, led by the Congress itself, had taken the initiative in the matter, though it is now being unfairly derided by Rahul Gandhi, the Congress president, as a Gabbar Singh Tax! This is ridiculous, to put it mildly.

I have been suggesting for quite some time that for the CBI, a governing council comprising the Prime Minister, concerned central ministers, and some chief ministers, by rotation could be constituted to oversee larger policy matters pertaining to the organisation. This would go a long way in reducing the resistance of states to the enactment of a separate law for the CBI. The constitutional mechanism of Inter-State Council ought to be used more effectively and purposefully to discuss and resolve Centre-state issues. With political maturity and statesmanship, innovative approaches can be developed to impart a new meaning and content to India's quasi-federalism.

PART FOUR

RHETORIC OF ZERO TOLERANCE FOR CORRUPTION

THE CANCER OF CORRUPTION

ERADICATION OF CORRUPTION has been a common and constant refrain of all governments which have come to power in the states and at the Centre since Independence. But, for the common person in the street, there has been no relief. The articles in this section bring this out fully. This was also borne out by the articles contained in my previous collection, *The Changing Times—A Commentary on Current Affairs* (2000). Why is it so difficult to eradicate corruption?

As I see it, the problem is of lack of not just the political will, which is often blamed, but, equally, if not more, the lack of administrative will among senior civil servants. A striking example of this was that rules were not framed for over thirteen years under the legislation on benami transactions. As a result, this important piece of legislation for dealing with corruption remained on paper. Further, literally thousands of cases are awaiting government approval for prosecution of officers involved in corruption. Creation of special courts for speedy disposal of corruption cases has been neglected, leading to such cases languishing for years together.

Let us now turn to the rhetoric of federalism which is heard so often to assert the autonomy of the state governments. I am unable to understand why there cannot be a national policy on eradication of corruption. The issues are common, the suffering of the common persons on account of corrupt practices of government functionaries are the same from one end of the country to the other. But, in the name of autonomy of the states, each state wants to have the freedom to deal with the problem (and in most cases not to deal) on its own. As a result, the central Whistle-blowers Act, for example, applies only to the central government establishments. Why should India not have a national policy on eradication of corruption?

Experience of last seven decades since Independence has brought out some pertinent concerns. To begin with, politics must be kept out in dealing with corruption cases. If this objective is to be achieved, anti-corruption organisations must be entrusted to Lokayuktas in the states and the Central Vigilance Commission (CVC) at the Centre. Appointment of Lokpal was unduly delayed by the Narendra Modi government. Now that Lokpal has been appointed, the Central Bureau of Investigation (CBI) and other anti-corruption agencies in the central government must be placed fully under the Lokpal.

An effective deterrent to corruption would be amendment of Article 311 of the Constitution to deny the protection to such of the government servants who are charged with allegations of corruption. Yet another effective deterrent will be to shift the burden of proof in corruption cases to those who are charged therein so that they will be presumed to be guilty unless they prove that they are innocent. Prima facie, this might appear to be harsh. But, corruption, which is a life-threatening disease for body politic, has to be treated to remove all its traces. In my book, *Good Governance Never on India's Radar* (2014), I have given a comprehensive twenty-six point programme for dealing with the menace of corruption and to make indulging in corruption prohibitively costly.

Another very disturbing facet is the nexus which has come to notice in major scams between the politicians, businessmen and the bureaucrats. As the coal scam showed, deliberate effort was made by the CBI to keep the then Prime Minister, who was also the Coal Minister at the time, and senior officers in the Prime Minister's Office (PMO) out of investigation. This was also seen in the 2G scam investigation. This gave a very wrong message that law does not apply equally to everyone and some are more equal than the rest—hardly the message to give if the rule of law is to prevail.

Yet another feature has come out prominently and unmistakably. The cases of corruption at the political level have received lenient treatment by the investigating agencies. The most prominent example was Bofors. Volumes can be written about how assiduous efforts were made to cover up and whitewash the inquiry, including by the Joint Parliamentary Committee (JPC). Most shocking was that even appeals were not filed where the decisions of the lower courts were questionable. The CBI filed an appeal in the Supreme Court against the order of the Delhi High Court after a lapse of several years and told the Court that the then UPA government did not permit it to file the appeal. The *amicus curiae* in the well-known *Hawala* case had suggested making a provision for appointment of an independent prosecutor by making a suitable amendment in the Constitution. But the Supreme Court had felt that the time for such a decision had not come. This fond hope of the Court has been belied by experience in several major cases so far. Time has now come to amend the Constitution to provide for appointment of an independent prosecutor in politically sensitive cases and major scams. The decision in this regard must be left to the Supreme Court, as the government, which would be an interested party, cannot be expected to take an initiative in the matter.

22

B.K. BANSAL SUICIDE AND SCOURGE OF CORRUPTION: ARE WE SERIOUS ABOUT ADDRESSING REAL ISSUES?

THE NEWS REPORTS OF suicide committed by B.K. Bansal, an official in the Corporate Affairs Ministry and his family members, following the raids and enquiries by the Central Bureau of Investigation (CBI), have shocked the country. Since there will be no question of a court case now, the final truth will come out, if at all, when the inquiry is conducted by the CBI in the allegations of excesses, maltreatment and atrocious behaviour of the investigating officers. But the larger issues posed by this case need urgent attention and should not be pushed under the carpet, as has been the case so far.

Corruption is like a terminal cancer in India. Irrespective of which political party is in power in the states and at the Centre, India has not found any answers to the affliction of corruption. In this matter, snail's pace has become a

---

Firstpost, 30 September 2016.

norm. The Law Commission in its 166th report (1999) had observed:

'The Prevention of Corruption Act has totally failed in checking corruption. In spite of the fact that India is rated as one of the most corrupt countries in the world, the number of prosecutions and more so the number of convictions are ridiculously low.'

The progressive deterioration in the working of CBI has been studied and commented upon by a number of committees and commissions which include, among others, the L.P. Singh committee, the Shah Commission of Inquiry in its report on the excesses in the Emergency, the National Police Commission, and the Estimates Committee and other Committees of Parliament, from time to time. The question of a separate legislation for the CBI had figured in Parliament way back in 1970 when Y.B. Chavan, the then Home Minister, had told Parliament that framing a legislation was being examined in consultation with the Law Ministry. Due to the opposition of the states, this subject has languished since then. After toiling for 14 years finally the Goods and Services Tax legislation is at last on its way to fruition but enacting a legislation for the CBI has not been pursued by any of the governments in power at the Centre.

Public memory is proverbially short. Highly adverse comments on the working of the CBI made from time to time by the Supreme Court have been forgotten. If this is the fate of the pronouncements of the highest court in the land, there is nothing much one can expect in a crucial area of governance, namely eradication of corruption.

The Narendra Modi government, on coming to power in 2014, has announced that it would be committed to the dictum of less government and more governance. An important ingredient of such a programme will have to do with eradication of corruption. But the ball is yet to start rolling.

I had comprehensively examined the various facets of this question in my book, *Good Governance Never on India's Radar,* and had suggested a national charter delineating 26 action points. I had also emphasised the need for introduction of the inquisitorial system on the pattern adopted by European countries, as opposed to the accusatorial system based on the British pattern adopted in India. This will meet with the repeated public demand in several cases that the investigation of the sensitive cases be carried out under the supervision of the higher judiciary. I had also urged that an independent directorate of prosecution should be established to pursue the major cases vigorously, without permitting any political influence to come in the way.

Yet another ingredient of the programme to fight corruption was to entrust the supervision of the CBI to an independent statutory authority, namely the Central Vigilance Commission (CVC). This suggestion was made by the Supreme Court itself in the Hawala case but has been resisted by the CBI. Neither has the government been keen on it for obvious reasons. If the Supreme Court finds it important to apply its full weight in the reorganisation of the BCCI in the interest of the game of cricket, there is no reason why matters pertaining to waging an all-out war against corruption be permitted to languish for lack of political will and by vested interests.

Public life in the country has become far too muddied over the years since Independence. The question of nexus between the politicians, bureaucracy and criminals has been talked about in hushed tones in the corridors of power. The N.N. Vohra Committee Report submitted in 1994 is brandied about in this connection. But the background papers on which its conclusions were based have not been made public yet. 'Dirty tricks departments' are no longer operative only in the government. Corporates are equally, if not more, in the game! Appointments of malleable officers at the behest of business houses have been a common practice in India for a long time.

In the recent years, allotment of portfolios of ministers too has been done on this basis. Consultancy firms are being employed to influence policy making in the government. Engagement of retired senior officers as consultants is a fig-leaf which is widely prevalent now. In the post-liberalisation environment, even eyebrows are not raised when corporate houses raise issues of their right to privacy against enquiries into their wrong-doings. Politicisation of higher civil services has made a mockery of the pattern of the British civil service adopted by India at its Independence. This brings out the very many nuances of the problem of tackling corruption in the higher echelons of the government.

Currently, some former secretaries to Government of India, with impeccable reputation for integrity and honesty, are being investigated by the CBI. From what is in the public knowledge, mostly, these cases pertain to matters which involve use of discretionary powers. Questions are often raised about the bureaucratic red tape and delays in decision-making processes in India. It is time we take note of the fact that this is because of our enviable system of transparency and accountability, not just to Parliament but also to the audit institutions, society at large by honouring the right to information, and openness to the media. Governments in a number of countries do not necessarily operate under these exacting standards. This has meant holding officers responsible for their actions, even long after their retirement. Further, the same standards of rectitude are not applied to the ministers and political executives. In allotments of coal fields, for example, ministers have hardly ever been held responsible.

In the notorious Adarsh Co-operative Housing Society case in Mumbai, successive Chief Ministers have been permitted to get away with a plea that they were misled by their officers! How such cases of decision-making at the highest level of government should be investigated and the evidence evaluated needs to be examined afresh. This is not a mere police function. Application of mind must be by an independent outside agency such as the CVC or the Lokpal, when established, before a case is filed in the court. Are we prepared to go to the basics? Without doing so, it will be futile to expect speedy decision-making and out-of-the-box thinking by the bureaucracy. Rather than remaining engaged with individual cases, it will be much more productive if we address these larger policy and institutional issues.

23

NEGLECT OF 1992 SCAM LED TO MALLYA, MODI FRAUDS

CLOSE ON THE heels of the Vijay Mallya scam involving a number of major banks, including the country's biggest bank, the State Bank of India, and the Industrial Development Bank of India, the country is rocked by another mega scam.

This time it is in respect to the second biggest bank in the country, the Punjab National Bank (PNB).

In reply to a question in the Lok Sabha, the government stated that during the four financial years 2013 to 2017, there were as many as 8,636 frauds in public sector and private sector banks in which an amount of Rs 26,922 crore was involved.

This should make anyone lose sleep. But, unfortunately, this does not hold good in respect to those in power! Something is certainly rotten in the state of Denmark.

There was the usual cacophony in the electronic media when the news broke. The blame game was about whether the previous United Progressive Alliance government should

---

Rediff.com, 7 March 2018.

be held responsible for the lapses or whether it is the Bharatiya Janata Party-led government which is remiss.

This in fact has become the standard pattern whenever the country is rocked by major scandals. Demands are also being made that a Joint Parliamentary Committee (JPC) should be appointed to go into the PNB scam.

Public memory is short and it is getting even shorter. Therefore, it might be worthwhile to recapitulate the experience of the JPC on the last bank scam in 1992.

Soon after the economic reforms were launched in 1991, the buoyancy in the stock market was mistaken as evidence of the success of economic reforms and its reception by the corporate world.

As a result, the Ministry of Finance as also the Reserve Bank of India failed to see that bank funds were being clandestinely used in the stock market by unscrupulous brokers.

There was an uproar in Parliament and the then Finance Minister Manmohan Singh, made a very uncalled for comment by saying, 'But that does not mean that I should lose my sleep simply because the stock market goes up one day and falls next day.'

This, in a sense, conveyed the approach of the government to the scam.

The JPC spent a lot of time in collecting information and literally truckloads of documents. It also made some very perceptive and penetrating observations on the functioning of the government, the supervisory role discharged by the RBI and several lacunae in it.

Referring to the then Finance Minister's flippant comment, the JPC sarcastically noted: 'It is good to have a FM who does not lose his sleep easily but one would wish that when such cataclysmic changes take place all around, some alarm would ring to disturb his slumber.'

The JPC had recommended: 'The Comptroller and Auditor General (C&AG) may be given a year's time to arrange for placement of staff in position and their training before starting on supplementary audit of all nationalised banks and financial institutions. Alternatively, the C&AG can take up the audit of all government banks and financial institutions in phases covering all of them within a period of two years from the date the necessary legal framework is created.'

The committee's observations and recommendations should have led to a number of important decisions pertaining to the supervision of the banking system, both by the Ministry of Finance and the RBI.

Unfortunately, this did not happen.

In fact, some officers against whom the committee had made severe criticism flourished in subsequent years.

Reference must also be made to yet another distinct feature of the functioning of the JPC. To give an impression that the committee's report was unanimous, the notes appended by a number of members were merely called 'notes' and not 'dissenting notes'.

For example, in the note submitted by a number of members including Jaswant Singh, George Fernandes, S. Jaipal Reddy, Gurudas Dasgupta and others, it was urged that certain matters must also be examined by Parliament (as the committee had not done so) when considering the report of the committee: Allegations relating to payment of Rs 1 crore by Harshad Mehta (to then Prime Minister P. V. Narasimha Rao); matters relating to the conduct of Romesh Bhandari, then the Governor of Tripura, etc.

Several other issues were similarly raised in the notes submitted by some other members.

As for the large amounts involved in the scam, all that the committee said was that these matters should be further investigated by the concerned government agencies.

It was not therefore surprising that Debashish Basu and Sucheta Dalal, the two journalists who had done commendable investigative work on the scam have noted in their book, *The Scam: Who Won, Who Lost, Who Got Away*: 'It was bad enough that gigantic scam took place. It is as incredible how ham-handed the scam investigation has been.'

In the meeting of bank chairpersons called by the then Finance Minister, Manmohan Singh had said, 'It was a collective failure of the banking system.'

Another term which was repeatedly used by government functionaries while talking about the scam was that it was a 'systemic failure'. As if for this collective or systemic failure no one could be held responsible.

The Action Taken Report submitted by the government to Parliament in July 1994 reflected this thinking and the Opposition parties boycotted Parliament for 16 days in July-August 1994.

The two recent major scams involving Vijay Mallya and Nirav Modi are a glaring proof of the neglect of the first bank scam.

It is against this background that one must ask a question whether appointing another JPC would serve any purpose, except that of window dressing.

If the intention is to take serious remedial measures, I would suggest that a high-level judicial commission of inquiry should be appointed under the Commission of Inquiry Act.

The commission should be asked to hold a wide-ranging inquiry concerning all aspects of the frauds perpetrated in the public and private sector banks.

It should also be requested to go into the functioning of the Ministry of Finance and the RBI over the years.

The commission could also examine whether the instrument of Letter of Understanding (LoU), introduced by the RBI, needs to be continued in such an unguided and unrestricted manner.

While appointing such a commission, the government should make a categorical announcement that the report of the commission would be published as soon as it is submitted to the government, without waiting for preparation of the ATR, and follow-up action on the recommendations would be taken expeditiously, within one year at the latest.

One issue which has come up time and again whenever banks have run into difficulties or have got involved in frauds is that of efficacy of the audit, whether the audit is by the statutory auditors or the RBI.

In most of these cases, it is not in public knowledge if any action was taken against the auditors for the lapses in the audit.

Action against the auditors is expected to be taken by the apex body of the auditors.

Over the years it is seen that apex bodies of several professions such as engineers, auditors, architects, advocates and so on, which are empowered under the relevant Acts of Parliament, have been remiss in discharging their responsibilities. This has led to a feeling of frustration and helplessness among the people.

In my book, *Good Governance Never On India's Radar*, I had advocated that Ombudspersons should be appointed for these professionals and their apex bodies. Such an effective grievance redressal mechanism will act as a valve in relieving pressures of discontent.

Transparent functioning of the Ombudsperson and her/his passing self-contained 'speaking orders' will go a long way in empowering citizens.

Finally, the truth, howsoever unpalatable it may be, must be faced. Bank nationalisation was undertaken by Indira Gandhi for purely political reasons and she made no secret of it when she spoke to I.G. Patel, the then Secretary, Economic Affairs, Ministry of Finance, with instructions for taking follow-up action.

The merits of the proposal were never examined before taking the decision. And neither have they been during the last five decades since nationalisation of banks.

A comprehensive study should now be undertaken to examine the extent to which these banks have fulfilled the objectives with which they were nationalised.

This flagship programme of the then avowedly socialist regime has been exploited fully by the ruling elite, whichever political party was in power.

The nexus between politicians, industrialists, large borrowers and bankers is legion in India. Crony capitalism has been in evidence all these years.

Nationalised banks have certainly served some purpose in terms of mobilisation of deposits, particularly from rural and semi-urban areas. But the credit delivery system of public sector banks in these areas has not been particularly effective or economical.

In fact, much greater responsibility in this regard is borne by the co-operative sector. The banks have been totally bureaucratised and politicised. The time has therefore come to seriously consider privatisation of these banks in a time-bound manner.

I hope the Narendra Modi government will set the ball rolling without any loss of time.

Taking effective remedial steps to ensure good health and credibility of the banking system is crucial to fulfilling India's ambitions as a rising power.

The latest report of Transparency International on the Global Corruption Perception Index continues to make a bleak reading so far as India is concerned.

India ranks 81 among 180 countries which is depressing. The World Bank's Global Investment Competitiveness Report 2017-2018 underlines the concept of government effectiveness.

It is an aggregate indicator that reflects, among others, perceptions of the quality of public services, the quality of civil service and the degree of its independence from political pressures, and the credibility of the government's commitment to its policies.

Gigantic bank scams in the recent years have clearly established the ineffectiveness of the government. The Modi government has been taking credit for improvement in respect of the ease of doing business in India.

But when I look at the scams I cannot help feeling that it is too easy to do business with banks in India, if one is a Harshad Mehta, Vijay Mallya or Nirav Modi and their tribe.

24

PNB SCAM OPENS PANDORA'S BOX: SERIOUS QUESTIONS ABOUT RBI ROLE AS REGULATOR, 'BUT WHO WILL BELL THE CAT?'

TALKING ABOUT THE Punjab National Bank (PNB) fraud, Urjit Patel, Governor, Reserve Bank of India (RBI), has said that there was 'anger, hurt and pain' in the central bank over the looting by some in the business community and the bank's helplessness in dealing with the situation as the regulator is constrained by inadequate legal powers to supervise and manage public sector banks, as it has no powers to remove Directors, management or supersede Boards of public sector banks.

Patel was in tune with the Hindutva idiom when he said, 'If we need to face the brickbats and be the *Neelakantha* consuming the poison, we will do so as our duty.' This timely statement needs to be examined closely since it has large policy implications and goes at the root of governance of not

---

The Citizen, 16 April 2018.

just the public sector banks (PSBs) but also other private and foreign banks.

The only other time when the Governor, RBI, had referred to the bank's limited statutory powers in defence of its role as a regulator was during the inquiry by the Joint Parliamentary Committee (JPC) on the bank scam in 1991. Deposing before the committee, the Governor, RBI, had stated: 'We are not in a position to proceed against the public sector banks except with the concurrence of the government. If we are to have a clear system perhaps we may have to amend the law in such a way that the RBI can take action against those chairmen also, whether in the public or private sector, but after giving a notice to them.'

Agreeing with the above observation, the JPC had recommended: 'The government should seriously examine the suggestion of the then Governor. The committee is of the view that if this entire system of selection and appointment of executives/directors is not totally revamped, our nationalised banking industry will not only [not] recover, it will pull our entire economy down with it.'

The JPC had also recommended that 'more deterrent and penal action should be taken in order to ensure that all banks fall in line with the guidelines/ instructions of the RBI.' The committee had suggested that 'the penal clauses in the Banking Regulation Act and other relevant Acts should be reviewed with a view to enabling the RBI to impose graded penalties and other types of punishments commensurate with the seriousness of the irregularities.

'It is also necessary to review all relevant legislations relating to banks and other financial institutions so that they keep pace with the technological changes and other developments.' (pp 205-206, 215 of JPC report) When the JPC report was submitted in December 1993, Manmohan

Singh was the Finance Minister. Unfortunately, no action was initiated by him to make legislative changes as above though this matter came entirely within the purview of the finance ministry.

Debashis Basu and Sucheta Dalal have brought out in their book, *The Scam: Who won, Who lost, Who Got Away,* that when the bank scam shook Parliament in late April 1992, the first reaction of the Finance Minister, who had earlier been Governor, RBI, was that the matter should be left to the RBI to handle. He was even reluctant to make a categorical statement in Parliament. Some members of the Opposition and of his own party seized upon the weakness and were baying for his blood. (p. 269) Manmohan Singh should have known that real powers to deal with the PSBs were with the government, i.e. Finance Ministry, and not with the RBI!

Granting that RBI's powers are limited, it will be useful to know in how many cases the RBI had brought serious lapses and irregularities in PSBs to the notice of the government and action was proposed against those responsible, and the decision taken by the government thereon. Was the advice rendered by the RBI overlooked by the government? If these matters had been in the public domain, there would have been some check on the government's handling of the PSBs.

During the last four decades, almost all major political parties have been in power in the Centre. The fact that legislative changes have not been brought about by any of them shows the vested interests they have in not letting go of the leverages of power.

It must also be noted that the public perception of the RBI being the supreme regulator of all banks (including the PSBs) has been perpetuated over the years by the RBI itself. This was also underlined by the committees appointed by the RBI such as the A. Ghosh Committee on Frauds and Malpractices in Banks (1992), Rashid Jilani Committee (1995) and so on.

The working paper No. 505 pertaining to frauds in the Indian banking industry prepared by the Indian Institute of Management, Bangalore, in March 2016 has raised important issues such as credibility of audit firms and credit rating agencies, lack of requisite standards of corporate governance and so on. None of these committees has talked about the handicap of the RBI due to lack of statutory powers to supervise the PSBs.

A related question is of restructuring of PSBs. M. Narasimham Committee's two reports submitted in 1991 and 1998 had, inter alia, dealt with this subject. But due to its large political overtones, the recommendations were shelved. The committee, appointed by the RBI to review governance of boards of banks in India, under the chairmanship of P.J. Nayak, has in its report submitted in March 2014 dealt with this issue, though, according to me, it was not a part of its terms of reference. The committee's report is problematic for various reasons.

The committee was asked to examine how the boards of the banks could be made more effective. It has come to the conclusion that it can be only if the government divests its ownership and control of the banks and entrusts this responsibility to a separate company to be set up for the purpose. It is not clear which stake-holders were consulted by the committee.

What is the guarantee that any such company will be kept away from government control? After all, the main question is of the political philosophy and ideology of the government. The committee's thinking is based entirely on enhancing the financial returns of the government. This can be a highly debatable objective. The committee is also anxious to remove three main constraints of PSBs, namely, the Vigilance Commission, the Central Bureau of Investigation (CBI) and the Right to Information (RTI).

I believe that whatever be the ownership pattern of banks, public accountability and transparency must continue to be their mainstay. I would not consider it advisable to keep the PSBs outside the purview of the RTI.

The definition of corruption and fraud advocated by the committee is also problematic. The committee has argued that fraud must manifest itself through existence of self-benefit. The committee is of the view that deviation from procedure must not constitute the sole basis for initiating criminal action. This would clearly be self-defeating.

It is as a result of the Nayak committee recommendations that the Bank Boards Bureau (BBB) was established by government in April 2016, under the chairmanship of Vinod Rai, former Comptroller and Auditor General of India (C&AG). Appointment of former C&AG as chairman should have been avoided. Constitutional functionaries such as C&AG must not be appointed in any government posts after retirement. Rai should also not have accepted this responsibility in the larger interest of constitutional probity.

The Bureau has recently been reconstituted. Unfortunately, enough information is not available in public domain to judge as to how far it has served the purpose of its creation. It is reported that Bureau's recommendations have been overlooked in some cases.

The Bureau is reported to have submitted a series of proposals to the government regarding its future work. These must be made public to give an opportunity to the civil society to express its views thereon. It must also be made mandatory to make public each recommendation of the Bureau which has not been accepted by the government and the reasons therefor.

The recent happenings in private sector banks such as ICICI, Axis Bank and so on too have raised questions about the role of the RBI as a regulator. At least in these cases, the

RBI cannot take an alibi of lack of statutory powers. The misdemeanours in some prominent private sector banks during the period following demonetisation of high denomination notes had shaken public confidence. In these cases too, the RBI's role and actions were far from reassuring. In some money- laundering cases too reportedly only fines were imposed on the banks.

It is high time the legal framework governing the banking industry is thoroughly reviewed and revised. But who will bell the cat? Our law-givers have no time to make laws!

PART FIVE

Rule of Law, The Police and The CBI

RULE OF LAW AND THE POLICE

INDIA'S CONSTITUTION LAYS special emphasis on Fundamental Rights of citizens which include, among others, equality before law; prohibition of discrimination on grounds of religion, race, caste, sex or place of birth; right against exploitation; and right to freedom of religion. But the main problem is of enforcement of these rights. Article 32 of the Constitution gives right to citizens to approach the highest court in the land for enforcement of Fundamental Rights but this is neither easy nor affordable for the common person. The instruments for day-to-day protection of citizens' rights are the law enforcement agencies such as the police and the CBI But it must be admitted that India has utterly failed in making these agencies accountable. Their image as exploitative arm of government has been so perpetuated in public mind that no citizen feels comfortable to approach the police for redressal of his/her grievances.

It is interesting to see that the image of police was the same during the colonial British rule. But, even after Independence, there has been no change in it. The working of the police has been looked into by scores of committees and commissions appointed by the state and central governments. The main problem is of rampant politicisation of administration in general and police in particular. But this is not the only concern. Communalisation of police, unjust and unfair treatment of minorities and deprived sections of the society such as the scheduled castes and scheduled tribes, landless labour, bonded labour, women and children, are matters of serious concern.

Blatant violation of human rights has emerged as one of the main concerns in the functioning of police in India. Custodial deaths and custodial crime have tarnished the image of the police. Fake encounters have become the normal mode of getting rid of alleged criminals. This 'street justice' makes the police the investigators, the prosecutors and the judge, erasing altogether the basic tenets of rule of law. Setting up of the National Human Rights Commission and similar bodies in the states has not been effective in controlling these malpractices.

Use of force as an investigative technique continues to be widely prevalent. Scientific techniques of investigation and using multi-disciplinary teams for investigation of crimes is mostly unheard of, except in metropolitan areas and large cities. Excessive use of force in crowd control during mass agitations and demonstrations has been a matter of concern for a long time. Separation of the law and order wing of the police from its intelligence and investigative wings has been recommended by a number of commissions and committees, but remains to be implemented.

Unfortunately, these concerns were not pressed in the public interest petitions filed in the Supreme Court. Their scope was confined to political interference in the postings, transfers and working of the police. However, the directions given by the Supreme Court, way back in 2006, on these matters have remained largely on paper. Major states are resisting the curtailment of their powers in these matters. Strictly speaking, non-implementation of the orders of the Supreme Court is nothing less than a break-down of the constitutional machinery. The constitutional remedy for it is the dismissal of the state government and imposition of President's rule. But this is unworkable as almost all political parties in power in various states are equally remiss in the matter. The issues therefore have to be addressed politically. A forum such as the Inter-State Council must be used to create a national consensus on the manner in which issues underlying police reforms are to be addressed. This will call for a statesmanship of the highest order which seems to be lacking.

Maintaining law and order and enforcement of the rule of laws are the primary duties of the state. Even in this age of globalisation and privatisation, police and administration of justice cannot be handed over to Ambanis, Adanis and the private sector. Budgetary constraints cannot be adduced as a reason for neglecting the legitimate funding requirements of these departments. One result of lack of adequate funding is the severe shortage of even rudimentary housing facilities for the police, leading to ghettoization and police residing in slums. Apart from its adverse impact on the morale of the police, this has led to a nexus between the criminals, bootleggers and the police. Excessively long duty hours and non-availability of even weekly offs due to inadequate police strength have been responsible for deterioration in the health and well-being of the police. This, in turn, has also adversely affected their interface with the public. It is unfortunate that there is little appreciation of the gravity of the problem and the urgency of its redressal.

Reference must be made to the related question of outdated criminal justice system in the country. This has led to low conviction rate in criminal cases. Other major concerns include: witnesses turning hostile, difficulties faced by people in registering their first information reports in police stations, repeated adjournment of court cases, anticipatory bail provisions, and widely prevalent practice of perjury. The witness protection programme has been approved by the Supreme Court only in December 2018. It is to be seen how well it is implemented.

Due to the increasingly poor image and credibility of the police, increasing demands are being made that investigation of cases should be carried out under the supervision of courts. In a few cases this demand has been conceded by the courts. But, due to pressure of other legitimate work, it will be difficult for the courts to take up this responsibility. I have therefore been advocating for some time that, to begin with, provision should be made to adopt, in important and sensitive cases, the inquisitorial system, as in several European countries (as opposed to the accusatorial system prevalent in India), under which investigation of cases is done under the supervision of judicial magistrates. The relevant laws need to be amended to introduce this new system on a pilot basis.

Yet another disturbing development is the demand voiced by litigants to shift the cases to courts outside the state due to pressures exerted in the state or the complicity of the police with the interested parties. This happened very rarely in the past. The courts have been permitting this on the merits of the case to restore a sense of confidence among the people in the justice system. But this too shows how serious are the underlying causes.

Some articles in this part deal with the steep downhill journey of the CBI which has brought down its public image, credibility and esteem. The politicisation of the institution began in the 1970s during Indira Gandhi regime. Each successive government, irrespective of the political party to which it belonged, has misused the CBI. Repeated castigation by the Supreme Court has not served any purpose. I have, therefore, argued that surgical steps need to be taken to bring about institutional and systemic reforms in the CBI. But these will never come about unless they are prescribed by the Supreme Court.

25

LET US NOT STOP THE POLICE FROM DOING ITS JOB

THE STALLED ATTEMPT of the Pune police to arrest some liberal activists has blazed a new trail and has raised disquieting questions which are far more important than merely the concerns arising out of the Bhima Koregaon violence.

Perhaps, it is for the first time that three courts in Delhi at three levels—a Magistrate's Court, the Delhi High Court and the Supreme Court—have taken cognisance of the matter the moment the activists were arrested.

The police had approached the Magistrate's Court for a transit remand to bring two of the arrested persons to Pune. The Delhi High Court and the Supreme Court have thought it fit to intervene and the Supreme Court has ordered that the persons arrested, not just in Delhi but also other places in the country, should be kept under house arrest till the case is disposed of by it.

Rediff.com, 3 September 2018.

The apex court has declared, 'dissent is the safety valve of democracy—if it is not allowed, the pressure cooker will burst.'

The observation made by the court is unexceptional but has created the impression that there was a deliberate attempt on the part of the police to stop dissenting voices in the country.

I find this somewhat disconcerting. It is time we go back to the basics.

It is true that the credibility and the image of police, both at the central and state levels, has suffered grievously in recent years, but this cannot be the reason for not permitting the police to act in this case.

If the rule of law is to prevail in the country, the police must be allowed to do its job.

After investigation, including interrogation of the persons concerned, the case will be put up in the court and the courts will have the last word to decide if there is any substance in the case.

Should the police be deterred from doing their work by seeking the intervention of the courts?

Should anyone, including the court, pre-judge the issues and the case?

There seem to be increasing instances of the courts stopping the police from interrogating the accused by taking them in police custody. The judgment as to whether custody is necessary for effective interrogation should be left to the police.

If there is misuse of powers, the police can be hauled up by the court but it would be frustrating the provisions of law if the police is not permitted to do their job.

I have been advocating for quite some time to do away with the provision of law for anticipatory bail *(The Changing Times, 2000,* pages 113-116).

The original purpose of incorporating Section 438 in the Criminal Procedure Code is being subverted by liberal recourse to this provision, particularly in high profile cases though interrogation of the accused in custody is often more successful during police investigation.

As the Punjab and Haryana High Court had held the investigation should not be stifled at the very threshold of investigation by granting anticipatory bail [*Gurbaksh v state of Punjab,* A. 1978 P&H (F.B.)].

The Supreme Court has also cautioned against its misuse. However, the experience is quite the contrary.

This was pithily brought out by a cartoon. A father proudly shows a statue of Mahatma Gandhi to his son and says, 'Gandhi had to undergo long spells in the prison in the freedom struggle.' The son innocently but pertinently asks, 'Daddy, why did he not take anticipatory bail?'

I have often argued in my writings that Naxalism should not be treated as a simple law and order problem and the underlying socio-economic causes must be addressed. But a line must be drawn between the advocacy for this well merited cause and supporting the ideology of violence to achieve the objectives.

Any encouragement for mobilisation of funds for the purpose, procurement and use of lethal weapons must be put down with a heavy hand. Often, there is a thin line between the proponents of the cause.

The police must be permitted to establish their case if any group of activists falls in the latter category. Prima facie, this is the issue in the present case.

As in the United States after the assumption of office by President Trump, in India too, the country is split in the middle, with *Hindutvawadis*, and liberals and secularists arraigned against each other.

It is as if 'either you are with me or against me'. Everything is either black or white. There are no shades in between.

As a society, are we becoming colour-blind? Analogies are being drawn with the Emergency during 1975-1977. This is ridiculous. In no way are the two situations even close to each other.

The very fact that the judiciary intervened so decisively in this case at the level of both the High Court and the Supreme Court so soon after the event and on one single day is proof enough that this comparison is not valid.

In fact, making such comparisons has been responsible for creating a very negative and destructive mindset in society.

In the national discourse on this case, one important aspect is being lost sight of. According to the Constitution of India, 'police' and 'public order' are subjects in the State List. The Union government is not even remotely concerned, except that in this case, the state and central governments belong to the same political party. But this is inevitable in a quasi-federal structure of India.

To ascribe motives to the actions of the state government, and that too at the so very early stage of police investigation will be counter-productive.

Let the law take its course. Let us not stop the police from doing its job.

India has the world's most powerful judiciary to uphold the Constitutional precepts and protect the citizens' freedoms.

26

WHY A REVAMPING OF THE CBI IS NECESSARY

WHEN ANY INSTITUTION becomes a law unto itself, it becomes imperative to ensure that it is made answerable and accountable to the society at large, and not just to the government. Over the years, disconcerting questions have arisen regarding the functioning of the Central Bureau of Investigation (CBI), irrespective of which government was in power.

Even the Supreme Court has exhausted its prolific vocabulary in castigating the functioning of the CBI. The latest case is of the CBI changing the 'look out notice' issued for Vijay Mallya from detaining him to just reporting his travels, which facilitated his flight to London. It brings out the totally arbitrary working of the CBI. Either the first notice was uncalled for or the second was totally unjustified.

The CBI has a chequered history which brings out all that is wrong with India's governance. Almost five decades ago, on April 29, 1970, the then Union Home Minister Y.B. Chavan had told the Parliament that a Central law for the CBI was

---

The Wire, 27 September 2018.

being prepared in consultation with the Ministry of Law. This proposal is still languishing! One knows that in India, things move at snail's pace, but in this case even the snail would have won the race!

In 1978, the committee appointed, under the chairmanship of L.P. Singh, former Union Home Secretary, had made wide-ranging recommendations to improve the CBI's working. As is the usual practice in such cases, the report was consigned to the archives.

This was followed by the recommendations of the Estimates Committee of the Parliament (1991-92). The committee had urged that a clear-cut policy should be laid down stating the purpose of CBI's functioning and had suggested a legislation defining its charter. The committee was firmly of the view that unless the CBI was given a statutory status and well-defined legal powers to investigate cases which have ramifications in states, its effectiveness would decline substantially and steeply.

The committee had further desired that the question of amending the Constitution for this purpose should be discussed with the states. The committee had underlined that the CBI was essentially an anti-corruption agency and therefore, the question of setting up a national police agency, distinct from the CBI, for investigation of criminal offences of national and trans-national importance should be examined promptly and with utmost seriousness, in consultation with the Chief Ministers of states. The committee had proposed that this new organisation should be placed under the Ministry of Home Affairs (MHA).

I was Union Home Secretary at the time. I felt that the recommendation of setting up a national police agency was sound and decided to pursue it further. As I had brought out in my memoirs, *Unfinished Innings* (1996), an issues paper for the committee of secretaries was prepared by the MHA, for taking follow-up action and putting up the proposals to the Cabinet Committee on Political Affairs. But the CBI was opposed to shedding any of its powers and functions and the then Prime Minister P.V. Narasimha Rao did not want the matter to be pursued. The reorganisation of the CBI thus proved to be a non-starter.

Exemption from RTI Act

Later, the functioning of the CBI figured prominently in the Jain hawala, 2G scam, coal scam and other prominent cases in which it had repeatedly come in for adverse notice. Its investigation of Bofors case raised a number of issues in public debate which have remained unanswered to this day. After the passage of the Right to Information Act, 2005, it was hoped that agencies like the CBI would be open to public scrutiny to some extent. But the CBI has conveniently managed to get itself exempted from the purview of the Act, and that too on the recommendations of the Committee of Secretaries!

The working of the CBI became totally politicised under Indira Gandhi's prime ministership. It will be recalled that the then CBI Director D. Sen was found guilty by the Parliament for obstructing four officers of industry ministry in collecting information for replying to a Parliament question on Maruti affairs and was sentenced to a prison term, along with the former Prime Minister Indira Gandhi and R.K. Dhawan, her private secretary. Sen had raided and arrested the four officers at the behest Indira Gandhi.

Since then, the CBI has become the hand-maiden of the government in power. This led the Supreme Court to pass orders in the *Jain hawala* case, saying the investigation should be pursued independently of the executive. But this remained confined only to that case and it did not stop the CBI from taking approval regarding its stand in other cases such as the 2G scam.

It is high time the CBI is mandatorily kept at an arm's length from the government while investigating politically sensitive cases. The Supreme Court had suggested in the *Jain hawala* case that the CBI should be placed under the supervision of the Central Vigilance Commission (CVC). As was to be expected, this was opposed by the CBI. The government too was not keen.

Problems within the CBI

At least two former Directors of the CBI are being probed for their nefarious role in influencing the investigations in high profile cases. The CBI is reported to be probing 26 of its own officers for graft. Another news item shows that its present director and special director are at loggerheads, making public allegations against each other. This is simply shocking and raises serious questions about the integrity and image of the premier investigating agency in the country.

Misuse of the CBI to settle political scores has largely been responsible for the state governments' opposition to enacting a Central law for the CBI. But unless the CBI is brought under a statute, it will be impossible to make it truly accountable for its actions and inactions.

Guidelines to watch over the CBI

Towards this end, I have been advocating for quite some time that a high-level governing board should be set up for the CBI in which, apart from the Prime Minister and the Union Home Minister, four to five Chief Ministers of states may be appointed, by turn, to give broad guidelines and keep a watch over the working of the CBI. This will instil a sense of confidence in the states and help in building consensus in favour of a Central law for the CBI. Second, the CBI should be bifurcated into an anti-corruption body and a national crime bureau. The latter should be entrusted with all matters pertaining to criminal offences with national and international ramifications. The present CBI, with its charter confined to anti-corruption cases, should continue to be under the Ministry of Personnel while the National Crime Bureau should be placed under the MHA.

Third, a comprehensive new central law should govern the working of the institutions. Fourth, the law should specifically provide for appointment of a special public prosecutor who will have full independence to deal with the politically and nationally sensitive cases and take a stand safeguarding public interest. Fifth, explicit charters may be laid down for both these organisations, with reference to which their work could be judged. Sixth, these organisations should be brought fully under the Right to Information law, with a stipulation that no information pertaining to any ongoing investigation can be made available, but that all information pertaining to cases which were withdrawn, or cases which were closed, or were dismissed by the court would be made available to the people. Such a social audit will go a long way in making both these institutions fully accountable.

Seventh, the law should lay down that such an annual social audit of the working of these organisations should be carried out by ten reputed, knowledgeable persons with background of law, justice, public affairs and administration and the audit report should be placed before the Parliament. Eighth, the selection of the Directors of both these institutions should be made by a committee presided over by the Prime Minister and comprise the Home Minister, the Lok Sabha Speaker and the Rajya Sabha Chairperson, Lokpal, when appointed, and leaders of Opposition in both the Houses. Ninth, the Directors should have a fixed term of three years. Tenth, after retirement, the Directors of both the institutions should be made ineligible for any appointment by the Central and state governments.

What is at stake is more than just the image and credibility of the CBI. India's image as a country committed to the rule of law itself needs to be refurbished nationally and internationally. The Narendra Modi government can send a powerful message by setting the ball rolling without loss of any further time.

27

HOW THE CBI CAN BE SAVED

PRIME MINISTER NARENDRA Modi, on assuming charge four years ago, had announced that his government would strive for less government and more governance. Little had he realised that this would be a daunting challenge to fulfil and it would remain one of his important unfulfilled promises. The print and electronic media has created an impression that the present infighting between the Director and Special Director of the Central Bureau of Investigation (CBI) and their levelling charges against each other is the most serious calamity in the CBI's history.

But this is far from true. Public memory is phenomenally short. Volumes can be written about the misuse of the CBI by successive governments and its high-handed, arbitrary functioning over the years since Independence, except for the years of Jawaharlal Nehru's regime as Prime Minister.

To recapitulate just a few instances: After the Emergency the then CBI Director was jailed by a Parliament resolution for having raided and arrested, on the directions of then Prime Minister Indira Gandhi, four officers of the industry ministry for showing the temerity to collect information about Maruti Udyog set up by Sanjay Gandhi, her wayward son.

Rediff.com, 31 October 2018.

The Justice Shah Commission of Inquiry set up to look into the excesses of the Emergency had observed that the chief of the CBI had lent himself to serve the ends which were 'other than strictly legal, constitutional or moral'.

A classic understatement! On return to power in 1980, Indira Gandhi issued orders for withdrawal and destruction of all copies of the Shah Commission reports.

This is perhaps the only case in recorded history where a report of the judicial commission of inquiry was destroyed by the successor government.

The two recent directors of the CBI are facing serious investigations for corruption charges and conflict of interest. Not long ago, a very senior CBI officer in Delhi was raided on corruption charges and he literally threw out sacks full of high denomination currency notes from his balcony in the high-rise building in R.K. Puram.

It was for the first (but certainly not the last) time that Delhi saw a torrential shower of currency notes! A recent news report mentions that at least 26 senior officers in the CBI are facing charges of corruption.

Misuse of the CBI has repeatedly come to public notice. Some prominent cases in this behalf include Bofors, the Commonwealth Games, 2G scam, coal scam and so on. It was the government of the day which was calling the shots, and no political party should be permitted to take a holier than thou attitude.

In the present imbroglio, too many uneasy questions have arisen. They concern the CBI, the Central Vigilance Commission (CVC) and the government itself.

- Why was the Special Director appointed when there were serious charges against him and the Director had brought these to the notice of the government?

- Why did it take this long to complete the inquiry against the Special Director?
- Why were the counter-charges made by the Special Director against the Director not looked into expeditiously?
- What was the government doing all this time when this infighting in the CBI was continuing?
- Was there a need to carry out the coup-like operation in the CBI office at midnight to send the two officers on compulsory leave?
- Why was the National Security Adviser brought in it? Why was the Cabinet Secretary sidelined?
- Why was the background and reputation of the interim Director not checked before appointing him in that post when he was also working in the CBI itself?

It is difficult to believe that the government was unaware of it. The CVC has also not come out unscathed in this sordid episode.

It is not therefore surprising that the Supreme Court has directed that the inquiry against the Director and the Special Director should be overseen by a retired judge of the Supreme Court.

I was surprised to read that the government advocate was trying to persuade the court not to insist on it. This was certainly not in keeping with the government's avowed claim that it was trying its utmost to be fair and transparent in the matter.

These are disturbing questions when the CBI and the CVC are working directly under the Prime Minister.

Palliatives suggested by High Courts and the apex court from time to time have not worked. For example, this 'caged parrot', as described by the Supreme Court, could not be handled by the CVC.

Setting up of a high-level selection committee for selection of the CBI director has not been successful as seen from the way the incumbent of the post has conducted himself. The much touted *hawala* case in which the Supreme Court gave a series of directions to give independence and autonomy to the CBI have also not worked.

The then Chief Justice of India, J.S. Verma, who had presided over the bench and had pronounced the *hawala* judgment, had himself expressed his deep disappointment at the reluctance of the CBI officers to exercise their authority independently. This was when Justice Verma was Chairman of the National Human Rights Commission. Answers must be found to this troubling experience.

Where do you go from here? The way forward is clear if there is a political will to take it. The important milestones are the following.

First, as the Estimates Committee of Parliament had suggested in its 13th report in 1992, in view of the vast increase in the workload of the CBI, it should be bifurcated, and the CBI's charter should be restricted to anti-corruption cases.

The investigation of major criminal cases having national and international implications, and national crimes spread over more than one state may be entrusted to a new National Crime Bureau and it should be placed under the Ministry of Home Affairs.

As brought out in my memoirs, *Unfinished Innings* (1996), I had initiated action in this regard when I was Union Home Secretary in 1992, but it had to be given up abruptly at the direction of the then Prime Minister P.V. Narasimha Rao who did not want any restructuring of the CBI.

Second, a new law may be enacted for the CBI.

This matter has been under consideration for the last five decades. This will also require a Constitutional amendment for which concurrence of the states will be required.

The states have been resisting this proposal due to the misuse of the CBI by the central government over the years by starting investigations against state leaders belonging to political parties opposed to the central government to settle political scores.

I have been suggesting for some time that a high-level governing board should be created for the CBI consisting of, apart from the Prime Minister and the concerned central ministers, a few chief ministers, by rotation.

This proposal needs to be placed before the Inter-State Council and its approval obtained.

Three, the charter of the CBI should be clearly spelt out in the new law so that the CBI's work can be assessed with reference to its charter.

Fourth, the CBI Director should have a fixed term of three years and he should not be eligible for any employment under the state or central government after retirement.

Fifth, the selection of the Director should be by a high-power selection committee comprising the Prime Minister, Chief Justice of India or a judge of the Supreme Court nominated by him, Lokpal (when appointed), and Leader of the Opposition (or of the largest party) in the Lok Sabha.

Sixth, the CBI should be placed under the Lokpal, when appointed. Till then, it should be under the CVC. Correspondingly, the anti-corruption bureaus in the states should also be placed under the Lokayuktas.

Seventh, the law should clearly lay down that the CBI should not be given any exemption from the Right to Information Act.

Eighth, the law should provide for social audit of the work of the CBI.

For this purpose, there should be a committee comprising jurists, retired judges, public persons, media and persons with experience of administration.

The annual report of this committee should be placed before Parliament. The report should, inter alia, cover conviction rate of CBI cases, review of cases closed by the CBI, CBI cases dismissed by the courts during the year, observations made by courts on the working of the CBI, and any other matters concerning the credibility and efficiency of the CBI.

This broad approach should also hold good for the new National Crime Bureau to be set up.

The very fact that enacting a central legislation for the CBI has been pending for the last five decades shows that unless there is a strong political will, the conundrum of the CBI shall continue forever.

Not a very encouraging note on which to end this account of grim reality.

28

POLICE FOR NEW INDIA

AFTER INDEPENDENCE, THERE has been a perceptible improvement in the functioning of several instruments of governance but police is the solitary exception. Its working has been marked by a steep deterioration. More shocking is the disdain of the police for the rule of law, which is supposedly its prime responsibility. Working of police has become notorious for lack of sensitivity to human rights, particularly of weaker sections of society, minorities, women, children, and other deprived sections such as bonded labour and landless labour. Equally shocking is the communal bias of the police which has created a feeling of insecurity among the minorities. Politicisation of police has reached its nadir. Every political party has used the police to increase its sphere of influence and the ruling party treats the police as its legitimate arm of exploitation.

A number of innovative measures adopted over the years have not worked in India. It was believed that police stations manned entirely by women would be able to address the grievances of women more sympathetically. But this has not

---

Dialogue Quarterly, April-June 2018.

proved to be true. It was believed that women police would be less prone to corruption than men. This too has been belied. It was believed that women police would be less prone to excessive use of force. This too has turned out to be a fanciful notion. It is time these concerns are looked into by experts.

The relevant issues are wide-ranging and complex and ought to be addressed holistically. Unfortunately, as in the story of the elephant and the seven blind men, mostly only one or the other aspect of this gigantic problem has received attention. It is interesting to see that there are a number of institutions which keep a watch over the working of the police—the judiciary, Women's Commissions, Scheduled Castes Commission, Scheduled Tribes Commission, Human Rights Commissions at the state and central levels, Parliament, state legislatures and the media. In spite of this close scrutiny, the credibility and image of police is the lowest among the public servants from one end of the country to the other. This needs to be recognised as a national calamity. CCTV cameras are no longer necessary to keep a watch over the wrong doings of police. Every smartphone in the hands of a common person is poised to record the atrocities committed by the police and their dereliction of duty. In the following discussion, I have attempted to touch upon a few constitutional, statutory and policy aspects which deserve urgent attention.

The issues pertaining to police reforms have been examined by scores of committees and commissions appointed by the central and state governments over the years. As is the usual practice, most of these have been consigned to archives. The most prominent of these studies was the report of the National Police Commission (NPC) which was appointed by the Janata government after the dreaded emergency. But, as soon as Indira Gandhi came back to power in 1980, she issued orders to withdraw the series of reports submitted by the NPC. It was only when the United Front government came to power that the then Union Home Minister Indrajit Gupta wrote to the states urging speedy follow-up action. But by then the political lethargy had set in and hardly any action was taken. Finally, a number of Public Interest Litigations (PILs) were filed in the High Courts and the Supreme Court. After considerable insistence by the petitioners, the Supreme Court gave directions for the restructuring of police departments in the states and the central police organisations. Though this was a step forward, it must be stated that it did not go far enough. The court directions were largely confined to safeguarding the police against political interference. Several other major concerns regarding the functioning of the police were totally left out in the submissions made to the court and consequently in the directions issued by the court. But, the most shocking aspect is the total disdain shown by most of the states to these directions. It is equally disconcerting that the Supreme Court has not hauled up any of the states for non-compliance of its orders. For example, the peremptory replacement of the Director General of Police by the Governor in J&K in September 2018 was in defiance of the Supreme Court directives. According to a news report, Chief Minister of Punjab Amrinder Singh believes that the orders of the court are not in keeping with the federal principles and increase the jurisdiction of the central government. He has announced that the Punjab government would be filing a review petition in the Supreme Court, though such attempts have failed in the past!

This takes us to the inevitable question of the review of Union-states relations. The Constitution of India largely followed the provisions of the Government of India Act, 1935, particularly on matters pertaining to relations between the Union and the states. The Seventh Schedule of the Constitution divides the responsibilities of the Union and the states in three lists—the Union List, the State List and the Concurrent List. The entries 'police' and 'public order' figures in the State List. This has severely restricted the charter of the Union government. It is imperative that this subject is transferred to the Concurrent List. This matter had come up for detailed examination on the basis of the recommendations of the four task forces appointed by the National Democratic Alliance (NDA) government following the Kargil War in 1999. The government had accepted the Cabinet Committee recommendations that the matter should be pursued by discussing it in the Conference of Chief Ministers and necessary proposals for amendment of the Constitution should be worked out. This was way back in 2002. We are now in 2018! Even discounting the 10-year UPA regime from 2004-14, one would have expected the NDA government under Narendra Modi to act on it energetically. Unfortunately, there has been no action on it at all. The urgency of the proposal can be seen even from the few instances given below.

First, in this continental size country with its multifarious problems of internal security, there is no provision for federal civil police. What we have are only the central paramilitary forces. The complex challenges of internal security, including of the national and international terror outfits, drug cartels and secessionist movements like Khalistan and Naxalism require that the central government is entrusted with the responsibility of police and public order on a concurrent basis. **Second**, the question of enacting a separate law for the Central Bureau of Investigation (CBI) has been under discussion for the last five decades. But the states have been objecting to it. I have dealt with this matter at some length in my article in *The Wire* (27 September 2018) titled *Why a Revamping of the CBI is Necessary*. As I have urged therein 'What is at stake is more than just the image and credibility of the CBI. India's image as a country committed to the rule of law itself needs to be refurbished nationally and internationally. The Narendra Modi government can send a powerful message by setting the ball rolling without loss of any further time. **Third**, it is imperative to authorise the Centre to *deploy* the central para-military forces in the states, as opposed to merely stationing them. In the recent past, this has become a major handicap for the Centre in dealing with law and order situation arising in major communal clashes such as in Ahmedabad and Godhra riots, the demolition of the Babri Masjid in December 1992 and the series of bomb blasts in Mumbai thereafter.

The political sagacity requires that these matters should be discussed in the larger national interest, keeping aside the rhetoric of federalism. It needs to be understood that, strictly speaking, India is not a federation. Article 1 of the Constitution clearly states that 'India shall be a union of states', though it has consciously adopted a number of federal features. But these cannot be permitted to undermine its basic tenet, namely, that it is a union of states. Therefore to argue that Indian federalism will be adversely affected by sharing the responsibilities of 'police and public order' between the union and the states is a gross misrepresentation. My next book, *India's Quasi-Federalism—Fault lines, Challenges and Opportunities*, on which I am currently working, will deal with these issues extensively.

The Inter-State Council established by V.P. Singh government in 1990, which has largely remained grossly underutilised and neglected, could be a useful forum for arriving at an amicable solution to these politically complex problems such as the transfer of the subjects 'police and public order' to the Concurrent List and restructuring of the CBI by creating mutual trust between the Centre and the states. In the Indian context, confidence-building measures (CBMs) are more important between the Union government and the states, than between India and Pakistan!

The question of infringement of human rights by police has become highly important over the years. The most repulsive of these are the custodial deaths. The utter disregard shown to the sensitivities on this subject by police in all states is shocking. The excessive use of force by the police in interrogation of accused and in crowd control, which is caught on smart phones of people, apart from the media, and shown in the 24x7 news on television, has created a widespread revulsion for the police. The so-called encounter killings have sullied the image of police. Abhinav Kumar, Inspector General, Border Security Force, in his thoughtful article '*Crime and Complicity*' (*The Indian Express*, 4 October 2018, p. 8) has written about the 'encounter culture' in Uttar Pradesh and has underlined that the 'encounter culture did not come out of nowhere'. But this is a not new phenomenon. Years ago, Bombay (now Mumbai) police took pride in its achievements in this regard. An inspector of police who was reported to have killed over hundred criminals in 'encounters' became a hero in real life and was later glorified in a Hindi film, which set up a very wrong example before not only the people but also the police. This is antithesis of the very concept of the rule of law. The recent instances of the police carrying an innocent woman on the top of their vehicle for interrogation, her falling off from the vehicle and making a run for home and shooting of an executive of a company for not stopping his car when asked by motorcycle riding police, have created terror psychosis in the country. Is this how the police are expected to behave in a civilised society? Whom are the police answerable for such atrocious conduct? The question of giving autonomy to the police will have to be discussed against this background.

The recent case of the attempt by Pune police to arrest five 'intellectuals' for their activities as urban Naxalites needs to be examined in depth, for it has serious implications for the functioning of the police. I had in my article titled, *Let us not stop the police from doing its job* (*rediff.com*, 3 September 2018) criticised the Supreme Court for its unjustified interference at the early stage of investigation by invoking its powers under Article 32 of the Constitution—'remedies for enforcement of [fundamental] rights'. While the majority judgment permitting the police to continue with the investigation has received wide publicity, the minority judgment of Justice D.Y. Chandrachud, which has cast serious aspersions on the police, has not been reported as extensively. Careful reading of the two judgments brings out how even highly trained judicial minds at the highest level take diametrically opposite views, based on their perceptions. The dissenting judgment shows how far the police have gone down in the perception of the informed sections of society. It is as if whatever police say or do can never be right. It was surprising to see that even the majority judgment further extended the house arrest of the five accused, rather than permitting the Pune police to arrest them. The minority judgment went even further and suggested setting up of a court-supervised special investigation team. There was widespread criticism of Pune police in a section of the media and by the so-called liberals for arresting the five intellectuals. Motives were ascribed for their actions. To avoid the backlash, Pune police held a press conference to give out their side of the story. But this too was faulted by the apex court. How should this one-sided game be played in the future? I am constrained by limitations of time and space to comment fully on all the issues arising out of this case but I feel that they need to be studied and debated. Both the majority and the minority judgments should be included in the syllabus of police training institutions and discussed in the basic training and refresher courses for officers at different levels. Such case studies will be much more productive in dealing with the day-to-day situations in the real world.

There is an animated debate in the country on enacting a common civil code but there has been no reaction to the very ill-considered decision of the government of India not to have an All India Police Act to replace the old, archaic Police Act of 1861. Even with the division of powers in the Seventh Schedule of the Constitution referred to earlier, the government of India could have taken the initiative to enact such a law as was done in the case, for example, of Urban Land Ceiling Act. Article 249 of the Constitution gives power to Parliament to legislate with respect to a matter in the State List in the national interest. Police and public order are the basic responsibilities of the government. While the states could be free to make any changes in the central law to suit the local requirements, I strongly feel that there are a number of precepts which should be considered sacrosanct and must form part of the national police act. Illustratively, these include basic structure of police at different levels, their designations, hierarchy of police structure, composition of police, fixity of tenure, representation for minorities, reservation policy, personnel policies, empowered staff selection committees, grievance redressal committees, thrust on human rights, minimum use of force by police, sensitivity in dealing with weaker sections, women and children, promoting communal harmony, upholding the secular fabric of society and maintaining the strictest standards of discipline. There can hardly be any difference of view on these basic prerequisites for a police force to meet the requirements of a new India. Why are we shying away from enacting such an act at the national level? Sadly, what is wanting is administrative and political will.

It is reassuring to see that the new Chief Justice of India Justice Ranjan Gogoi has indicated that he would soon unveil a plan for initiating judicial reforms to redress the frustrations of the people with the judicial system we have inherited and then perpetuated over the years. I had dealt with this subject in a 100-page chapter titled *Judicial Reforms Nowhere in Sight*, in my book, *The Judiciary and*

Governance in India (2008). I would like to invite attention here to only a couple of suggestions made therein. In the recent years, the credibility of police has gone down to such an extent that there are repeated demands made that investigation of cases be carried out under the supervision of the High Court or the Supreme Court. Similar demand was made in the case of five intellectuals referred to above. Justice Chandrachud, in his dissenting judgment, has upheld this demand, though the majority judgment did not consider it necessary that the investigation should be taken over from the Pune police. In my abovementioned book, I had recommended that the inquisitorial system, which is in vogue in a number of European countries such as France and Germany, as opposed to the adversarial system prevalent in India, should be introduced on a pilot basis to have the police investigations carried out under judicial magistrate's supervision. Justice V.S. Malimath Committee, in its report on reforms of criminal justice system (2003), had noted that the inquisitorial system is certainly efficient in the sense that the investigation is supervised by the judicial magistrate which results in a high rate of conviction. The committee on balance felt that a fair trial and, in particular, fairness to the accused, are better protected in the adversarial system. However, the committee felt that some of the good features of the inquisitorial system can be adopted to strengthen the adversarial system and to make it more effective. This includes the duty of the court to search for the truth, to assign a proactive role to the judges, to give directions to the investigating officers and prosecution agencies in the matter of investigation and leading evidence with the object of seeking the truth and focusing on justice to victim. This effectively will hit the nail insofar as police prosecutions are concerned. This single reform will go a long way in redressing the grievances of the people.

The other critical reform, which is necessary, pertains to the problem of perjury. In a number of recent cases of communal violence in Godhra and elsewhere, love jihad, encounter killings and rape, the enormity of the problem has repeatedly come to the fore. Perjury has been made a criminal offence under Sections 193 to 195 of the Indian Penal Code. As is well known, perjury can contribute to the wrong person being convicted while the true criminal and the perjurer walk on the street in freedom. The Malimath Committee found that, unfortunately, the legal provisions are rarely resorted to and perjury has become a routine feature in courts. The committee has stated that the court's response to the serious problem of perjury is rather one of utter indifference. The committee had recommended substantial enhancement of punishment for perjury and a summary trial of such cases. The committee had also recommended that a law should be enacted for giving protection to the witnesses and their families on the lines of the laws in the USA and other countries. Much remains to be done in this critical area.

Reference must be made to two other reforms which are imperative to smoothen the work of the police and to make it more effective. These pertain to arbitrary withdrawal of cases by state governments for political purposes, and the increasing recourse taken to the provision of anticipatory bail by the financially well-off and politically powerful persons, frustrating the efforts of the police to interrogate the accused in custody. I have been writing about it for several years but the vested interests for retaining the status-quo have prevailed.

The institutional mechanism to keep a watch over the work of the police can be only as effective as the political will of the elected government in power. Unfortunately, there is lack of political and administrative will in this regard in various states and the Centre. This is evident from the fact that several commissions such as the Minorities Commission, the Human

Rights Commission, and Women's Commissions are not fully operational or not effective enough in exerting pressure. In several states, the citizens' grievances commissions are non-existent. This needs to be remedied. Citizens themselves will have to exert pressure to bring this about.

Reference must also be made to yet another instrument in the hands of the citizens to keep a close watch on the police. It is the right to information enacted in 2005 to empower the citizens to seek information on the working of the police. Unfortunately, this instrument has started becoming blunt for two reasons. First is that the government has been making liberal use of the provisions to exempt the working of the police from the purview of this Act. I have dealt with this at length in my article on the CBI referred to above. The second is the apathy of the citizens themselves. It must also be underlined that in several states the Information Commissions have been rendered ineffective due to the posts of Information Commissioners lying vacant or the posts being filled by persons on political considerations. This proves once again that mere enactment of a law is not enough. It is equally important that it is implemented vigorously to realise the underlying objectives.

I find that most often, the thrust of writings on police reforms is mainly on curtailment of political interference in the working of the police and giving autonomy to the police in their work. Both these are no doubt important but, in the Indian context, a few other aspects are as important, if not more important to increase the morale, effectiveness and commitment of the police. Foremost among these is proper provision for police housing. In most of the large cities and metropolitan areas, due to grossly inadequate government housing, the police have to live in slums, hutments and *juggi-zonpadis*. Whatever housing is available in police lines, its upkeep and maintenance is in shambles for lack of funds.

The long daily working hours for police are simply inhuman. In Mumbai, for example, till very recently, the police did not get even a weekly off. When, in 2017, for the first time, the then Mumbai Police Commissioner, Datta Padsalgikar, introduced the weekly holiday for the police, he deservedly became an iconic figure in the Mumbai police. And this is at the time when the state government employees and officers are demanding a five-day week! The basic requirements such as proper housing and weekly rest is certainly not too much to ask for, but it does not figure in the discussion on police reforms. Are we not missing something important in the process?

The police as the upholder of the law of the land is the face of the government but in the recent years, the fear of police is nowhere to be seen. There are frequent cases of attacks on police, blackening of their faces and even beating them up. There have been shocking cases of taking liberties and misbehaving with women police. This degradation of the police is undoing of the civilisational values and culture. But these concerns hardly ever figure in the discussion on police reforms.

Note must also be taken of the police sacrificing their lives in the fight against Naxalites and terrorists. Hundreds of police lose their lives in this manner each year. Questions are hardly ever raised about whether their families have been taken care of, their children's educational and other needs are catered for and so on. All police personnel must be provided insurance cover against such calamities. These are matters of serious concern in the Indian context and have implications for the morale of the police. Should they not find a mention in the discussion on police reforms?

But this is one side of the story. The other equally important aspect relates to rehabilitating and refurbishing the public image of the police. If public perception about the police is to be changed radically, and the police are to become the friendly and reassuring face of the law, some radical changes will have to be made in the recruitment, training, and mental make-up of the police. How to bring this about is a question to which there are no easy answers. Psychological tests will have to be devised to judge the mental make-up, equanimity and fairness of the incumbents from the recruitment stage and at frequent intervals thereafter in their long career. Eminent social science institutions in the country must be empanelled for devising and carrying out the tests. Collaborative assistance of well-known foreign institutions must also be sought without any hesitation.

The sharp deterioration in the working, rectitude and image of the police, coupled with the serious threats to internal security, is a daunting challenge. The question is whether India is prepared to meet this challenge. Drum-beating has already begun for the state assembly elections due in a few states and the Lok Sabha elections in 2019. But in the noisy, acrimonious debates on TV channels, the press and social media, police reforms hardly ever figure, though they are so vital for the survival of civilisational values and the rule of law in the country. Where are we headed?

29

CBI VS CBI: NOTHING LESS THAN SURGERY IS CALLED FOR

WHILE PUTTING FORTH the say of M.K. Sinha, Deputy Inspector General of the Central Bureau of Investigation (CBI), before the Supreme Court, his advocate prefaced it by saying that what he had to submit was shocking. The Chief Justice is reported to have said that nothing would shock the court any more.

This may be so for the court but millions of ordinary citizens like me are shell-shocked with the revelations!

The question, in this most unsavoury chapter, is not just of the CBI's survival as an institution but of the survival of the rule of law itself, which is part of the basic structure of the Constitution. The Supreme Court has adjourned the hearing of the case to November 29. In the meanwhile, it will be appropriate to set out what and how much is at stake in the outcome of this case.

At the outset, it must be stated that the extent and nature of political interference which has been noticed in this case is not the first instance of its kind. But, we, as a society, have

---

The Citizen, 21 November 2018.

deliberately pushed it under the carpet and have turned a blind eye to it. Efforts made to invite the attention of even the higher judiciary to it by way of Public Interest Litigation (PIL) have not succeeded.

My own PIL, filed in the Supreme Court [writ petition (c) No. 69 of 2004], is a case in point. The court dismissed it at the admission stage itself! I am happy that with this high-profile case, at last national attention has been drawn and riveted on the underlying issues. I hope that the Supreme Court will go into the basics of the issues and will not confine itself merely to resolving the infighting in the CBI.

A close scrutiny needs to be made of the way the higher civil services, charged by the Constitution with the running of the administration, have been enslaved by whichever political party has been in power. The protection, given to them under the Constitution at the behest of far-sighted Sardar Vallabhbhai Patel, has been completely eroded. What has happened in the CBI is only the tip of the iceberg.

It was the first Administrative Reforms Commission which recommended that the CBI should be transferred from the Ministry of Home Affairs (MHA) to the Department of Personnel and Training (DoPT) under the Prime Minister. I have never been able to understand the logic of it. But, Indira Gandhi, then Prime Minister, who was keen on concentrating all power in her office, took full advantage of it and transferred the CBI to the DoPT.

External intelligence too was taken out of the Intelligence Bureau (IB), which was under the MHA, and shifted to the Cabinet Secretariat which is directly under the Prime Minister. The politically manoeuvred control of both these organisations by the Prime Minister's Office has repeatedly come to adverse notice over the years. It therefore needs to be examined whether these organisations should be shifted back to the MHA, where they legitimately belong.

The selection of Director CBI has now been entrusted to a high level committee comprising the PM, the Chief Justice of India and the Leader of the Opposition.

Right from beginning, I have argued that it is wrong to involve the CJI in the selection process. Such selections done entirely on the basis of confidential records of officers do not necessarily lead to selection of the most deserving officers, whether it is for the post of Central Vigilance Commissioner, Chief Election Commissioner or CBI Director.

This procedure undermines the important principle of separation of powers between the judiciary and the executive.

As seen in recent years, the selections made by this committee have been challenged in the Supreme Court, making it untenable for related PILs to be decided by that court. It is for the same reason that I have been contesting the point made in the present case by some people that Director CBI should not have been asked to go on leave without the approval of the selection committee as above.

As for the Leader of the Opposition, while he should be on the committee for selection of incumbents for the above posts, he should not be involved in other administrative decisions such as of sending an officer on leave. These fine distinctions must be maintained.

Reference must also be made to the direction of the court to entrust the inquiry against the CBI Director to the CVC. Looking to the background of the case, it was unlikely that the CVC's findings would be perceived as unbiased. I had therefore argued that the inquiry should be overseen by the Supreme Court. Fortunately, in spite of the opposition of the government, the apex court had asked a retired judge of the Supreme Court to be associated with the inquiry. According to one news report, the judge has submitted his separate findings to the Supreme Court. If true, this is a welcome development.

It is a matter of concern that practically anyone associated with the government, including those holding constitutional and statutory positions, is being viewed with suspicion.

The credibility of the government is as low as during the regime of Indira Gandhi, particularly in the emergency in 1975-77. This is a major challenge facing the country. It has been alleged that several functionaries in the government such as the National Security Adviser (NSA) have interfered in this case.

At the same time, the Cabinet Secretary, who is the head of the civil service, has been sidelined. This has serious long-term implications for the integrity and cohesion of the apparatus of governance. Urgent remedial steps need to be taken before things go out of hand.

Another worrisome factor is the state governments withdrawing their approvals given to the CBI to operate in their states. This again is not new. Partly, it may be due to the impending Lok Sabha elections in 2019. Partly, it could also be to protect the interests of supporters of the political parties in power in these states. But, answers must be found to the fears and suspicions of the states if a central legislation for the CBI is to come into being.

I have been advocating for some time that a governing board should be appointed for the CBI on which, apart from the Union Home Minister (after the CBI is transferred to the MHA) and three central ministers, three chief ministers of states should also be appointed by rotation to create a sense of confidence in the apolitical, unbiased working of the CBI. The subject of enacting a central legislation for the CBI must be brought up before the Inter-State Council for very early approval.

Experience so far has fully brought out the importance of having an independent and competent prosecution agency. Unfortunately, in the *hawala* case, the Supreme Court did not accept the suggestion of the amicus curiae for the appointment of an authority akin to the special or independent counsel in the United States for the investigation of charges in politically sensitive matters and for prosecution of these cases.

The court had felt: 'We are of the view that the time for these drastic steps has not come. It is our hope that it never will, for we entertain the belief that the investigative agencies shall function far better now, having regard to...the directions which are contained in this judgment. The personnel of the enforcement agencies should not now lack the courage and independence to go about their task as they should, even where those to be investigated are prominent and powerful persons.' As I had brought out in my book, *Good Governance Never On India's Radar* (2014), these fond hopes were belied even before the ink on the judgment was dry. The present controversy shows the depth to which the CBI has fallen.

I have also been advocating that the new legislation for the CBI should provide for an annual social audit of the working of the CBI by a committee of eminent legal experts, retired judges, persons knowledgeable in administration, and representatives of the media and non-governmental organisations. This report must be placed before Parliament each year. A beginning needs to be made even before the passing of a new law for the CBI. There will be no better way to restore the credibility and image of the CBI.

Finally, and most importantly, the CBI should be brought under the control of the Lokpal, when he/she is appointed. The appointment of the Lokpal has been unduly delayed by this government for no justifiable reason. Similarly, the anti-corruption outfits in the states should also be brought under the Lokayuktas.

I hope the Supreme Court will consider giving unambiguous, time-bound directions on all these issues.

However, a word of caution is necessary. The experience of implementation of the directions of the Supreme Court in regard to police reforms given in 2006 has been far from reassuring and they have largely remained on paper though over a decade has elapsed since then. The apex court has been far too accommodating and has not hauled up the defaulting states.

Let us hope the position in this case will be different and the apex court would ensure expeditious steps by the Centre and the states. The Court's time is too precious and must not be permitted to be frittered away.

30

BULANDSHAHR VIOLENCE: POLICE-POLITICAL NEXUS GENERATES DEEP FEAR IN LAW ABIDING CITIZENS

MOB VIOLENCE AND repeated incidents of lynching in the country have created an atmosphere of fear and insecurity among law abiding people. What is at stake is not just the maintenance of public order but the very survival of a civilised society.

If lasting solutions are to be found, the following four basic questions, which have been staring India in the face, must not be ignored any further.

The foremost concern is about what we have done to the **police apparatus in the country.** Police is no longer looked upon by the common person as an upholder of the rule of law but has become an extended arm of exploitation by the political party in power.

The image and credibility of the police has reached its nadir. No amount of exhortation by statutory commissions and the

---

The Citizen, 9 December 2018.

higher judiciary has made any difference to the conduct and behaviour of police. This is largely due to the support which the police receive from the political party in power. This nexus between the politicians and the police has become the bane of the system.

This is evident from the fact that even the directions given by the Supreme Court to the state governments way back in 2006 regarding the restructuring of police departments have not been implemented by most states. Some of the directions were aimed at reducing the political interference in the functioning of the police.

The Bulandshahr tragedy brings out how important these directions would have been and why the states are resisting implementing them.

The police being under the influence of the political party in power is evident in the Bulandshahr case. It was interesting to see that the senior police officer addressing a press conference soon after the event in which a police inspector was killed, assiduously evaded answering questions about the association of persons named in the first information report with the political party in power in the state and its associate organisations.

It is shocking to see that the police investigation is concentrated on the killing of cows than on the murder of the police inspector. Efforts are also being made to divert attention from the gravity of the offence by putting forth a theory of conspiracy. As if the murder of the police officer could not have been avoided because of conspiracy!

There is reasonable scope to believe that investigation in such cases may come under political pressure.

I have been advocating for some time that in such sensitive and communally charged cases, inquisitorial system, as prevalent in several European countries, be adopted. Under this system, the courts and its adjuncts (the examining magistrate and the public prosecutor) exercise full control over the investigation and the presentation of the case at the trial. Relevant laws must be amended to permit the courts to order adoption of this system, as the state governments which are interested parties will not be inclined to permit this procedure.

This brings me to the next question of the need to separate **religion from politics.** The major ailments afflicting India's body politic require that this issue is addressed urgently. But it has been consciously neglected by all political parties, though a resolution on the subject moved by Ananthasayanam Ayyangar was passed by the interim Parliament on 3 April 1948 almost unanimously, with only one member opposing it. Separating religion from politics was considered to be so basic for India's survival that the resolution was passed even while the Constitution was being debated. Unfortunately, suitable provision was not made in the Constitution itself at the time. The then Prime Minister Jawaharlal Nehru had extended full support to the resolution.

Since then, the country has witnessed several serious catastrophes arising from the intermixing of religion and politics. Demolition of the Babri Masjid by a frenzied mob of lakhs of *kar sevaks* in December 1992, the massacre of 3,000 Sikhs in Delhi, Kanpur and other places in 1984, horrendous communal riots in Godhra, Ahmedabad and Mumbai over the years, to name just a few, and the unabashed lynching by cow vigilantes in the recent years have brought home repeatedly the urgency of taking action to separate religion from politics.

To do so will, however, require a Constitution amendment which will call for a two-thirds majority in both the Houses of Parliament and its ratification by more than half of the state legislatures.

During the prime ministership of Jawaharlal Nehru, Indira Gandhi and Rajiv Gandhi, the ruling Congress party had a massive majority in Parliament and this would have been possible but no action was taken by them. Now it would be possible to bring this about only if all, and not just the so-called secular parties, take a principled stand on the subject.

It is disappointing to see that even in the talks of building up a grand alliance, *mahagathbandhan*, of all secular parties, no one dares to talk about the need for a time-bound action plan for separation of religion from politics. I wonder how long India will have to wait for undertaking this basic political reform which is so crucial for the survival of secular democracy in the country.

This brings me to the next imperative of safeguarding **the secularism in India.** In this multi-religious, multi-lingual, multi-cultural, multi-ethnic country, even at present, minorities account for 20 per cent of the total population. This percentage is expected to stabilise at about 30-35 per cent in the coming years. Can India afford to neglect or treat as second-class citizens such a large portion of its population? Should religious beliefs and practices of Hindus be inflicted on the other communities?

Both Jawaharlal Nehru and Mahatma Gandhi were opposed to imposing a ban on cow slaughter. As I had brought out in my book, *Secularism: India At A Crossroads* (2016), even V.D. Savarkar, who was a staunch proponent of Hindutva, had ridiculed the concept of protecting the cows.

As for the legal sustainability of the ban on cow slaughter, there are two strong, diametrically opposite views. Justice P.B. Gajendragadkar, former Chief Justice of India and former Chairman of the Law Commission, had invited attention to the observation of the Supreme Court itself that where Directive Principles of State Policy came in conflict with the Fundamental Rights, the latter must prevail over the former.

The Supreme Court has upheld the ban on cow slaughter by reversing its long held view to the contrary. This judgment ought to have been challenged by filing a review petition. But, even the UPA government did not want to be seen as opposing the ban on cow slaughter. Whatever the outward pretentions, the so-called secular parties are reluctant to come out openly against the demands of Hindus, howsoever unreasonable they may be.

But, even now it is not too late to raise the issue in the Supreme Court. After all, secularism has been declared as a part of the basic structure of the Constitution and nothing can be done to undermine or dilute it. If this is to be the reality, a question needs to be raised whether ban on cow slaughter and secularism can go together. I believe that the issue needs to be reopened and placed before the Supreme Court once again.

Mob violence and vigilantism have taken a foothold in India after the BJP came to power at the Centre and in a number of states and started aggressively asserting its Hindutva ideology. These pernicious forces can be controlled only by addressing the basic issues discussed above. Mere window dressing will be futile.

PART SIX

Economic Reforms Gone Astray

ECONOMIC REFORMS MIRED IN POLITICS

ECONOMIC REFORMS WERE initiated when India was on the verge of bankruptcy in 1991. But, even in that dire situation, reforms had to be ushered in clandestinely, by back-door. With the political baggage of socialism widely prevalent in almost all political parties and intellectuals, no clear-cut agenda of economic reforms and the time-frame for its implementation was ever placed before the country by the government. This has continued ever since. There has therefore been no public debate and discussion on the pros and cons of reforms. This is particularly true of Parliament and the state legislatures. The states have in fact, till recently, been led to believe that this subject is outside their jurisdiction and is solely in the purview of the central government.

The reforms in the power sector bring out how wrong was this contention. The entry 'electricity' is in the Concurrent List of the Seventh Schedule of the Constitution. Due to inadequate funding of the sector by the states, severe power shortages were being experienced all over the country.

When the central government started making investments in the generation and transmission sector in a big way in the

1970s, instead of welcoming the move, the states raised a number of objections. Same thing happened when the power sector was opened to the private sector. The approval of the Enron power project, involving the largest foreign direct investment at the time, against all cannons of propriety and without following the procedures for competitive bidding etc., dragged the Maharashtra State Electricity Board into bankruptcy. The power purchase agreement was so one-sided as to raise questions about the concept of globalisation and permitting foreign direct investment in a public utility sector. When the matters became totally unsustainable, the Maharashtra government appointed a high-level expert committee under my chairmanship to examine how the project could be renegotiated and made workable. The report of this committee was an eye-opener to the blind advocates of economic liberalisation. The travails of Enron project are brought out in an article in this book

The Modi government has actively pursued significant economic reforms. This effectively meant dismantling the elaborate architecture of socialistic pattern of economy erected by Indira Gandhi in her heydays and perpetuated over the years since then. There are still many strong adherents of that ideology and economic reforms meet with considerable resistance, whether it is permitting the private sector entry into mining sector, disinvestment from public sector undertakings, reform of public sector banks and so on. Labour reforms is a mine-field and no government so far has shown courage to make even a modest beginning. The Modi government took a long overdue decision to privatise Air India which has been plagued by mismanagement, governmental interference and overstaffing, to name just a few of its ailments. It was interesting to see even a Parliamentary Committee opposing the privatisation initiative! Of course, the government itself had laid down such difficult conditions for the future working of the privatised entity that it was most unlikely that any sane private sector company would dare to take over this loss-ridden, loss-making entity. But this brings out once again how most decisions about economic reforms lack broad political consensus and become lethal weapons in electoral politics.

The outstanding examples of this are the two prominent initiatives, taken by the Modi government, namely, demonetisation of high value currency notes and introduction of Goods and Services Tax (GST), which have created a political storm. As for demonetisation, I have been a strong supporter of the idea for various reasons brought out in my articles. The fault was of the RBI and the Ministry of Finance in not taking advance action to meet all contingencies. It should not have been difficult to foresee the difficulties. A point was made by critics that the RBI was not consulted. It must be stated that there is no reason to believe that the RBI was not consulted but on such an issue, the final decision has to be of the government's, and not the RBI's. When the taxation inquiry committee under the chairmanship of the former Chief Justice of India, N.N. Wanchoo, had made a recommendation in 1971 of demonetisation, it was debated and approved in a series of meetings held in the Ministry of Finance at which the then Governor, RBI was fully involved. The recommendation was finally rejected only at the level of the then Prime Minister Indira Gandhi. Shockingly, her reason was that it would adversely affect raising of funds by the Congress party for the elections! I have brought out the details of this in my memoirs, *Unfinished Innings—Recollections and Reflections of a Civil Servant (1996)*. It was necessary to take a politically courageous decision to give a shock treatment to the country. There would always be two views on the subject. But it is important that informed public debate on the subject is divested of politics and all facets are fully understood in the discussion.

The story of GST is stranger. The initiative in the matter was taken by the then UPA government. It was opposed at the time by the BJP but when it came to power in 2014, the BJP pursued it vigorously. Now, the UPA is in Opposition and has opened a tirade against it. Rahul Gandhi, president of the Congress party, has gone to the ridiculous extent of calling it a Gabbar Singh tax (bandit's extortionary tax)! I am firmly of the opinion that this is one of the most significant steps taken by India in its struggle for economic liberalisation. It is the first successful instance of cooperative federalism taking roots in the country. When the Constitution was framed, no one could have imagined India taking such a giant leap forward for establishing one market for this continental size country.

Another instance of totally inconsistent position of the two political parties on yet another major reform was the introduction of the Aadhaar identity card. This initiative was taken by the UPA government to bring about direct transfers of subsidies to beneficiaries by eliminating intermediaries and pilferages in the process. With all its drawbacks, the scheme had something to commend itself. The BJP which was then in the Opposition had vehemently opposed the move but after it came to power, it became its strongest votary. Working of Indian democracy is indeed strange and impossible to fathom!

Politics in India has pervaded all walks of life. One had hoped that after 70 years of Independence, political parties would become more mature. But the reality is quite the opposite. Let us hope that at least on matters pertaining to major economic reforms, political parties will come together on a common minimum programme. For, what is at stake is the lifting of India's millions from poverty, dealing with the massive problem of unemployment, and achieving double-digit rate of growth of economy. Needless to say, India's quest to become a global power is dependent on it.

31

DABHOL (ENRON) POWER PROJECT – AFTERSHOCKS

IN PERHAPS THE largest corporate scandal in the world, the Enron empire in the USA collapsed in 2001 after ruining the lives of millions of its employees and shareholders. It is noteworthy that, in spite of the complexities of the financial transactions of the company, the web of shell companies it had created and the extraordinary political clout of its president Kenneth Lay, criminal cases against the top executives of the company were pursued vigorously, and in less than five years, several top executives were convicted to undergo prison terms running into several decades. Lay died of heart attack soon after his indictment and before the sentence could be pronounced. In sharp contrast is the position in India where all those involved in the approval of the Enron power project, which unjustly tarnished India's image internationally, led to series of arbitration proceedings and court cases, and resulted in a huge financial loss to the exchequer, have not even been held accountable. The ruling political and bureaucratic elite

---

Economic and Political Weekly, 26 August 2006.

seem to believe that the ghost of the Enron project and the monumental failure of governance in its approval can by exorcised by reviving it at any cost and renaming it the Ratnagiri power project. The settlement reached with the two foreign equity holders and the international banks and financial institutions is far too generous. In addition are the large subsidies doled out at the cost of the unsuspecting tax payer to hide from public scrutiny how totally unviable was this project.

To begin with, it would be useful to recapitulate the salient features of the project. It was to be a base load project with an installed capacity of 2,184 MW and was to use LNG as feedstock. Phase I of 740 MW was commissioned on 13 May 1999 and when the project was mothballed on 29 May 2001, construction of Phase II of 1,444 MW was at an advanced stage. This was the largest private sector power project taken up in the country by a foreign investor at an estimated cost of $ 3,000 million. The power purchase agreement (PPA) entered into by Enron with the Maharashtra State Electricity Board (MSEB) was totally one-sided and the cost of power was so high that it would have meant financial ruin, not just of the MSEB but also the Government of Maharashtra (GOM), which had given guarantees for the timely payment for the power purchased by the MSEB.

The GOM appointed an expert committee on 9 February 2001 to examine the project and suggest a way out. Apart from three other members, the authors of this article worked as the chairman and member of the committee respectively. The committee submitted its report on 10 April 2001 in which it, inter alia, recommended that the project should be restructured by negotiating it afresh to bring down the cost of power. The committee had underlined that this would mean all concerned parties taking a 'hair cut', i.e., making substantial concessions. The settlement reached by the Centre needs to be examined in this background.

The argument advanced by the Dabhol Power Company (DPC) and its proponents that the MSEB rescinded the contract with the DPC due to its inability to pay for power is mischievous and misleading. Under the contract, the MSEB had to make 'capacity payment' to the DPC, on the basis of the rated base load capacity declared to be available by the DPC for each availability period, irrespective of whether energy was actually delivered by it to the MSEB or not. Accordingly, the MSEB had made a huge payment of Rs 2,180 crore to the DPC from May 1999 till May 2001, when the dispute between the parties arose on account of the material misrepresentation made and non-fulfilment of commitments given by DPC in the PPA, which had guaranteed that the power plant had the capacity to ramp-up from cold start (i.e. when the plant is completely shut down for over 12 hours) to 100 per cent load within a period of 180 minutes. The DPC repeatedly failed to fulfil this obligation when the MSEB asked the DPC plant to be brought on line and as a result was liable to pay a rebate of Rs 401 crore to the MSEB. The DPC refused to adjust this amount against the payment which was due to it from the MSEB and instead insisted that the MSEB should make full payment for the power purchased by it and the question of breach of the PPA obligation should be referred to an international arbitration. This was a totally indefensible position taken by the DPC and when the MSEB declined to go along, the DPC stopped the supply of power to the MSEB. In the settlement agreed to, the MSEB appears to have been forced to give up the claim for this large amount altogether.

The details of the revival package worked out between the concerned parties such as Bechtel, General Electric, Indian and foreign financial institutions, the MSEB and others in

July 2005 are still not in the public domain. Though Phase I of the plant was partly restarted and power therefrom sold to the MSEB, details of the new PPA are not known. The tariff at which power from the rechristened (Ratnagiri) plant is to become available is not clear. Approval of the Maharashtra Electricity Regulatory Commission (MERC) has not been taken for the purchase of this power nor has it been established that it is according to the criterion of merit order dispatch, which requires that power must be purchased by a distribution agency based on its cost, with the cheapest power being drawn first. At the commencement of negotiations, the GOM had laid down a condition that it would take power from this project at a tariff not exceeding Rs 2.40 per unit. Later, the GOM relented and agreed to a higher price of Rs 2.80. Now the figure being talked about is Rs 5.30 or even more. It is not clear if this is to be the cost at the bus-bar. In that case, the cost to the consumer would be even higher taking into account the transmission and distribution losses. If the application of the Maharashtra Power Distribution Company for purchase of power from this project had come before the MERC for approval, all details of the financial restructuring could have come in the public domain and it would have been possible to contest some of the terms of the settlement. It would have also enabled quantification of diverse subsidies which tax payers all over the country have to bear to artificially bring down the power tariff for this project.

It is believed that the settlement was agreed to by the government under duress, mainly due to the apprehension that the arbitration proceedings launched by the multinational equity holders under bilateral agreements with some countries were likely to go against India. To what extent such fears were justified is debatable. Whether the legal firms selected to represent India's interests were sufficiently experienced, competent and qualified is also not clear. It is far from clear why the MSEB and the GOM did not offer to purchase the 65 per cent equity held by Enron during the bankruptcy proceedings in the court in New York when it was available for a mere $20 million. We had publicly raised this issue way back in June 2004.[1] The government has never clarified the position, even to date.

The negotiating position of the government would have been strengthened immensely if the judicial commission of inquiry, which the authors of this article had recommended, in spite of the opposition of the other three members of the expert committee, had been permitted to go ahead. The authors had forewarned that, 'If the judicial inquiry also establishes that there is exercise of undue influence that had resulted in any decision that was against the public interest, the relevant provisions of the contract law may have to be invoked for legally reviewing the existing contractual commitments with the DPC and taking all necessary steps that would subserve the public interest, without the GoM/MSEB having to incur any contractual liability.'[2] In spite of opposition from vested interests, it was due to the considerable public pressure that the GOM appointed a commission under the Commissions of Inquiry Act, 1952, under a retired judge of the Supreme Court on 7 November 2001. The commission was asked to submit its report in six months. The appointment of the commission was opposed not only by Sharad Pawar, who was the chief minister at the time the project was originally approved, but even by the NDA government at the Centre by filing a petition in the Supreme Court under Article 131 of the Constitution. Unfortunately, the Supreme Court gave an *ex parte* stay on 9 April 2003 restraining the commission from proceeding further with the inquiry. It was shocking to see that the state government neither took care to file a caveat in the Court not to hear the matter without issuing a notice to it nor did it make any effort to get the stay vacated. Even after the United

Progressive Alliance (UPA) government came to power, it too was not interested in the inquiry by the commission and the stay continued indefinitely. Finally, when the much extended term of the inquiry commission came to an end in 2005, the state government quietly buried the commission by not extending its term. After thus deliberately weakening its own case by not permitting such a high level judicial commission of inquiry to function, the Centre has entered into a settlement package, which according to the sketchy information available in the public domain so far, is as one-sided as was the original PPA of the project.

The fair price of equity of the foreign promoters was not more than $320 million. If the written down price of the 65 per cent equity held by Enron ($20 million) is taken into account, this was even lower. But, Bechtel and GE, who had purchased the Enron equity at this throwaway price had been given much more than their equity investment though the project had become sick and had been shut down as unviable. In any project which becomes sick, it is the equity holders who have to take the maximum hit. In the present case, apart from giving up its claim of Rs 401 crore referred to earlier, the MSEB, which had 15 per cent equity in the project, had to forego its investment totally. Question also needs to be asked as to what sacrifices the Indian and foreign financial institutions were forced to make. After all, they were no less responsible for not carrying out the financial scrutiny of the project properly. Instead, they relied solely on the generous guarantees of the state government and the counter-guarantees by the Central government. Even a rudimentary examination of the basic features of the project should have made it clear to any analyst that it had no chance of success and that it would mean a financial ruin for the MSEB and the state government. But, as is the common experience, multinational firms, in their pursuit of maximising their profits, hardly ever exhibit any social commitment or concern for the interests of their much weaker joint sector partners from developing countries. The role of the Indian and foreign financial and legal consultancy firms appointed by the MSEB too left much to be desired. With all the political rhetoric of the ongoing economic reforms and the talk of disinvestment in PSUs, restructuring of the Dabhol project has meant nothing but the nationalisation of a badly conceived and designed largest private sector power project in India funded by a notorious multinational. The PSUs such as the NTPC and the GAIL, which were not earlier prepared to touch the project with a barge-pole, have been coerced into taking over and running the project, reminding one of the heady days of social control over the commanding heights of the economy. This is yet another example of 'privatisation of profits and nationalisation of losses'!

When the scandal is of such monumental proportions, it is no wonder that the 'much educated' ruling politicians, and bureaucrats are going out of their way to shower concessions on this project to bring down its nominal tariff as much as possible, with hidden subsidies. The state government has already announced a series of concessions such as of stamp duty, sales tax and so on. The Centre has extended project-specific concessions such as of customs duty waiver for the naphtha to be imported for the project, waiver of capital gains tax, income tax concessions, grant of mega power project status and so on. It has even decided to refund the import duty levied on the project! Tax concessions are hardly ever given retrospectively for a specific project. But, political reputations and interests of so many influential power elite are involved in the instant case that no price is too high to pay to save them. According to some tentative estimates, the burden of subsidy for this project which will have to be borne by the tax payers may be as high as Rs 10,000 crore over the next few years. No second-hand power project anywhere in the world would have cost as much. The authors of this article, who had raised their voice against the project, were branded by its proponents as enemies of Maharashtra who were responsible for plunging the state in darkness!

Scandalous cases like this make the government worry about the Pandora's box which the Right to Information Act would force it to open and the skeletons which would tumble out of it. It is therefore no surprise that demands for information pertaining to this project and its judicial inquiry are stone-walled, whichever political parties are in power at the Centre and in Maharashtra. It is an eloquent commentary that Parliament has had no time or inclination, all these years, to discuss this project, whether in its previous or the present incarnation, and the failure of governance as broad, across different governments at different points of time, at both the state and Central level, and at both administrative and political levels, which it personifies.

Notes

1. Madhav Godbole, Resolving Dabhol Tangle, *Economic and Political Weekly*, June 5, 2004, pp. 2329-2334.
2. Government of Maharashtra, *Report of the Energy Review Committee*, April 2001, pp. 84-85.

32

MODI HAS BEEN LET DOWN BY BUREAUCRACY

PRIME MINISTER NARENDRA Modi must be acclaimed for taking the courageous decision to demonetise high denomination notes.

During the last 70 years since Independence, every political party has indulged in the rhetoric of fighting black money, but there has been no concrete action, except for the demonetisation by Morarji Desai's Janata Party government in 1978.

However, since the government fell soon after and there was no follow-up action, its impact was limited.

The National Institute of Public Finance and Policy, in its report, *Aspects of Black Money in India*, had estimated black income generation at 18 per cent to 21 per cent of the Gross Domestic Product (at factor cost) for the year 1983-1984. There has been steep increase in black income since then.

The Direct Taxes Inquiry Committee (1971), popularly known as the Wanchoo Committee, in its interim report, had recommended demonetisation of high value currency notes.

Rediff.com, 28 November 2016.

The report was discussed in a series of meetings with the then Finance Minister Y.B. Chavan, on whose personal staff I worked at the time, and it was decided that the recommendation should be acted upon.

In view of the importance of the subject it was decided that the Finance Minister should first discuss the matter with then Prime Minister Indira Gandhi before further steps were initiated.

When Chavan called on Indira Gandhi and explained what he had in mind, she asked him only one question: 'Chavan*ji*, are no more elections to be fought by the Congress party?'

Chavan got the message and the recommendation was shelved. (Madhav Godbole, *Unfinished Innings,* 1996, pp 87-88)

Against this background, Modi must be complimented for taking a normally unthinkable step which would change the face of this country.

It is sign of political maturity that common people all over the country have welcomed the move and supported the objectives underlying it.

However, it is evident that they have been put to tremendous hardships and inconvenience.

The print and electronic media is bringing out the enormity of their privations every day. The question therefore needs to be asked whether preparatory actions for demonetisation could have been chalked out more thoroughly, thoughtfully and with a greater foresight. Several lacunae are evident.

The government has stated that the planning for this momentous step had begun 10 months ago. The government thus had enough time to make the scheme as fool-proof and workable as possible.

Unfortunately, this does not seem to have happened and there are too many yawning gaps which have led to tremendous misery and inconvenience all around.

None of the measures below would have compromised the secrecy of the operation in any way. With the nationalisation of banks in 1969 and encouragement of the cooperative sector in development, the spread of banking has been far and wide, including in the rural and semi-urban areas.

This factor ought to have been taken into account while devising the scheme of demonetisation.

The decision of the government to exclude cooperative banks from the implementation of the scheme has raised many awkward questions.

The prime cause of this is the dual control on supervision of these banks by the RBI and the state governments. I firmly believe that all banks must be brought under the RBI's sole supervision. Let us hope this issue will be addressed with earnestness at least now.

Non-availability of new notes in sufficient quantities on the day of demonetisation is also shocking and totally inexcusable. Specious reasons are being advanced for delays, including in recalibration of Automated Teller Machines (ATMs). Delays in bringing these machines into operation could have been easily foreseen and taken into account.

Since large areas in the country are still without ATM facilities, orders could have been placed in advance for new ATMs taking into account the configuration of the new notes of the denomination of 500, 1,000 and 2,000. The old ATMs after their recalibration could have been sent to the areas in which this new facility is yet to be provided.

The perceptions of people in the very sensitive exercise of demonetisation should also have been given due weightage.

Thus, the explanation given by the government for the running of colour from the new 2,000 rupee note, that if the colour runs, it is a genuine note, is ludicrous, to put it mildly.

The requirement of additional staff in banks could also have been anticipated and a scheme put into effect for re-employment of retired employees of the banks for a fixed duration.

For a continent-sized country like India time limits provided for conversion of old notes, and payment of bills should have been long enough so as to create a sense of assurance among the people that there is no need to run to the banks and ATMs immediately.

As an exceptional measure, the banks could have been kept open for all 24 hours to cater to the demands of people who have offices and work schedules to attend and can do their banking transactions only after office hours.

This is also true of large numbers of people in the business, informal sector, daily wage-earners and others.

It needs to be reiterated that demonetisation is (hopefully) a once in a life-time phenomenon and the follow-up actions also need to be taken care of as an exceptional measure to ensure smooth changeover to the new system.

The experience so far is a shocking example of how a critical scheme of national importance can be brought into disrepute by inefficient and badly designed implementation.

Finally, the war against black money must not end with demonetisation.

The government must announce in no uncertain terms that this is just the beginning and a series of steps would follow to bury the ghost of black money for ever.

Even in this regard the record of performance of successive governments is hardly anything to write home about.

Benami transactions, for example, have continued unabated despite the law on the subject which has remained on paper for years together.

There is rightly a perception among citizens that large loan defaulters and law-breakers have the protection of the political elite and have therefore gone scot-free.

The nexus between criminals, politicians and bureaucrats has been conveniently overlooked by the government. The frightening phenomenon of corruption has never been addressed with any seriousness by any government.

A comprehensive national policy needs to be adopted for eradication of corruption (Madhav Godbole, *Good Governance Never on India's Radar*, 2014, pp 213–17). The rhetoric of 'zero tolerance for corruption' is as empty and meaningless as 'the law will take its own course'.

The unfinished agenda for dealing with black money is formidable. But the wheel does not need to be reinvented.

The question is whether we, as a nation, are prepared to put our shoulders to it to make it move.

33

A CITIZENS TRIBUNAL SHOULD LOOK INTO THE FAILED GAMBLE OF DEMONETISATION

THE RESERVE BANK of India's (RBI) annual report for 2017-18 revealed that 99.3 per cent of demonetised currency notes have come back to the banking system. Everyone is asking, where has all the black money gone? This is particularly embarrassing with the 2019 Lok Sabha elections round the corner. The Narendra Modi government's demonetisation move has already been deeply mired in electoral politics. But efforts must be made to look at the pertinent issues, keeping politics aside for a while.

Modi's decision in 2016 was the second time India has witnessed demonetisation after independence. The first was in January 1978, when the Janata government was in power. It was opposed by the then RBI Governor I.G. Patel. But the government decided to go ahead anyway, as the move was primarily aimed at Indira Gandhi's Congress, which was flushed with funds, particularly during the emergency. It was

The Wire, 10 September 2018.

also meant to eliminate the possible use of high denomination currency notes for financing illegal transactions. There was reportedly a quantum jump in high denomination currency holdings in 1975-76 and 1976-77. The then Finance Minister H.M. Patel, while moving the Bill in Lok Sabha on March 21, 1978 had stated that high denomination bank notes were being used extensively for illicit transfer of money for financing transactions which were harmful to national economy. Replying to the brief discussion, the Finance Minister stated that 'the purpose of demonetisation was to ascertain whether the money was legally held and the liability of income tax discharged on it'. Interestingly, only 68 per cent of the demonetised currency notes were returned to the banking system then, compared to 99.3 per cent after 2016. Even then, Finance Minister Patel called it 'not worthwhile' till the conditions which encouraged black money were destroyed, otherwise there is 'little point in grappling with shadows'.

The 2016 decision

The decision-making process which led to demonetisation on November 8, 2016 will remain a state secret for a long time to come. But there is enough evidence to show that cash currency holdings did not form any significant portion of black money, which is primarily held in shares, gold, jewellery and real estate, often as benami holdings. A Finance Ministry white paper in 2012 showed that for the period 2006-2012, cash seized during searches and seizures ranged only from 3.75 to 7.3 per cent of total undisclosed income.

There has been serious debate in the country on the wisdom of demonetisation. But I believe that it was a courageous decision which needed to be taken to give a shock treatment, particularly to the black economy, and to create a national resolve to eradicate black money. However, the objectives enunciated by Prime Minister Modi while announcing the decision—diverting the large unaccounted black money stashed in cash to government through RBI surpluses which may be generated, dealing a mortal blow to the spread of fake currency and terrorist funding—have been belied.

But, as a saving grace, my hopes that demonetisation would be followed by a number of other steps to deal effectively with black money have been substantially realised. Strengthening and activating the Benami Transactions (Prohibition) Act which was lying in disuse for over a decade, identifying hundreds of shell companies and initiating proceeding against them, introducing a transparent system for auction of mining rights of coal and other natural resources, bringing in bankruptcy code, amendment of the Corruption Act, encouraging and promoting cashless transactions, pursuing cases against clandestine bank account holders in Switzerland and other tax heavens will help tackle black money. The nearly 71 per cent surge in income tax returns filed till end of August 2018 would not have been possible without creating a new climate for tax compliance in the country. Thus, demonetisation became just one of the steps meant to create a national climate.

Political parties and black money

Unfortunately, in the all-party meeting called by the Election Commission in August 2018 to consider electoral reforms, the BJP did not lend its support to the suggestion to put a ceiling on expenditure of political parties, though this is one of the main reasons of black money. As election results in some states soon after demonetisation showed, in spite of the persistent campaign by a section of the print and electronic media, the common person in the street had stood by the government, in spite of the privations and severe difficulties. But that is all the more reason why the failure of demonetisation gamble needs to be studied in depth.

Prima facie return of most of the currency to the banking system is impossible to accept at face value. Does it mean that there was no black money at all? Or that the whole system has become so corrupt and rotten to the core that all black money has been neatly converted into white without leaving any traces behind? Immediately following demonetisation, there were unnerving reports in the media about the manner in which short-cuts had been found, stacks of new bank notes were being carted away, and how the system had been totally undermined. The government had made tall claims that all such transactions would be fully investigated, and persons found guilty will be brought to book. What happened to these claims? It is shocking to see that no worthwhile cases of black money have been unearthed and no big players in the game identified and proceeded against.

Most importantly, the pain suffered by common people must not be forgotten. As I have written more than once, most of these privations could have been avoided if sufficient advance planning had been done and preparatory actions taken. The RBI and the Ministry of Finance must be held squarely responsible for these lapses. But who will bell the cat? For obvious reasons, the government will be most reluctant to open the can of worms and the Opposition parties would like to fully exploit the situation.

In this pre-election year, every issue gets politicised. Even the introduction of the Goods and Services Tax (GST), which was such a long overdue reform and in which all political parties came together to realise the dream of cooperative federalism for the first time since independence, is now being ridiculed as 'Gabbar Singh Tax'! Much is being made of the economy's slow-down, but it must not be forgotten that sectors such as real estate were flourishing on black money. Temporary slow-down in such sectors need not be unduly magnified.

In a poisonous and politically vitiated atmosphere, how to analyse objectively the failure of demonetisation is a million-dollar question. Normally, in a democracy, the Parliament is the highest forum of grand inquisition. A joint parliamentary committee (JPC) is a potent instrument to investigate such major national lapses. However, experience of successive JPCs has been grossly disappointing, whether it was Bofors, bank scam or 2G scam. It will therefore be futile to appoint another JPC on demonetisation. In fact, a parliamentary committee which has been debating this issue for months has still not been able to finalise its report due to sharp differences among its members along party lines! All this is quite exasperating.

Against this background, I would suggest that a high-level Citizens Commission be appointed to look into the colossal failure of demonetisation. The initiative for the purpose will have to be taken by a reputed, non-political organisation. The composition of the commission will also have to be totally apolitical and comprise persons of highest integrity and standing in society. The Citizens Commission on 1984 anti-Sikh riots in Delhi comprising S.M. Sikri, former Chief Justice of India, as chairman is a case in point. This commission's report was much more credible than several other commissions appointed by the government. The Concerned Citizens Tribunal headed by Justice V.R. Krishna Iyer, former judge of the Supreme Court, in respect of Godhra riots in 2002 also did a commendable job to expeditiously bring out the national concerns underlying communal riots. In India, currently, it is next to impossible to keep politics out of anything, but if calamitous decisions are to be avoided, politics must be kept aside to draw lessons for the future. The menace of black money is going to be with us for a long time. It is therefore important to know what went so terribly wrong with the demonetisation exercise. It will be best to entrust this responsibility to a Citizens Tribunal.

PART SEVEN

National Security - Increasing Concerns

MULTI-DIMENSIONAL NATIONAL SECURITY

WHEN ONE TALKS of national security, what comes to mind is the nation's defence preparedness and its armed forces. But, with the advances in science and technology, globalisation, economic integration, large and continuous movement of people and cargoes across the oceans, air space and land borders and increasingly complex societal changes the world over, the word security has acquired complex connotations. All aspects of a nation's life are now perceived as covered therein. Any weakness in any of them can be exploited by the enemy in the event of conflict and war. A chain is only as effective as its weakest link. This is borne out by the articles contained in the book.

India with its large size and its multi-religious, multi-lingual, multi-ethnic diversity, has a complex set of security concerns. Its often noisy, chaotic, multi-party democracy has added to the difficulties. The partition of the country at the time of its Independence has left behind bitter memories of communal strife. As a result, often, public discourse on some issues such as illegal migration from Bangladesh acquires communal overtones. The lingering Kashmir tangle has become a permanent item on the agenda of unresolved issues. Added to this are the issues of federalism and Centre-state relations.

Let us begin with the last-mentioned issue. When the Indian Constitution was framed over 70 years ago, the founding fathers were working in the atmosphere of frightening communal riots, movement of millions of people across the borders from one country to another, gigantic problems of food shortages, and intense Cold War in the international forums. One primary concern of the founding fathers was to ensure the unity, integrity and cohesion of the country comprising not only the erstwhile British India but also 550 princely states. The country had to cope with, and discard, by bringing about agreement of all minorities, systems such as religion-based separate electorates which had contributed to creating an ever-widening divide between the Hindu and Muslim communities and the partition of the country. With such gigantic challenges, a large number of people in India and abroad believed that India will not be able to reach an agreement on a Constitution. But this is what India was able to do. And it has been able to work under the Constitution all these years by making amendments where necessary.

In the process, India had to inevitably make certain compromises. But these were meant to strengthen the tenets of parliamentary democracy, secularism, rule of law, and separation of powers. With the adoption of country-wide Goods and Services Tax, India has given proof of its co-operative federalism.

With the experience gained of the working of the Constitution so far, some changes in the constitutional arrangements between the Union and the states have become necessary. The experience of serious communal riots such as in Ahmedabad, Godhra, Meerut and Mumbai, among others, have shown that it is imperative to have both the Union government and the concerned state government working conjointly to contain such communal situations. This is further borne out by the destruction of the Babri Masjid in which the state government was complicit. The Union government had to watch the situation helplessly. The only option the Union had was to dismiss the state government and to impose President's rule. For various reasons, the then Prime Minister P.V. Narasimha Rao dithered, in spite of the advice of the Ministry of Home Affairs that President's rule be imposed in the state. It is therefore imperative that the entries 'police' and 'public order' are shifted from the State List to the Concurrent List of the Seventh Schedule of the Constitution. This will empower the Union to deploy the central police forces in the states under its own supervision, and also to deal with and intervene more effectively in cases of terrorism. Enacting a central legislation for the CBI, which has been languishing for years together due to the resistance of the states, would also be possible.

The problem of illegal migration from Bangladesh has been grossly neglected over the years due to sheer vote bank politics. It was only when the issue was raised before the Supreme Court in a Public Interest Litigation that the Court came down heavily and chastised the central government by saying that illegal migration was like invasion of India and must be dealt with on a war-footing. In spite of this direction of the Court, the issue continued to be neglected. Even the Assam Accord was kept in cold storage for years together. It is only now that the full implications of the national register of citizens nearing completion in Assam are being realised but that too not wholly. If the problem of illegal migration is to be taken to its logical conclusion, such citizenship surveys will have to be carried out in all the states where the illegal migrants have dispersed. They include, among others, Uttar Pradesh, Delhi, Rajasthan, Gujarat, Maharashtra and some north-eastern states. No thought has been given yet to how the 'stateless persons', to be declared in due course, are to be treated. As usual, the government, of whichever political party it may be, seems to be inclined to push the problem under the carpet. This shows how the national security can be compromised seriously, in a democracy, by neglect of the issues by the government and lack of vigilance by the people at large.

Another problem which has met similar fate is that of neglect of India's international borders. After the Kargil War, the central government had appointed four task forces—for internal security, [international] border management, management of defence, and intelligence apparatus—to take a close look at India's security system. I was the Chairman of the task force on border management. The task forces were asked to submit their reports within three months. Thereafter, a group of ministers was asked to interact with the concerned ministries, organisations and chairpersons of the task forces and to make suitable recommendations to the Cabinet. For the first time in the history of the Government of India, this exercise was completed in a record time and the government decisions were placed before Parliament in February 2001 under the title, *Reforming The National Security System: Recommendations of the Group of Ministers*. Unfortunately, many of these decisions were sidelined by the UPA government, which came to power in 2004, during its long tenure of ten years.

Special attention may be invited to the breach of coastal security, in particular, when the dastardly attack was launched on Mumbai by the Pakistani terrorists on 26 November 2008. The government of Maharashtra had appointed a high-level committee to go into the handling of this event and to draw lessons for the future. It was shocking to see that the UPA government forbade the committee from looking into the role of central agencies and organisations such as the Research and Analysis Wing (R&AW), Intelligence Bureau

(IB), the Indian Navy, and the National Security Guards, among others. Neither was any inquiry of its own ordered by the central government. Such a partisan attitude resulted in the weaknesses and lapses of these organisations remaining unidentified and unrectified. The inquiry by the Maharashtra government also became a futile exercise.

The larger issues pertaining to the governance of the country which also have a close bearing on national security must not be lost sight of. The foremost among these is to preserve the secular fabric of the country. Keeping India at peace with itself will largely depend on taking care of its minorities and creating a sense of confidence and belonging in them. This is the biggest challenge facing India's security.

34

SECURING INDIA'S BORDERS – THE WAY AHEAD

Introduction

I AM GRATEFUL TO the Institute for Defence Studies and Analysis (IDSA) for inviting me to deliver the Y.B. Chavan Memorial Lecture. My gratitude is for more than one reason. I had known the founder of the Institute, K. Subrahmanyam, rather well since the days he was doing the ground-work for setting up the Institute. His deep understanding of strategic issues and wide-ranging interests have been responsible for the pre-eminent position enjoyed by the IDSA over the years. Also, I had the privilege of working closely with Y.B. Chavan as his Private Secretary for over three and half years during 1968 to 1972 when he was Union Home and Finance Minister. Chavan was one of the most outstanding Home Ministers this country has seen. An able administrator, statesman and astute parliamentarian, he was cast truly in the mould of Sardar Vallabhbhai Patel, the first Home Minister and Deputy Prime

---

The 5th Y.B. Chavan Memorial Lecture, 3 December 2014.

Minister of India. Chavan had the rare distinction of being in charge of three major Ministries, namely, Defence, Home and Finance in very critical times. Chavan steered the Home Ministry through really turbulent times marked by political instability, growing threat of Naxalism and student unrest, and severe strains on centre-state relations. I have seen at close quarters the keen interest Chavan took in the working of the IDSA. Coming here to give this lecture has meant refreshing old, fading memories and reliving through those difficult times.

India's Borders

Management of international borders for a country like India is a challenging task with its land border of 15,106.70 km spread over 92 districts in 17 states. All states except Madhya Pradesh, Chhattisgarh, Jharkhand, Delhi and Haryana are frontline states. In addition, India has a vast coastline of 7,516.6 km touching 13 states and union territories (UTs). India has 1,197 islands accounting for 2,094 km of additional coastline. Reference must be made to 51 Bangladeshi enclaves in India and 111 Indian enclaves in Bangladesh.

Perhaps, no other country has such varied borders—thickly populated borders such as of Punjab and Bangladesh, sea coast, islands, desert stretches, marshy lands, creeks, snow-bound areas, forests such as on Nepal and Myanmar border, and so on. This brings out the real challenges in guarding of borders and also the large extent to which the state governments are concerned with and have to be involved in any strategy for management of borders.

First Comprehensive Review Following Kargil War

The subject of border management came up for comprehensive examination in the Government of India for the first time only after the Kargil War, with the government setting up four task forces to look into the problems pertaining to national security. One of the task forces was on border management, headed by me. In my talk today, I propose to deal with a few policy issues pertaining to border management. The areas of air defence, coast guard and border roads are excluded from its purview.

Perfunctory Follow Up Action on Task Force Recommendations

It is gratifying to see that, as a follow-up of the recommendations of Task Force on Border Management (TFBM), Department of Border Management was created in MHA in January 2004, though unfortunately, it does not seem to have made much difference to action on the pertinent issues.

The first thing which strikes one is how little the people at large know about this crucial subject. The government's excessive preoccupation with maintenance of secrecy is responsible for it. The task force on border management had, while submitting its report, recommended to the government that its full report should be made public to increase public awareness of the issues. Unfortunately, the government did not agree and only the report of the group of ministers (GOM), which contained only the recommendations of the task force which were accepted by the group, was made public. It is high time, this approach is reviewed. It is only by creating public awareness and close involvement of the people at large that interests of safeguarding national security can be served best. The importance of this assertion can be evident from some instances referred to hereafter.

Equally important is the question of follow-up action on the decisions of the Group of Ministers. The predecessor-successor complex in the government is so acute that generally decisions taken by the previous government of different political colour are put in cold storage so as not to give credit to it. This seems to have happened so far as border management is concerned. It is a travesty that national security was undermined in the process. Now that the NDA government is back in power, I hope concerted action would be taken for speedy follow-up action.

The task force was anxious that guarding of borders should not be neglected by withdrawing border guarding forces for internal security or other duties such as VIP security. The ITBP seems to have been drafted for VIP security duties in recent years. Same is true of some other border guarding forces. The task force had emphasised that the state governments may be persuaded to expand their police forces so as to reduce the draft on central forces. The task force had also recommended the strengthening of other forces such as the CRPF (Central Reserve Police Force), and the CISF (Central Industrial Security Force) to take over VIP security duties. It was suggested that a firm policy may be announced by the central government. This does not appear to have happened so far.

Illegal Migration from Bangladesh

As will be discussed later, the problem of illegal migration from Bangladesh is far too serious but the common man in the street is not aware of its full implications. As a result, the campaign which was launched by the Shiv Sena–BJP government in Maharashtra in 1995-96 to detect and deport illegal migrants in Mumbai was frustrated due to the opposition of the then Left Front government in West Bengal. Maharashtra police had, for once, been successful in obtaining the orders of the magistrate under the Foreigners' Act to deport a batch of illegal migrants. Armed with this order, the Maharashtra police party had escorted the migrants to West Bengal to take them to the Bangladesh border, but their efforts were frustrated in Kolkata itself. The West Bengal government refused to give any assistance to Maharashtra police. There were public demonstrations and even stone pelting by Leftist parties. As a result, the Maharashtra police had no alternative but to return to Mumbai with the illegal migrants and to release them in the city to live happily thereafter!! The situation would have been quite different if illegal migration from Bangladesh had not become a vote-bank issue with communal overtones. I am not aware of any other instance of any other state government making efforts of rounding up illegal migrants and pursuing their cases in the court, except for the stray cases in the North East.

The gravity of illegal migration from Bangladesh hardly needs to be over-emphasised. It has changed the composition of several areas not only in the states adjoining Bangladesh but also in far-off places like Delhi. It was not therefore surprising that an illegal Bangladeshi migrant was appointed as a special executive magistrate in Mumbai. It is only after public outcry that the order was cancelled. Fears are being expressed that if the present trend continues, India may be faced with a demand for second partition. The illegal migrants are so well assimilated that in Nagaland, for example, illegal migrants are known as 'Naga Mias'. In parts of Assam, it has led to repeated large-scale racial and communal violence. According to present estimates, over three crore Illegal Bangladeshi migrants are residing in India. Earlier, in a Public Interest Litigation (PIL) the Supreme Court and very recently in November 2014, the Delhi High Court have castigated the central government for neglecting the issue and not taking any worthwhile action. (*Loksatta*, 7 November 2014)

The same public apathy is evident in the employment of illegal migrants from Bangladesh in low-paying jobs in the North-East and other states. It is seen that local persons are not prepared to take up certain types of jobs. Ready availability of illegal migrants seeking employment is a boon to the local people. Such labour is not unionised, is hard-working and diligent and is often prepared to work for long hours, in contravention of local labour laws. The question of passing a central legislation to prohibit employment of illegal migrants in any trade, profession, economic and commercial activity, service industries, etc. needs to be pursued vigorously. Since migrants are now spread over not only in the north-east but also in far-off states such as Delhi, Gujarat, Maharashtra, Rajasthan, and so on, such a law will have to be passed by Parliament to have all-India application.

Illegal migration from anywhere, and particularly Bangladesh, is due to both push and pull factors, which would continue to operate in the foreseeable future due to disparity in the development in India and Bangladesh. It would be futile to lose sight of this reality. The Task Force on Border Management (TFBM) had therefore suggested that a system of work permits should be introduced under which a certain number of persons will be permitted to enter India for a specified period of time. The main advantage of adopting this policy would be that authentic information will be available regarding the number of persons who are permitted to enter the country in search of employment. At the end of the stipulated period, the person will have to leave India. The Group of Ministers was not inclined to agree and felt that this will open the flood-gates for migrants. But this apprehension seems to be baseless. A number of countries are operating such schemes with reference to their neighbours. I would suggest that this proposal should be seriously considered to find a long-term solution to the problem.

The task force report had invited particular attention to the striking proliferation of madarsas on the Indo-Bangladesh and Indo-Nepal borders and their serious implications for the overall security situation. The task force had also underlined that partly this was due to non-establishment of primary and secondary schools by the concerned state governments in the border areas. This left no option to the parents but to send their children to the madarsas. The large funding of some of the madarsas and places of worship through funds received from abroad, often through hawala and other clandestine channels, was also highlighted by the task force. Though over a decade has elapsed since the submission of the report, these issues have continued to be neglected and have reportedly come up again in the investigations by the National Investigation Agency (NIA) in the Burdwan bomb blast inquiries in October-November 2014.

The confiscation of large quantities of illegal arms and ammunition in Burdwan in West Bengal in October 2014 and the alleged laxity of state police in the matter has come in for considerable comment. The representatives of the ruling Trinamool Congress party have stated that the fault is due to the porous Bangladesh border and the neglect of the concerned central government agencies to safeguard the border properly. This is a typical case of shifting the blame and finding a scapegoat. But the basic thrust of the argument in terms of the importance of safeguarding the border cannot be lost sight of. The terrorists involved in a number of recent heinous crimes have confessed that they were trained by Lashkar-e-Taiba (LeT) in Pakistan and had used Bangladesh and Nepal for clandestine cross-border journeys. This, once again, highlights the importance of putting in place a mechanism for assessing the work of border guarding forces, referred to above. It is imperative that the data in regard to performance appraisal of forces is in the public domain and made available under the Right to Information Act.

A section of intellectuals in Bangladesh has been arguing on the basis of the concept of *lebensraum* or living space to claim that Bangladesh has a right to the living space around Bangladesh to accommodate its increasing population. Over the years, the reality is much worse than what this totally unacceptable concept seems to convey. The living space thus claimed is not just in the adjoining areas but also all over India in far-off states such as Delhi, Maharashtra, Madhya Pradesh, Rajasthan, Uttar Pradesh and so on. Now some political parties in Bangladesh are even advocating the setting up of a union of Bangladesh and West Bengal. It is high time India awakens to these horrendous impending dangers.

Overstaying Visitors

Another instance of public apathy is equally disconcerting. Overstaying visitors from Bangladesh and Pakistan has been a matter of serious concern for a very long time. The Ministry of Home Affairs (MHA) had, therefore, reissued a circular some years ago to make it obligatory on a person, with whom a foreigner may be staying, to inform the police if the foreigner overstayed beyond the visa period. These unexceptional instructions too had to be withdrawn due to the clamour in the English media. This shows pitiable lack of awareness in the country on matters of interest crucial to national security. The government also did not make any effort to explain the position to educate the public opinion and preferred to meekly submit to public pressure and withdraw the instructions.

Aadhaar Card—Misconceived Scheme

The Aadhaar card scheme launched by the government of India may have some merit in terms of establishing the linkages of the persons with disbursement of subsidies, identification of beneficiaries under various welfare schemes, plugging loopholes in implementation of various development programmes and so on. But, the scheme is clearly counter-productive in terms of detection of illegal migrants whose number now exceeds over 30 million, even by a conservative estimate. Under the scheme, any resident of India, irrespective of whether he is an Indian citizen or not, is eligible to get an Aadhaar card. And the process of obtaining the card is so simple that all illegal migrants can easily get such cards. Since this card is being accepted as a proof of one's residence, it is bound to become a 'passport' for his citizenship. According to a news item (*IE*, 20 September 2014), the Prime Minister has directed that passports be linked to the *Aadhaar* data in order to prevent duplication of work and ensure maximum utilisation of the collected information. According to yet another news item, the central government is likely to make Aadhaar card mandatory for issue of passport. (*The Indian Express*, 11 November 2014) This will make it easier for illegal migrants to obtain Indian passport. The whole governmental system seems to be working to make their life in India as comfortable as possible! The concerned bill—The National Identity Authority Bill, 2010—is still languishing in Parliament for want of consensus among political parties. Even though the bill is yet to be passed, thousands of crores of rupees are being spent on the scheme each year. This is a travesty of parliamentary democracy. I had hoped that the NDA government on assuming power in May 2014 will review the scheme as it undercuts the efforts of identification and deportation of illegal migrants. Unfortunately, the NDA government has extended its full support to the scheme. This is an outstanding example of how ministries in government of India have been working at cross purposes even in matters involving national security. On the contrary, as brought out by the 124th Report of the Standing Committee of the Ministry of Home Affairs presented to the Rajya Sabha on 20 March 2007, the Multi-Purpose National Identity Card Scheme has been languishing since 2003.

Importance of Border Trade

Any programme of border management must encourage border trade so as to reduce the scope for clandestine activities. The flourishing illegal trade in cattle on Bangladesh border is a case in point. The number of cattle seized in each of the three years from 2010 to 2012 is over 1.25 lakh and the number of persons arrested is nearly 400. This must represent a miniscule percentage of actual smuggling of cattle and the corruption it must lead to. Cow slaughter is banned in India. The Supreme Court decision in the matter itself needs to be reviewed. But, there is no reason why export of cattle to Bangladesh should not be legalised. By doing so, it will not only lead to considerable accretion of foreign exchange but stop clandestine practices in the border areas and in the border guarding forces.

Importance of Evaluating the Performance of Border Guarding Forces

This leads me to an important recommendation of the task force which pertained to evaluating the performance of border guarding forces. The task force had recommended the principle of 'one border one force' with a view to making the border guarding forces accountable for their actions and inactions. It was suggested that the evaluation criteria and mechanism should be carefully worked out and annual evaluation of each border guarding force should be carried out sector-wise and made public. No information is available in the public domain on the action taken in this behalf so far.

Border Fencing and Demarcation of No Man's Land

Over the years, considerable emphasis has been placed on border fencing and flood lighting, particularly on the Bangladesh and Pakistan borders. One aspect has however been neglected all along. The Bangladesh border is an artificial border in most parts and often divides a village or even a residential house in two. In such a situation, safeguarding the border becomes impossible. Efforts will have to be made to re-demarcate the border in selected places by mutual agreement between India and Bangladesh. But this process has been rendered next to impossible due to the Supreme Court decision in the *Berubari case* involving exchange of enclaves between India and Bangladesh. The apex court decided in the said case that every such transfer of land or settlement will require amendment of the Constitution, making the whole process highly politicised and time-consuming. One can imagine how contentious and controversial will be any settlement of China border, leave aside the enclaves in the Bangladesh border areas.

A facet of border management, which has been neglected all these years, is of demarcating a no-man's land along the border so as to keep it fully sanitised and to safeguard it from any human activity. Creation of such a strip would make the task of border guarding forces so much easier. This is particularly necessary in some segments of the Bangladesh and Pakistan borders but due to financial implications and the likely problems in resettlement of the population, this subject has been put on the back burner all these years. With recent unprovoked firing on civilian population in the border areas in Punjab and Jammu & Kashmir, demand has been raised by the affected people themselves to have them resettled in the other safer areas. It is high time priority is given to this aspect for time-bound action.

Coastal Security—The Weakest Link

As is well known, a chain is only as strong as its weakest link. One of the weakest links in border management pertains to coastal security. It is seen that the programme of coastal security is being implemented in nine coastal states and four coastal union territories since 2005. The programme involves setting up of 73 coastal police stations, 97 checkposts, 58 outposts, and 30 operational barracks, and to equip them with 204 boats, 153 jeeps and 312 motorcycles. However, the available data on the subject is disconcerting. Praveen Swami in his article 'India's marine police programme floundering' (*The Hindu*, 4 August 2011) has brought out how the ill-trained and unequipped crews are unprepared to deal with terrorist threats, how police boats are 'floating hell' and have not even been provided with toilets, and how the programme is marred by poor planning.

Maharashtra is an outstanding case in point. This state had the dubious distinction of suffering heavily due to utter neglect of coastal security. The 13 serial explosions in Mumbai on 12 March 1993 which killed 257 persons were due to contraband bomb-making material brought in on the Ratnagiri coast. The involvement of customs staff, police and others has been well documented. All concerned persons should have been dealt with in an exemplary manner. But the cases were permitted to be dragged on in the courts for years. There is no reason why provisions of Article 311 of the Constitution could not be invoked to take exemplary action which could have had a deterrent effect on others for creation proper climate.

A Classic Case Study

Attention must also be invited to the daring and dastardly attack by Pakistani terrorists on Mumbai by sea route on 26 November 2008 which killed 170 people, including 25 foreign nationals, 18 security personnel and five sailors on high seas. V. Balachandran, a highly respected IPS officer who had worked with in the Research and Analysis Wing (RAW) and Cabinet Secretariat and who was a member of the two-man inquiry committee appointed by the state government, has stated: The 26/11 Mumbai attacks were marked by several new features.[1] For the first time, heavily armed terrorists invaded India through sea route and engaged in active combat for almost 68 hours. All earlier attacks on Mumbai were explosions through timed devices. It was also for the first time that so many foreigners were killed, mostly in five star hotels. Mounting of simultaneous attacks by terrorists on five targets totally confused an unprepared Mumbai police and public, much like the 11 September attacks in the USA. The psychological damage and panic created in civilian population resulted in severe public anger resulting in the resignation of several senior politicians, including the state Chief Minister and the Union Home Minister.

The saga of the attack reads like a crime novel. The preparations for the attack were carried out in great detail. It was in January 2008 that two Indian nationals handed over rough target maps to LeT leadership. This information was fed into five GPS sets procured by the LeT. Fake Indian identity cards were prepared for ten terrorists (in five 'buddy pairs') who were taught the Hindi spoken in Mumbai. Cell phones were obtained for them in fake names by payments made in other countries. Five cell phone handsets used by terrorists and abandoned in Mumbai were found procured from China.

The fully trained terrorists left Pakistan waters on 23 November 2008 in a Pakistani vessel *Al-Hussaini*. Each was armed with one AK-47 rifle with 240 bullets, 10 grenades, one 7.62 pistol with 14 rounds, one Nokia cell phone, RDX laden improvised explosive devices (IED) and dry fruits. The group had a satellite phone. On entering Indian waters off Saurashtra coast, they hijacked an Indian vessel *MV Kuber* with five crew members. Four of them were led away in *Al-Hussaini* and reportedly killed. One was taken to Mumbai coast as a guide, until the last four nautical miles, and then killed. They then inflated the rubber boat with a foot pump, transferred all equipment and abandoned *Kuber* with the dead sailor, reaching the Mumbai shoreline around 8:30 p.m. on 26 November. On landing in the thickly populated Machimar Nagar (Fishermen's colony) opposite Badhwar Park Railway officers' quarters, they split themselves into five groups and went towards target areas. Some hired taxis while one team walked up to the target area. The rest is history... The killing of senior Mumbai police officers seriously demoralised the entire police force which was engaged in combating operations for 68 hours.

Balachandran has emphasised that the attacks unveiled a number of innovations in terrorist methodology. The most important was the handlers' ability to direct action from a foreign country. Next was their ability in utilising India's free electronic media as guide for further killings. The elaborate subterfuge which the handlers organised in their communications with terrorists was yet another innovation.

The two-man committee was aghast to see the state of coastal security. The committee has noted that despite receiving as many as six alerts between August 2006 and April 2008 about the likelihood of resort to sea route by terrorists, no significant steps had been taken to beef up coastal security by having regular interaction with the Coast Guard although the Government of India had notified on 22 Sep 2003 the Coast Guard as the Lead Intelligence Agency (LIA) for coastal/ sea borders.

It was well known that the patch work joint patrolling started from 1993 (after the serial bomb blasts in Mumbai) had not worked. Nothing other than convening meetings seems to have been achieved as is evident from the information given to the committee by the Director General of Police (DGP), Maharashtra. The difficulties of coastal patrolling require serious attention as Maharashtra has a coastline of over 720 km and Mumbai is an island surrounded by sea and densely forested mangrove creeks.

The committee found that arrangements for monitoring security along the coast continued to face several impediments despite some recent decisions at higher levels of the Government of India and the Maharashtra authorities.

The Government of India had notified the Navy as a designated authority responsible for overall maritime security with both coastal and offshore security under its control. However, the exact responsibility of the State Marine Police has not been made clear. The committee felt that it would be impossible for the Maharashtra state police including Mumbai city police to undertake the task of coastal security within their jurisdiction.

It was brought to the notice of the inquiry committee that on 05-01-2009 the state government issued a GR sanctioning funds for hiring boats for patrolling. But, the question was not merely of boats but training of policemen in sea operations. Present training by Coast Guard for a few weeks is totally inadequate.

Also, present arrangements of the Mumbai police, where four police stations are notified as responsible for coastal policing have led to certain degree of confusion among the police stations about the role of the local police stations having jurisdiction over the land but not over adjacent water—a few feet away. One cannot make a fine distinction between illegal activities on land, i.e. up to sea shore high water mark and what takes place a few feet inside in the waters.

The committee was of the view that present arrangements were of a cosmetic nature. This observation was based on assessment made by officers in the field, who may have to face consequences of lapses, if any, in future. This must be sorted out by the administration keeping in view practical implementation

The DGP told the committee that the coastal security plan introduced by the Government of India since 1993 was not working well because several agencies have to contribute to its success. According to these instructions local police have to cover shore to 12 nautical miles, Coast Guard 12 to 200 nautical miles and the rest by the Navy. For sea patrolling the

Customs had to lend boats, staff had to be provided by police, LMGs to be mounted by Navy etc. One by one, agencies, other than the police, dropped out. Navy which in 1993 agreed (Home Department minutes dated 7-4-1993) to provide 8 ships for coastal patrolling withdrew in 2006 by establishing 'Quick Response Teams' at Murud and Ratnagiri. This was not adequate as evidenced by 26/11 attacks. The DGP said that all these difficulties had been voiced on several occasions.

The committee was also told that coastal patrolling was not adequate since the local police did not have high speed boats, did not have trained marine police and were not able to do patrolling during monsoons or rough seas. Besides, the training by Coast Guard/Navy is only for a few weeks which is not enough for the policemen to acclimatize with the problems of operating on the seas.

The committee found that the resources available with Mumbai police were not adequate to conduct sea patrolling so as to intercept the boat used by terrorists and hence nothing perhaps could have been done on receipt of such intelligence alerts.

The committee felt that senior police inspector, Cuffe Parade, should have set up some effective police presence on the sea front including Badhwar Park.

The committee was of the view that there was some confusion about the geographical limits of the jurisdiction of the newly created Marine Police stations along the coastal line. This became evident in the case of the incident regarding Machimar Nagar. The committee has recommended that DGP/ Commissioner of Police should clarify the matter so that local police stations are clear of their role.

The only saving grace was that, unlike in many other earlier terrorist attacks in India, during this incident, there was real time operational cooperation between foreign and Indian intelligence agencies in tracking down communications between terrorists and their handlers. This helped immediate tactical planning for counter measures. Foreign cooperation also actively helped in securing scientific evidence in tracking down the source of procurement of equipment used for the attack. But this was after the event and cannot be a substitute for close attention to safeguarding of borders.

As for the strategic failures of the government machinery, Balachandran has brought out that even though the central agencies received a series of intelligence alerts from 2006 that the LeT was training teams for sea-borne commando attacks on multiple targets including luxury hotels in Mumbai, they did not lead to capacity building by the local police in Maharashtra state. No efforts were made to strengthen sea patrolling. The state police were responsible for guarding 12 nautical miles from the shore line, Coast Guard from 12 to 200 nautical miles and the rest the Navy. Owing to several reasons, the state of Maharashtra, which has 720 km of coastline, could not set up satisfactory coastal security. The central government also failed to order the Coast Guard to keep vigilance despite terror alerts since 2006. Special anti-terrorist squads created in Maharashtra to confront terrorists in the wake of earlier bomb attacks also proved inadequate. The terrorists used 'area clearing weapons' like grenades against which the local police had no suitable equipment to counter.

Prior to the attacks, the central and state governments neglected 'open source intelligence' on such attacks. They failed to verify press reports that a suspected LeT vessel with terrorists was intercepted in March 2007 off Mumbai by Coast Guard. Similarly, the Mumbai police failed to analyse capacity-building by the terrorist groups concerned and their implications for Mumbai's own security following the Kabul Serena Hotel attack (January 2008) or Islamabad Marriot attack (September 2008).

The government's response was also disappointing in that it took (almost 11 hours) for the National Security Guard (NSG), the specially trained commando force to counter terrorist attacks, to arrive at the scene since they had to be flown from a location near Delhi. By the time they arrived, most of the killings and arson had already taken place. The Army and Navy contingents who were deployed in the interim to help the local police proved ineffective in resisting the heavily-armed and well-trained terrorists. Even the NSG only managed to clear the last terrorists in the afternoon of 29 November. The poorly equipped local police took heavy casualties in the process but contributed most to containing the damage.

I have given these extensive details since they pertain to the most recent case study which is so closely related to the subject of border security. Three shocking points pertaining to the above inquiry need to be noted. First, the inquiry was intrinsically incomplete as it pertained only to the actions of the Mumbai police. The role of central government agencies such as the Research & Analysis Wing (RAW), Intelligence Bureau (IB), National Security Guard (NSG), Navy, and the Coast Guard was kept out of the purview of the committee. It is not known if the central government carried out any inquiry in the matter as this would have been a useful case-study for all concerned. The people have a right to know how these agencies functioned and what needs to be done to avoid such lapses in the future. But, this is not for the first time that the central government took holier than though attitude. In the notorious Enron power project, the Centre refused to cooperate with the high level inquiry committee appointed by the state government, under my chairmanship. In fact, the then NDA government went to the extent of obtaining from the Supreme Court an *ex-parte* stay for the judicial commission of Inquiry set up by the state government under the chairmanship of a retired judge of the Supreme Court! This tendency of hiding its lapses and misgovernance in the name of safeguarding one's turf and secrecy needs to be deprecated.

The second shocking feature was the refusal of the state government to make the report of the two-man committee public under the ridiculous plea that it would adversely affect the criminal trial of Ajmal Kasab, the only terrorist who was arrested and finally executed under the orders of the court. In the process, the shortcomings of the state agencies and remedial actions which needed to be undertaken were kept away from public scrutiny. Some public spirited persons went in a PIL to the Bombay High Court but the state government stonewalled it on the pretext of national security! Finally, under intense public pressure, the report was placed on the table of the legislature on the last day of the session. The report has been marked confidential and has not therefore come in for public scrutiny. Such efforts are totally counter-productive. The cause of national security is certainly not served by such tactics. And the third, no action was taken against anyone for the lapses in this case which resulted in such a large loss of precious lives, destruction of public property and the loss of public confidence in the government's ability to ensure national security.

Lack of close cooperation and reluctance to share information among agencies operating on the border is a long-standing problem. The Task Force on Border Management had, inter alia, underlined the importance of institutionalising the arrangements for exchange of intelligence at various levels. In the anxiety of each organisation to guard its turf and not permit another agency to share in the credit for any operation, no progress has been made in the matter so far, even though nearly 15 years have elapsed since the submission of the report. The states always seem to complain that the intelligence alerts received by them are not specific enough and are therefore non-actionable. It must be appreciated that by its very nature, intelligence on sensitive issues is, in most cases, non-specific and often general. The skill lies in piecing together such intelligence and to build a coherent picture out of it. Experience has shown that there is considerable scope for capacity-building in this area.

Some Larger Policy Issues

Finally, I would like to dwell on an issue which has considerable bearing on national security as also the law and order situation in the country. The founding fathers of the Constitution had not visualised that making water-tight compartments between the responsibilities of the states and the Centre would create such enormous problems in a gigantic country like India. According to the Constitution, public order and police are entirely in the domain of the states. This has created enormous problems in dealing with the menace of inter-state crime, organised crime, drug trade, clandestine activities along the borders, and so on. It is time the Constitution is amended to make police and public order concurrent subjects. This will strengthen the hands of the central government substantially. Now that the BJP has a clear majority in Lok Sabha and the people's mandate to give good governance to the country, I hope the central government will make strenuous efforts to build an all-party consensus for the passage of the necessary Constitution amendment.

It is equally important to pay attention to the restructuring of the state and police departments in the states and at the Centre. It was as far back as 2006 that the Supreme Court laid down guidelines on this subject in a public interest litigation filed by the Common Cause and Prakash Singh. Unfortunately, these guidelines have not been implemented by most of the large states and also the central government.

Ultimately, the success of border management will depend on how efficiently the police functions in the country. It is a pity that even the orders of the highest court in the land have not been implemented so far. This is a shocking commentary on the state of governance in the country.

In conclusion, I would like to underline once again the importance of reducing to the barest minimum secrecy in dealing with matters pertaining to management of international borders. It is only by the closest surveillance of the people at large that borders can be safeguarded. Second, the importance of close cooperation of the states in these endeavours cannot be over-emphasised. I hope this Y.B. Chavan memorial lecture will help in inviting attention to these crucial issues.

Notes

1. V. Balachandran, Dealing with the Aftermath of Attacks: Lessons from Mumbai and Elsewhere on What to Do and What not to Do, *National Security and Intelligence Management: A New Paradigm*, Indus Source Books, Mumbai, 2014, pp. 258-261.

35

INDIA'S INTERNAL SECURITY WOES

INDIA'S INTERNAL SECURITY woes are becoming more complex and explosive each day. But there is hardly any awareness of it and the national life grinds and moves on from one 'breaking news' to the next. Clearly, issues pertaining to national security, unity and integrity will have to be given the highest priority over everything else. Balachandran's book does a yeoman service in inviting attention to the complex and wide-ranging issues which have been put on the back burner all these years. Importantly, it brings out how they are being dealt with in a number of countries. But there are no 'one size fits all' solutions. As the experience so far has shown, merely grafting imported policies, practices and procedures does not necessarily work.

India's Constitution must be given credit for binding together this multi-religious, multi-lingual, multi-racial, and multi-cultural country as one nation, decisively disproving many prophets of gloom in India and abroad. In hardly any

---

Foreword to V. Balachandran's book, *Keeping India Safe: The Dilemma of Internal Security*, 2017.

other developing country are the tenets of parliamentary democracy, secularism and the rule of law so firmly entrenched. Crucial institutions such as the judiciary, the higher civil services, the Election Commission of India, the Human Rights Commission, print and electronic media and statutory regulatory bodies have imparted strength to all national endeavours.

When the Indian Constitution was being framed, many considered India to be only a geographic entity, rather than a nation, comprising, apart from the British India, over 550 princely states which had voluntarily merged with India. Such a feat was not achieved anywhere in the world. The holocaust of the Indian partition was a horrendous experience and the founding fathers of the Constitution did not want a repetition of it in the future. This was reflected in their persistent efforts to provide for a strong central government. But equally strong was the desire of the provinces for sufficient freedom and autonomy. The over-riding concern was to have a Constitution which would be acceptable to all provinces and diverse sections of society. As a result, several compromises had inevitably to be made. These included, among others, 'police and public order' being made subjects in the State List in the Seventh Schedule.

Unfortunately, during the last 67 years since the adoption of the Constitution, political oneupmanship has overtaken the sober, mature politics during the freedom struggle. As a result, the political rhetoric of federalism has come in the way of even considerations of national security and unity. This has been seen in the opposition of states to enacting of laws for the Central Bureau of Investigation (CBI), railway police, and a federal police. Even enactment of a *model* legislation for *Lokayuktas* is being opposed. Efforts at enacting a legislation to deal with serious communal violence and giving the central government a larger role in dealing with such communal strife have been stymied. Based on the findings of the four high-level task forces on national security set up by the GOI after the Kargil War (This author was the Chairman of the task force on border management), important recommendations made by the Group of Ministers and approved by the Cabinet to initiate the process of consulting the states for amending the Constitution to increase the powers of the central government to deal with extraordinary situations have been languishing since 2002.

This author has been suggesting for quite some time that the opposition of states to passing of a central legislation for the CBI could be addressed by setting up a high-level steering committee comprising the representatives of the Centre and the states to oversee the functioning of the CBI. The federal council comprising representatives of the Centre and the states being created for policy matters pertaining to the Goods and Services Tax is an innovation which could be replicated for a number of institutions pertaining to internal security.

Dr B.R. Ambedkar, Chairman of the Drafting Committee and the then Law Minister, had rightly emphasised in the closing speech of the Constituent Assembly in November 1949: 'However good a Constitution may be, it is sure to turn out bad because those who are called to work it, happen to be a bad lot...The Constitution can provide only the organs of state such as the legislature, the executive and the judiciary. The factors on which the working of those organs of the state depend are the people and the political parties they will set up as their instruments to carry out their wishes and their politics. Who can say how the people of India and their parties will behave...It is therefore futile to pass any judgment upon the Constitution without reference to the part which the people and their parties are likely to play.' How ominously prophetic have been the observations of Ambedkar!

But, even without amendment of the Constitution, a great deal can be achieved if available instruments of governance are used effectively and apolitically. But, the record of premier central agencies such as the CBI and the National Investigation Agency (NIA) has been a disappointment, irrespective of which political dispensation has been in power. The police departments of the state governments are also in shambles. It is shocking that even the directions of the Supreme Court, in the *Prakash Singh* case [WP (civil) No. 310 of 1996], issued on 22 September 2006, have not been implemented by most states, though over a decade has elapsed. There can be no more eloquent commentary on the state of governance in the country. The grievances and public outcry in respect of the Armed Forces Special Powers Act can be addressed not by amendment of the Act to dilute the protection for the armed forces but by ensuring that the Act is invoked sparingly and for very short durations.

Balachandran has brought out how the central government made efforts to see that the actions and inactions of its agencies were not probed by the inquiry committee on 26/11. This was no different than the resistance of the GOI to the probe by the high-level technical committee of experts appointed by the government of Maharashtra (2000) to examine how the highly controversial Enron power project which cast unsustainable burden on the state was approved and to suggest the ways for dealing with the situation. In that case, the GOI went to the extent of getting an *ex parte* stay from the Supreme Court to the hearings of the judicial commission of inquiry, presided over by a former judge of the Supreme Court, appointed by the government of Maharashtra. If lessons are not to be learnt from the monumental mistakes of the past, we will be destined to repeat them in the future.

While some woes of internal security are due to the gaps in the Constitution, many more are due to the failure of governance for which only the administrative and political systems are to blame. The agenda of unfinished tasks so comprehensively and lucidly discussed by Balachandran should impel wider and informed public debate on the subject. In a democracy, there can be no better way of overcoming the woes.

36

SAVING THE NATIONAL REGISTER OF CITIZENS FROM THE 'BENGAL TIGERS'

A FEW WEEKS AGO, West Bengal Chief Minister Mamata Banerjee roared, 'They say they will start the exercise [National Register of Citizens] in Bengal. I want to see who dares to do that. We are Bengal tigers. It will not be so easy. Before you start anything here, remember that your days will be finished in 2019.'

We know that India is a country of stark contrasts. In Tripura and Jharkhand, politicians are anxious that the NRC be taken up in their states immediately. Tripura has approached the Supreme Court for the purpose, while the Chief Minister of Jharkhand, Raghubar Das, has requested the Union Home Minister for urgent action. Das has vowed to deport all foreigners residing illegally in the state.

Manipur, has gone one step ahead of Assam and passed a law proposing that all those who settled in the state after 1951 be barred from being recognised as permanent

---

The Wire, 27 October 2018.

residents. They will either have to leave or seek special entry and work permits. This is the inevitable result of the neglect of the subject by successive Union governments since Independence. The Assam Accord was reluctantly signed by the Rajiv Gandhi government in 1985 to bring to an end a long period of violence and insurgency. But the accord remained inoperative and it was only in 2013 that action to compile the NRC began. Five years later, it is still mired in controversy.

The main question is whether we, as a nation, are committed to address the question of undocumented migration with any seriousness of purpose. It is futile to be under the misconception that the problem is confined only to Assam. It is shocking that states like West Bengal and Bihar have continued to deny the existence of the problem.

As Union Home Secretary, I was concerned a great deal with massive migration from Bangladesh. I convened a meeting of the Chief Secretaries of the concerned states on March 24, 1992 to discuss a package of measures to be adopted on an all-India basis. It came as a surprise to me that even at an official level, there was reluctance on the part of some states, and particularly West Bengal and Bihar, to deal with the problem firmly. This was clearly at the behest of the political direction of the state governments. I pursued the matter further and persuaded S.B. Chavan, Union Home Minister, to convene a meeting of the chief ministers.

Accordingly, the meeting was held on September 28, 1992. In the background paper circulated for the conference, it was highlighted that Assam, West Bengal, Bihar, the north-eastern states and some other states in the country including the Union Territory of Delhi had been severely affected by the problem. The paper had underlined the fact that undocumented migrants seemed to be 'using West Bengal as a corridor to migrate to the other parts of India. Parts of Bihar have been affected seriously. Large numbers have come to Delhi and have settled down in several other areas.'

A comprehensive package of nine measures was proposed to deal effectively with this gigantic problem. It was, however, shocking to see that the then Chief Minister of West Bengal, Jyoti Basu, and of Bihar, Lalu Prasad Yadav, were reluctant to approve the press note of the conference proceedings. Indeed, Chavan had to exert a great deal of pressure to persuade them to do so. It is interesting to see that the stand of the Chief Minister of West Bengal on the subject has not changed even though the Communists have been ousted and Trinamool Congress has taken over.

This subject came up for close examination again after the Kargil War. The then NDA government led by Atal Bihari Vajpayee had appointed four task forces in 2000 to look into issues pertaining to the national security system. I was the Chairman of the task force on border management. The task force had estimated that there were about 15 million undocumented migrants from Bangladesh, mainly spread across Assam, West Bengal, Bihar, Tripura, and Meghalaya. Maharashtra, Rajasthan and Delhi had also been significantly affected.

The reports of the four task forces were carefully considered by the group of ministers on national security and their recommendations, on approval by the Cabinet, were placed before Parliament in February 2001 titled, 'Reforming the National Security System'. Attention must be invited to a few of the important decisions placed before Parliament, which unfortunately have largely remained on paper.

First, non-citizens should be issued an identity card of a different colour and design. As is seen, this decision has been totally disregarded while issuing Aadhaar cards which make no distinction between undocumented migrants, non-citizens and citizens, thereby complicating the problem of detecting and dealing with migrants.

Second, a work permit scheme was to be introduced for foreigners wanting to work in India. This seems to have been forgotten altogether.

Third, children of illegal migrants born in India automatically become Indian citizens. The Citizenship Act was to be amended to rectify this.

Fourth, attractive financial incentives were to be given for information leading to the successful deportation of undocumented migrants.

Fifth, and most importantly, the government was to work on enactment of a refugee law in consultation with the Law Commission, the National Human Rights Commission, state governments, and others to take into account the humanitarian interests of refugees as also the security and other concerns of the government.

Unfortunately, virtually all of these recommendations—and the important issues they were meant to address—have been totally sidelined.

In the light of the Assam NRC, a number of questions have been raised nationally and internationally about stateless persons, how they would be treated and so on. There has been complete silence on the part of the government, as if this problem is not there at all, though it is staring us in the face. This issue had been flagged way back in 2001 but neither the NDA government nor the UPA government has taken any interest in the subject. It is imperative that this issue is debated and discussed nationally. Parliament must find time to get it examined in depth through one of its committees. The Law Commission must also be asked to give its considered views on the subject. Unless a satisfactory answer is found to the question of the future of refugees or stateless persons, no political party will muster courage to take a firm stand on the question of undocumented migrants.

In sum, it must be appreciated that the Assam NRC is just the beginning. Similar action will have to be taken in a number of states. While the West Bengal government headed by the TMC is fiercely opposed to it, the silence of Bihar's NDA government and Delhi's AAP government is deafening. What does it show of our national commitment to the cause? We cannot push the problem under the carpet by merely politicising and communalising the issues, as has been done so far by almost all political parties.

It is high time a national consensus is evolved, particularly on the questions of identifying illegal migrants and enactment of a refugee law. It will be totally short-sighted and counter-productive to make this an issue for scoring political brownie points. I also hope that the usual ploy of leaving the issues to the Supreme Court will not be resorted to. That will be a clear proof, once again, of failure of democracy in this country.